Sensual Relations

Sensual Relations

*Engaging the Senses in
Culture and Social Theory*

DAVID HOWES

The University of Michigan Press

ANN ARBOR

Copyright © by the University of Michigan 2003
All rights reserved
Published in the United States of America by
The University of Michigan Press
Manufactured in the United States of America
∞ Printed on acid-free paper

2006   2005   2004   4   3   2

A CIP catalog record for this book is available from the British Library.

Library of Congress Cataloging-in-Publication Data

Howes, David.
    Sensual relations : engaging the senses in culture and
social theory / David Howes.
        p.   cm.
    Includes bibiographical references and index.
    ISBN 0-472-09846-2 (cloth : alk. paper) — ISBN 0-472-06846-6
(pbk. : alk. paper)
        1. Ethnology—Papua New Guinea.   2. Senses and sensation—Papua
New Guinea.   3. Body, Human—Social aspects—Papua New Guinea.
4. Papua New Guinea—Social life and customs.   I. Title.

GN671.N5 H69   2003
305.8'009953—dc21   2003005021

For Constance Classen

Contents

Illustrations

Foretaste

This book is about the life of the senses in society, and the challenges posed to both classical and contemporary social and cultural theory by reflecting on the ever-shifting construction of the sensorium in history and across cultures. The title, "Sensual Relations," indicates that the focus will be on the interplay of the senses rather than on each sense in isolation. Too often studies of the senses will consider each of the five senses in turn, as though sight, hearing, smell, taste, and touch each constituted a completely independent domain of experience, without exploring how the senses interact with each other in different combinations and hierarchies.

Too often, as well, the senses are considered from a purely physical and personal psychological perspective. Sensory experience is presented as physical sensation shaped by personal history. Writers on the senses reminisce about the favorite smells of their childhood or marvel at the finely tuned ear of the musician (e.g., Ackerman 1990; Gonzalez-Crussi 1989) with little notion of how sensory experience may be collectively patterned by cultural ideology and practice. Sensation is not just a matter of physiological response and personal experience. It is the most fundamental domain of cultural expression, the medium through which all the values and practices of society are enacted. To a greater or lesser extent, every domain of sensory experience, from the sight of a work of art to the scent of perfume to the savor of dinner, is a field of cultural elaboration. Every domain of sensory experience is also an arena for structuring social roles and interactions. We learn social divisions, distinctions of gender, class and race, through our senses. The aim of this book is hence to show how sensual relations are also social relations.

In the last few decades there has occurred a remarkable florescence of theoretically engaged (and engaging) work on the senses in a wide range of disciplines: from history and philosophy to geography and sociology, and from law and medicine to literature and art criticism.[1] These works come after a long dry period in which the senses and sensuality were bypassed by most academics as antithetical to intellectual investigation. According to the latter perspective, sensory data was just the gaudy clothing that had to be removed to arrive at the naked, abstract truth. Already in the nineteenth century the Symbolist champion of multisensoriality, Charles Baudelaire, inveighed against the "modern professors" who had "forgotten the color of the sky, the form of plants, the movement and odor of animals" (1962: 213). Many academics are now eagerly rediscovering how colors, movements, and odors may themselves be crucial vehicles for cultural meaning and not merely picturesque trappings.

This sensual turn in scholarship is therefore partly a reaction against the incorporeality of conventional academic writing.[2] It is also a challenge to what has been called the hegemony of vision in Western culture. This dominance is primarily due to the association of sight with both scientific rationalism and capitalist display and to the expansion of the visual field by means of technologies of observation and reproduction—from the telescope to the television. The power and prominence of vision in the contemporary West have understandably attracted a great deal of academic attention. The other senses, and particularly the so-called lower senses, have, by contrast, been underrepresented and undertheorized in contemporary scholarship.

Despite the current interest in extending the sensory bounds of scholarship, sight is still undoubtedly the star of academic research on the senses. While the image of sight as the medium of a monolithic, rationalist worldview has been successfully shattered by recent work in the humanities and social sciences, it retains its sensory dominance through myriad scattered reflections (Jay 1988, 1993). Constance Classen writes in *The Color of Angels:*

The concept of sight, like an object reflected in a room of mirrors, has assumed so many different guises in our culture that it can provide us with the illusion of a complete sensorium. Paintings, photographs and films, for example, are said by some critics to represent and evoke non-visual sensations so well, that the non-visual senses can scarcely be said to be absent from these media. In many contemporary academic works sight is so endlessly analyzed, and the other senses so consistently ignored, that the five senses would seem to consist of the colonial/patriarchal gaze, the scientific gaze, the erotic gaze, the capitalist gaze and the subversive glance. (1998: 143)

Even critiques of the dominance of sight tend to remain within the realm of vision and rarely consider what alternatives to hypervisualism might lie within other sensory domains, or emerge from combining the senses in new ratios. More work evidently needs to be done to encourage academics to break free from the spell of the specular and look, not beyond their noses, but *at* their noses and all the rest of the human sensorium.

Anthropology has done the most to promote and theorize a full-bodied approach to sensory experience and expression (Strathern 1996: 200; Lock 1993; Herzfeld 2001). A partial roll-call of sensually minded scholars in anthropology would include Edmund Carpenter (1972), Alfred Gell (1977, 1995), Anthony Seeger (1981, 1987), Steve Feld (1982, 1988, 1996), Nancy Munn (1983, 1986), Michael Jackson (1983a, 1989, 1998), Paul Stoller (1989, 1995, 1997), Constance Classen (1990, 1993a, 1993b, 1997), Marina Roseman (1991), Carol Laderman (1991), Bob Desjarlais (1992, 1997), Michael Taussig (1993), Vishvajit Pandya (1993), Nadia Seremetakis (1994), Susan Rasmussen (1995, 1999), Penny Van Esterik (2000), Tim Ingold (2000), Adeline Masquelier (2001), Judith Farquhar (2002), and Kathryn Linn Geurts (2003) as well as the present writer (Howes 1986 et seq.).

The anthropological investigation of cross-cultural variations in the elaboration of the different senses has increasingly made it clear that sensory experience may be structured and invested with meaning in many different ways across cultures. The present book is centered in the anthropological endeavor to explore and theorize the cultural formation of the senses. It is divided into three parts. The first part examines the history of anthropological investigations into the senses, from measuring the sensory acuity of "savage races" in the late nineteenth century through to the late-twentieth-century development of a meaning-centered "anthropology of the senses" (including the detour represented by the rise of the textual model of cultural analysis in the 1970s). The second part explores how the anthropology of the senses may be applied to particular cultures, in this case, the cultures of two geographically distinct areas of Papua New Guinea—namely, the Massim and Middle Sepik River regions. The last part of the book discusses how the insights gained through this approach enable us to rework our understanding of classic social and psychological theory, specifically, the theories of Marx and Freud.

Marx and Freud have both been taken as theoreticians of the senses—Marx for his materialist approach to human consciousness, Freud for his work on sexuality. It is true that the young Marx held that "the *forming of the five senses* is a labor of the entire history of the world down to the present" (1987: 109). It is also true that the young Marx railed against the alienation of the senses in nineteenth-century bourgeois society, and envisioned an alternative society in which the senses would be liberated from the tyranny of private property and "become directly in their practice *theoreticians*" (107). He was distracted from elaborating further on these tantalizing statements, however, by his growing preoccupation with analyzing the specular character of the commodity-form in his life-work, *Capital.* It may well also be the case that the severe physical discomfort caused by the boils that mercilessly erupted all over his body alienated Marx from his own sensuous existence and disinclined him to write further on the subject of the cultural formation of human sensoriality. The recession of the senses in the mature Marx, and the link between this and his theory of the dematerialization of the commodity in capitalist exchange, will be the subject of chapter 8. In effect, the senses (like commodities) become "ghosts" in Marx's mature theory, haunting his work but too insubstantial to grasp.

Sigmund Freud is another classical theorist whose work

promised to foreground the sensorium as an object of study, but failed to realize that promise and even (at least in the case of some senses) had the reverse effect. Influenced by contemporary theories of biological and social evolution that placed smell, taste, and touch at the bottom rungs of physiological and cultural development, hearing at the middle, and sight at the top, Freud assumed that within the psychological development of the individual the "lower" senses would similarly be left behind or subordinated to a large extent as a person grew into maturity. The sense of smell was particularly denigrated by Freud. With regard to sexual stimulation, for example, Freud wrote that in the case of (normal) humans the role of olfaction has been completely taken over by vision. Freud's "denial of nasality" in his mature work was due partly to his antagonism toward his former friend and colleague Wilhelm Fliess, who made the nose central to his sexual theories, and partly (similarly to the case of Marx) to his own extensive nasal complaints. Freud's nose and the sensory deficiencies of his theory of psychosexual development will be the subject of chapter 7.

If Marx and Freud were deficient in good sense, where may one look to find it? Here the anthropological material from Melanesia plays a key role.

Melanesian Sensory Formations

Melanesia has long been considered an important testing ground of Freudian theory. Bronislaw Malinowski rocked the psychoanalytic establishment of the 1920s when he questioned the universality of the Oedipus complex on the basis of his ethnographic research in the Trobriand Islands (1924). Opinion has remained divided as to whether Oedipus should be counted in or out of the Trobriands ever since. Chapter 7, in addition to presenting a sensuous critique of Freud's theory of psychosexual development, proposes a solution to the Trobriands Oedipus debate based on a reanalysis of the sensory and social organization of the Trobriand psyche.

Just as sensory material from Melanesia challenges the classificatory schemes of Freudian theory, so does it raise questions about the limitations of Marxist theory. Marx apparently conceptualized the sensory characteristics of commodities solely in terms of their use-value: a thick coat is useful for keeping out the cold. Melanesian cultures afford powerful examples of the ways in which symbolic values may be invested in the sensory characteristics of commodities quite apart from their "usefulness" as objects—the rattling sound of a string of shells that speaks of its owner's "thunderous" renown, the rotting smell emanating from a yam storehouse that signals its owners' surplus productivity and proven generosity. Such symbolic sensory values abound not only in the classic "gift economies" of Melanesia but also in the Melanesian reception of consumer capitalism.

Melanesia is the home of the "cargo cult" (Worsley 1970; Lindstrom 1993). According to reports, these cults involved native peoples attempting to ritually ensure the delivery of a desirable cargo of Western products by imitating European practices and destroying their own crops, traditional sacra, and so forth. This suggests a society that would be highly receptive to the attractions of Western-style consumer capitalism. Rather than simply being slavish consumers of Western goods, however, Papua New Guineans creatively discover uses and meanings for imported products that go far beyond anything their manufacturers might have imagined (Lederman 1986; Liep 1994). In the Melanesian "mode of domestication," it is the sensory characteristics of commodities—the whiteness and fragrance of baby powder, the texture of cast-off plastic bags—that inspire new, indigenous values and uses. In a number of ways, therefore, Papua New Guineans subvert the instrumental logic of late modern capitalism and manage to keep their senses about them. Melanesia hence provides a valuable context in which to complete and critique Marx's all-too-brief account of the sensory regime of capitalist society, as chapter 8 will show.

Aside from its potential contributions to Freudian and Marxist theories, the ethnography of Melanesia contains much material relevant to the elaboration of an anthropology of the senses. For example, the geographical diversity of a country such as Papua New Guinea provides many sensory environments, from the salience of smells and sounds and relative occlusion of vision in the rain forests of the interior (Feld 1982) to the "open, joyous, bright" expanse of the sea in coastal areas, like that of the Massim region of Milne Bay Province, where special importance is attached to the kinesthetics of seafaring (Malinowski 1967: 95; 1961; Chowning 1960). Other sensuous geographies include the Middle Sepik River region, with its swampy valleys and rugged mountain ridges, and the barren tracts around Port Moresby, where the hills have been completely denuded of forest. Melanesia thus presents a good context in which to explore the phenomenon of "emplacement," or sensuous reaction of people to place.

Melanesia also presents a vital context in which to explore the sensual dimensions of social exchange, following Nancy Munn's exemplary analysis of the social and cultural values embedded in the sensory characteristics of exchange objects (what Munn [1986] calls "quali-signs of value") in *The Fame of Gawa*. According to this approach, the "spiritual bonds between things" (as well as persons) spoken of by Marcel Mauss in his classic study of the gift economy are also *sensual bonds*. This recognition opens the way for the study of gift exchange as a "total sensory phenomenon" as well as a "total social phenomenon" (Mauss 1966: 1; Nihill 2000). Interestingly, one of the first casualties of this new approach is Malinowski's "big picture" of the interisland network of ceremonial exchange known as the Kula Ring. As we shall see in chapters 3 and 4, instead of trying to simply picture the Kula, Malinowski should have listened to its aural dynamics and scented its aromas.

The ethnography of Melanesia contains many intimations of alternative epistemologies (Barth 1975; Tuzin 1980; Gell 1995; LiPuma 2000). Stephen Feld (1996) has coined the term *acoustemology* to refer to the way in which the Kaluli people of Bosavi reckon time and space by reference to auditory cues and entertain a fundamentally acoustic view of the structure of their physical and social universe. Andrew Strathern (1989) records that the Melpa speakers of Mount Hagen distinguish three primary ways of knowing: seeing (direct knowledge), hearing (education, hearsay), and doing or experiencing (cult participation), and rank them in that order (see further Eves 1998: 36–37). Michael O'Hanlon (1989), by contrast, reports that the neighboring Wahgi are sometimes reticent about believing the evidence of their senses; they defer to what other people say about an event. The question of the relation of the verbal to other "nonverbal" (or sensual) registers of communication needs to be resolved. This is one of the central questions of the anthropology of the senses and will be addressed in chapters 2 and 6.

Most of the societies of Papua New Guinea remain oral or residually oral societies, because government-sponsored literacy campaigns have met with uneven success. According to the theory of oral mentality proposed by the media theorists Marshall McLuhan (1962) and Walter Ong (1982), therefore, aurality and the sense of hearing should be central to Melanesian civilization. Yet the Middle Sepik region excels in the production of "visual art." Indeed, among the Kwoma, who inhabit the Ambunti District of East Sepik Province, there is an overwhelming emphasis on visual display (and concealment). Western society is not, therefore, the only "society of the spectacle" (Debord 1977). How is such "eye-mindedness" to be squared with orality theory? How does orality theory have to be rewritten (maybe even jettisoned) in light of such departures from the expected? More important, how are the senses articulated to each other in cultural practice even in the most ocularcentric of societies, like that of the Kwoma? These questions will be explored in chapters 4, 5, and 6.

Finally, Melanesia has been the site of some very probing reflections on the construction of the self (e.g., Leenhardt 1979; Munn 1986; Battaglia 1990), partly because of the challenge that the "relational person" of Melanesia is deemed to pose to the standard Western conception of the autonomous individual (LiPuma 2000). On one account, the model of "intersubjective gazing" is what gives Melanesian notions of personhood and agency their distinctive form.

> Every act reveals an individual, but at the same time is motivated by a concern to anticipate and meet the expectations of someone else's regard. In any relation there is an imagined reciprocity of gazes, with each person perceived as the cause of another's agency . . . Instead of a relation between subject and object, one therefore has a relation between two subjects, who each act with the other in mind. (Reed 1999: 50; Strathern 1988)

I would question the adequacy of this model, at least for the Massim and Middle Sepik River regions, where the ethnographic record and my own experience of interpersonal relations suggest that all of the senses are involved, though in different mixes, in social and self-perception. The issue of the relationship between what Nancy Munn (1986) calls "the scale of self-constitution" and specific local ways of sensing (or "sensory orders") will be explored throughout the chapters of Part 2.

Precursors to the Anthropology of the Senses

Before this Foretaste becomes an aftertaste, I would like to signal how the relational approach to the study of the senses advocated here is both indebted to and departs from the work of two precursors to the anthropology of the senses, Marshall McLuhan and Claude Lévi-Strauss.

It is to McLuhan that we owe the idea of the sensorium as a combinatory and cultures as consisting of contrasting "ratios of sense perception." As he wrote in *The Gutenberg Galaxy*:

> It would seem that the extension of one or another of our senses by mechanical means, such as [the wheel as an extension of the foot, the book of the eye, the telephone of the ear], can act as a sort of twist for the kaleidoscope of the entire sensorium. A new combination or ratio of the existing components occurs, and a new mosaic of possible forms presents itself. (1962: 55)

Brilliant as many of McLuhan's readings of the impact of new media on Western thought and society may be, the technological determinism of his theory needs nonetheless to be tempered by the recognition that the body is humanity's first instrument or tool (Mauss 1979), and cultures develop practices or "techniques of the senses" (Howes 1990a) that need not have any exterior or extracorporeal form. Indeed, a primary weakness of McLuhan's theory is that all societies that lack the technology of writing are typed as "oral societies" and held to be subject to the same "tyranny of the ear." In point of fact, there is a great deal of diversity to the sensory emphases of oral societies—and to those of literate (visual) cultures too for that matter (Classen 1993b, 1998).

Furthermore, McLuhan imputed various characteristics to the

senses in an a priori fashion: visuality was associated with linearity and neutrality, while aurality was associated with multidimensionality and emotivity. The cultural meaning of the senses, however, is not simply derived from any presumed inherent psychophysical characteristics, but elaborated through their use (Classen 1990; Leavitt and Hart 1990). What one soon finds out from studying such uses is that different cultures accentuate different characteristics of each sensory field—for example, color over line in the domain of vision, hardness over smoothness in the domain of touch—just as they elevate and elaborate or suppress the different senses themselves.

Taking these criticisms into account, what I think we can retain from McLuhan is the importance of studying how the senses are distinguished, characterized, and customarily combined in a given culture. Such intersensory relationships will inflect the form of social relations and the manner in which the universe is perceived and ascribed meaning, or in other words "sensed."

The work of Claude Lévi-Strauss represents another vital opening in the direction of an anthropology of the senses. In *Mythologiques*, Lévi-Strauss extended the model of structural linguistics to the study of the sensory codes of myths. According to structural linguistics, words only signify by virtue of the differential relations in which they stand to other words in a language or "code." Building on this insight, in "Fugue of the Five Senses," Lévi-Strauss shows how a series of Gê myths employs contrasts between sensory qualities—thus "rais[ing them] to the point of having a logical existence"—in each of the five basic sensory codes to transmit the same message having to do with "the origin of man's mortality" (1969: 147–63, 164). In the final analysis, according to Lévi-Strauss, all of the codes are intertranslatable because the relations *between* the signs in each sensory modality or code are homologous.[3]

One difficulty with Lévi-Strauss's approach to the senses is that the sensorium is not exclusively structured like a language. Sensory phenomena can be highly meaningful in ways that are ineffable. Lévi-Strauss's preoccupation with discovering binary oppositions is also problematic. Sensory values may interact with each other in much more complex forms than that of simple binarisms.

Judith Farquhar has identified a further difficulty arising from the strictures of the structuralist account of signification.

> The analytic power and tidiness of structuralist analysis in the Lévi-Straussian manner gratifies me as an anthropologist even as it annoys the eater in me, for explanatory power about signification seems to be gained at the expense of poetry—the flavors and pleasure—inherent in everyday reality. The structuralist analyst works through the concrete to reach the logical, leaving the charms of mundane experience far behind. (2002: 57)

While Farquhar still seems to adhere to a division between the conceptual sphere of the mind as the realm of abstract logic and the sensuous domain of the body as the irrational location of pleasure, her criticism nevertheless highlights Lévi-Strauss's penchant for rapid flight from sensory experience to perch in the "higher" regions of structural analysis. The social roles of the senses also tend to be bypassed in Lévi-Strauss's constant search for the operations of "mind" (i.e., cognitive codes). However, the life of the senses is not simply a matter of logic, but of experience.

The ultimate difficulty with the structuralist paradigm, perhaps, is that it imposes a consensus model on the operations of the senses, whereas a conflict model could prove equally germane and illuminating. Lévi-Strauss was inspired in his use of a consensus model by "the poet," Charles Baudelaire. The latter imagined the senses to be joined in idyllic harmony (see "Correspondences" in Baudelaire 1975). Not so another poet of sensuous experience, Wordsworth:

> I speak in recollection of a time
> When the bodily eye, in every stage of life
> The most despotic of our senses, gained
> Such strength in *me* as often held my mind
> In absolute dominion. Gladly here,
> Entering upon abstruser argument,
> Could I endeavour to unfold the means
> Which Nature studiously employs to thwart
> This tyranny, summons all the senses each

To counteract the other, and themselves,
And makes them all, and the objects with which all
Are conversant, subservient in their turn
To the great ends of Liberty and Power.

(1959: XII: lines 127–39)

As appears from these lines, Wordsworth thought the "natural" state of the senses to be one of mutual dependence and interplay or "counteraction," yet we live under "this tyranny" of vision. To free himself from the despotic reign of the eye, the poet endeavored to "summon *all* the senses," believing that to overturn or otherwise transform the conventional Western hierarchy of sensing could prove both empowering and liberating.

There is no "natural" state of the senses among humans, however, we can only ever know the senses as socialized (Classen 1993b: 37–49). It is therefore necessary to substitute "cultures" for Wordsworth's "Nature" in the preceding lines. Furthermore, there is nothing to prevent the ear or the nose from being any less tyrannical than the eye in some other cultural formation of the senses. Taking these criticisms into account, what I would like to retain from Wordsworth is his insight into the conflict of the faculties, or politics of the senses. The senses are not always in agreement with each other. At times conflicting messages are conveyed by different sensory channels, and certain domains of sensory expression and experience are suppressed in favor of others.[4]

Interestingly, the conflict model of the sensorium is supported by the work of the evolutionary psychologist Thorne Shipley in his *Intersensory Origin of Mind.*

> Since the various senses are evolved to model the spatio-temporal intensity distributions of different physical energies in nature, it is natural that they come to evoke different models of nature. The co-ordination of those differences . . . is what the mind was evolved to do. . . .
>
> Sensory arguments ("Surely, that mouse did not really roar!") rather than sensory agreements are at issue. Ultimately, what we take for reality is some sort of compromise among the evidence of the senses, as sifted by critical reason. But if the senses had

always agreed as to what is really there, conscious mind would probably not have been found necessary for survival. (1995: 18)

Of course, few psychologists would venture as far as Shipley does in positing an intersensory origin for brain functions. The psychology of perception as practiced in the West concentrates on the study of the senses in isolation from each other—the better to control (uncontrollable) "variables" (Stein and Meredith 1993: xii–xiii). Alternately, psychologists attempt to map neuronal connections and therefore proceed in ignorance of the diverse social connections among the senses that other cultures have dreamed up and put into practice (Howes 1990a; Howes and Classen 1991; Classen and Howes 1996a).

There exist many different social models for ordering and inter-relating the senses (and, as in the case of Wordsworth, many different individual challenges to those social models). Each of these models reveals a different twist of McLuhan's "kaleidoscope of the sensorium," with different sensory values and practices coming to the fore. In what follows, I shall explore this social interplay of the senses in Melanesia, and examine its ramifications for various fields of theory in Western academia.

Lake Memphremagog, Quebec
August 2002

Acknowledgments

For their advice, encouragement, and own contributions to the sensual turn in anthropological understanding, I wish to thank Gilles Bibeau, Ellen Corin, Bob Desjarlais, Steve Feld, Annette Green, Michael Herzfeld, Christine Jourdan, the late Roger Keesing, Lawrence Kirmayer, Michael Lambek, John Leavitt, Ken Little, Margaret Lock, Roger McDonnell, Rodney Needham, Jérôme Rousseau, Paul Stoller, and Jojada Verrips. I have also derived much stimulation from conversations with friends and colleagues at Concordia University, Montreal, most notably Jim Drobnick, Jennifer Fisher, Homa Hoodfar, Joseph Smucker, and Anthony Synnott. My thanks as well to all the other researchers and students who have worked with me in the context of the Varieties of Sensory Experience project, the Concordia Sensoria Research Team, and the Culture and Consumption Research Group, especially Kregg Hetherington, Jean-Sébastien Marcoux, Elysée Nouvet, and Anke Schwittay.

For the generous hospitality, the stories, and many stimulating sensations I enjoyed while in Papua New Guinea, I am indebted to the people of Tongwinjamb and Ambunti, East Sepik Province, and of Bwaiowa and Dobu in Milne Bay Province, as well as Colin Filer, Andrea Mandie, Linus Digim'Rina, and Father Bernard McGrane for facilitating my introduction to the two regions.

For the financial assistance that made possible different branches of the research reported in this book, I thank the Social Sciences and Humanities Research Council of Canada, the Fonds pour la Formation des Chercheurs et l'Aide à la Recherche du Québec, Concordia University, and the Olfactory Research Fund.

For the maps and diagrams I thank Derek Parent and Larry Dionne respectively. Special thanks to George Classen for the splendid line-drawings and for much other assistance. I also greatly appreciate the patience and enthusiasm shown by my editors at the

University of Michigan Press, beginning with Susan Whitlock and ending with Ellen McCarthy.

For the innumerable ways in which they have nourished and sustained me throughout this endeavor, warm thanks to my mother, my father, Didi, Emilia, my sister and brothers, and my children, Jonathan and Emma. Finally, my deepest thanks go to Constance Classen for inspiring me with her own work and working together with me to define the field of the anthropology of the senses.

The idea for this book grew out of my doctoral dissertation at the Université de Montréal, which was written under the direction of Gilles Bibeau. An earlier version of chapter 1 was presented at the Twelfth International Congress of Anthropological and Ethnological Sciences in Zagreb, Yugoslavia, in July 1988, and first published in *Culture*, vol. 11, in 1991. An earlier version of chapter 7 formed the basis of several talks, most notably at the Warburg Institute in May 1999, and the German Historical Institute in Washington, DC, in October 2001. The first part of chapter 7 initially appeared as an article in *Psychoanalytic Psychology*, vol. 14, in 1997; and the second part as a chapter in *Nose Book: Representations of the Nose in Literature and the Arts*, edited by Victoria de Rijke, Lene Ostermark-Johansen, and Helen Thomas (Middlesex University Press, 2000). I wish to thank the various audiences and anonymous reviewers for their responses, and the copyright holders for their permission to reproduce these texts (in modified form) here.

I wish to thank Penguin Putnam and Routledge for permission to quote extensively from Bronislaw Malinowski, *Argonauts of the Western Pacific* (New York: E. P. Dutton, 1961). Finally, I thank Walter Gruen for permission to use Remedios Varo's painting, *The Creation of the Birds*, as the cover illustration. An androgynous, owl-like figure sits at a drawing table. The figure's palette is composed of colors that have been distilled from the night air by means of an elaborate alchemical vessel. In one hand, the figure holds a prism that focuses a moonbeam onto the page; in the other hand is a stylus (attached to a violin), which she/he uses to draw a series of birds that take flight. Varo's painting marvelously conveys the theme of the crossing of the senses which recurs throughout this book.

PART I

Making Sense in Anthropology

CHAPTER I

Taking Leave of Our Senses

A Survey of the Senses and
Critique of the Textual Revolution in
Ethnographic Theory

Anthropology's engagement with the sensuous has shifted over the last century and a half from a concern with measuring bodies and recording sense data to an interest in sensing patterns, then from sensing patterns to reading texts, and finally from reading texts to writing culture. In the course of the latter shifts, the content of anthropological knowledge has changed from being multisensory and social to being spectacularly stylized and centered on the individual ethnographer. The result is that ethnographic authority now depends more on the "reflexivity" with which one writes than the accuracy with which one "represents" a culture (e.g., Clifford and Marcus 1986; van Maanen 1988; Geertz 1988; Stoller 1994; Marcus 1998; Lassiter 2001). In the conclusion to this chapter it is suggested that anthropologists have become too self-conscious about "getting themselves into print," as Clifford Geertz (1988) would say, and need to start being more conscious of the effects of the "model of the text" and the medium of print *on* consciousness.

A Measure of Sense

Anthropologists of the nineteenth and early twentieth centuries had a fascination with the physical and sensory characteristics of the populations they studied. Much of this fascination was motivated by the contemporary concern to classify people as belonging to distinct racial types (Synnott and Howes 1992). Another fundamental reason for this fascination, however, was the long-standing philosophical conceit that associated Europeans with the mind and reason while identifying non-Europeans with the body and senses. When perusing the literature or going into the field, anthropologists expected and actively sought out evidence of "savage sensuality" that would support this identification of non-Europeans with the realm of the body and senses.

Many of the first encounters of Europeans with the peoples of Africa, the Americas, and Oceania occurred in the context of voyages of exploration and cartography. It is not surprising, therefore, that not only the lands, but also the bodies of the peoples living there were subjected to measurement and mapping in order to take their place within the European *mappus mundi*. A typical example of this extension of cartography to the body is the twenty-seven measurements taken of an Andaman Islander captured in a British naval expedition of 1858, including the length of the arm, the breadth of the nose, the interior and exterior distances of the eyes, and the circumference around the calf (Tomas 1996: 88; see further Bijlmer 1923).

In fact, in the very act of measuring the body parts and registering the sensory acuity of "primitive" peoples, anthropologists were constituting themselves as rational Europeans and their subjects as sensuous savages. The Europeans had a monopoly over the scientific tools for measuring, testing, and recording, while their subjects often had (or at least were expected to present) only their immediate corporeal being. For example, the test equipment for measuring sensory discrimination carried on the Cambridge anthropological expedition to the Torres Strait in 1898 included "color tests, eye tester, diagrams, . . . scents, syren whistle, hand-grasp dynamometer, induction coil and wire, marbles, dynamo-graph, pseudoptics, diaspon, musical instruments," and so on (Kuklick 1991: 142). Here then was the equipment to investigate almost all the sensory domains of indigenous experience, though not to fathom their social and symbolic significance.

Since sight and hearing were traditionally linked with intellectual activity and civilized behavior in European culture, while taste, touch, and smell were associated with animality, it was imagined that "primitive" peoples would show a predilection for the "lower" or "animal"—in short, "primitive"—senses. In the eighteenth century, one already finds treatises describing the tactile aesthetics or exceptional olfactory abilities of "savages." These become commonplace in the nineteenth century, supported by anecdotal descriptions from explorers and travelers. The natural historian Lorenz Oken went so far as to invent a racial hierarchy of the senses. In his scheme the European "eye-man" was at the top of the scale, followed by the Asian "ear-man," the Native American "nose-man," the Australian "tongue-man," and, at the bottom, the African "skin-man" (Classen 1997: 405).

Influenced by such social hierarchies of the senses, one of the main hypotheses that the Torres Strait expedition sought to test was that the "primitive" senses would be especially developed among such a "primitive" people as the Torres Islanders. Although the data itself was inconclusive, it was interpreted to support this hypothesis. William McDougall, whose task was to study the muscular and tactile responses of the Islanders, determined that their "power of tactile discrimination is about double that of Englishmen" (cited in Richards 1998: 149). Charles Myers, who was in charge of testing olfactory capabilities, concluded that the evocative power that odors apparently held for the Islanders constituted "yet another expression of the high degree to which the sensory side of mental life is elaborated among primitive peoples" (1903: 184).

The *Reports* of the Torres Strait expedition (Haddon 1903) reinforced the classic European concept of the opposition of body and mind, savagery and civilization. "If too much energy is expended on the sensory foundations," as was deemed to be the case with the Torres Islanders, "it is natural that the intellectual superstructure should suffer" (i.e., remain undeveloped), wrote W. H. R. Rivers (cited in Richards 1998: 147; see also Kuklick 1998: 174–75). This inverse relation between sense and intellect was held to be true not only of indigenous peoples but also of Europeans with a "primitive" frame of mind. Thus the scientific community considered the nineteenth-century artistic interest in the aesthetic potential of odors (e.g., among the Symbolists) to be conducive to, or else the result of, mental degeneracy (Classen 1998: 118–21).

While often permeated with racist assumptions and limited by a fixation with scientific measurement, the anthropological literature of the late nineteenth and early twentieth centuries is nonetheless often rich in sensuous ethnographic detail. The olfactory vocabularies or the gustatory codes, the body techniques and general sensory ambience (which many later anthropologists would simply overlook, or treat as picturesque trivia) are carefully noted in many of these now forgotten monographs (Bleek and Lloyd 1911; Bijlmer 1923). Though they may have been included in the first place as signs of racial distinction, they nonetheless signal the importance of investigating a wide range of sensory domains of expression, and they provide a tantalizing indication of the vitality and sophistication of sensory symbolism across cultures.

Disciplining the Senses: An Eye or an Ear

After World War I there was a decline in interest in exploring the sensorium in anthropology. The study of the senses was disadvantaged by its close association with the categorization of racial types. Such sensory phenomena as fragrances, flavors, and textures were furthermore deemed to be rather frivolous subjects for study. Attention to these sensory domains seemed to denote a sensationalist interest in exotica on the part of the ethnographer. The study of social systems—kinship terminology, political structure, land tenure—characterized much of the "serious" anthropology of the day. This trend became even more marked after World War II.

The senses were not entirely eliminated as a field for anthropological inquiry, but their range was narrowed down to two: sight and hearing. This narrowing was due in part to the assumption that sight and hearing are the least subjective of the senses and therefore the most suitable for scientific investigation. Supporting this focus on sight and hearing was the development of influential technologies of reproduction. Among the range of sensory phenomena, the only ones that could be recorded by these technologies were sight and sound. Cameras and phonographs were quickly pressed into service as tools of anthropological data collection (Grimshaw 2001; Brady 1999). Such devices reinforced the association of sight and hearing with rationalism by appearing to register cultural expressions in a direct, unmediated, objective fashion. As these technologies necessarily excluded all other sensory phenomena, they also presented cultures as purely visual or auditory manifestations. Thus what seemed to be real was a world devoid of scents, savors, temperatures, and textures.

It can further be argued that by working primarily or only with sensory phenomena that could be recorded, anthropologists were seeking to control and contain the subjects they studied, to reify them and turn them into museum or laboratory specimens. Smells may be disruptive and elusive; touches, interactive and personal; sights and sounds, however, can be mechanically detached from the people who produce them and can be controlled at the will of the observer.

In a well-known phrase, Marshall McLuhan argued that the transition from orality to literacy gave Western society "an eye for an ear" by precipitating a shift from an oral-aural to a visual sign system (McLuhan and Fiore 1967: 44). As anthropologists with a sensuous turn of mind increasingly channeled their interests into either "visual" anthropology (including the anthropology of art) or "auditory" anthropology (including linguistics and the anthropology of music), they can be said to have given the cultures they investigated "an eye *or* an ear."

Anthropologists tended to classify non-Western cultural phenomena in terms of the familiar disciplinary divisions of Western culture. For example, practices or objects with apparent aesthetic dimensions were classified either within the domain of visual arts or within that of music. Once thus classified they were analyzed using criteria drawn from those fields in the West: line, form, melody, and so on. Furthermore, in the West a visual artist or scholar of art is rarely also a musician or scholar of music, as these fields require different abilities and training. Similarly, within anthropology, an anthropologist of art is rarely also an ethnomusicologist. The sensory specialization required within Western culture thus came to be reproduced in ethnographic practice, and sensory and social domains that may be inseparable in the culture under study came to be divided up along conventional disciplinary lines. An anthropologist may have either an eye or an ear.

The systematization of knowledge within anthropological linguistics, ethnomusicology, the anthropology of art, and visual anthropology has generated many valuable insights into the visual and aural forms of diverse cultures, but at the cost of sensory exclusionism. This refers to the manner in which "other" sensory domains are customarily eliminated or evoked only indirectly in each of these subdisciplines of anthropology. For example, the tactile qualities of a weaving, which may be of immense importance to the culture concerned, are excluded when the work is analyzed in terms of its visual aesthetics and reproduced as a photograph or drawing. The visual image is retained and may be tremendously powerful in itself, but all the invisible threads that tie it to a larger cultural tapestry of textures and scents and sounds are snipped off. The example may also be given of Navajo sandpainting, which for the Navajo involves essential elements of touch and movement, but for Westerners is customarily transformed into and appreciated as a static work of visual art (Classen and Howes 1996a: 89). Similarly, the dynamic, multisensory context in which a song is performed disappears when only the musicological elements are analyzed or only the recorded voice is heard.

Sensory exclusionism has played a particularly formative role in the domain of psychological anthropology (with certain exceptions to be discussed in the next section). Consider Paul Berlin and Brent Kay's monumental study, *Basic Color Terms.* According to some (e.g., Brown 1991), this study put an end to the long-standing debate over the relativity of perception by showing that there exist certain universal "focal colors," the evidence for this being that people from twenty different cultures were able to distinguish between such colors (when presented to them in the form of tinted chips) no matter how many color terms their respective languages possessed. However, this leveling of difference was only the first step in Berlin and Kay's two-step argument. Based on a further survey of ninety-eight different languages, Berlin and Kay concluded that there is a progressive order to the sequence in which basic color terms enter languages, and that it is possible (in view of this order) to plot the various languages of the world on a single "evolutionary" scale. In their own words:

The overall temporal order [to the encoding of perceptual categories into basic color terms] is properly considered an evolutionary one; color lexicons with few terms tend to occur in association with relatively simple cultures and simple technologies, while color lexicons with many terms tend to occur in association with complex technologies. (1969: 101)

Those languages in which the color lexicon consists of just two terms, "light" and "dark," like that of the Dani of Irian Jaya, occupy the lowest rung in the Berlin and Kay scale, whereas the English language, which possesses the full complement of eleven "basic" terms—and more—occupies the highest rung.

The main problem with Berlin and Kay's evolutionist assumptions and conclusions is that they were never in fact put to the test. For example, it was never asked whether the apparent paucity of the Dani color vocabulary might be attributable to a Dani preference for "physical thinking" (after Luria 1976) over "visual thinking," which would present as a bias in favor of transposing visual imagery into object or tactile imagery.[1] Nor did Berlin and Kay ever consider whether the alleged simplicity of the color vocabularies of the oral (read: nonliterate) cultures they surveyed might not be offset by the complexity of these same cultures' other sensory vocabularies.

To pursue the last point a bit further, if Berlin and Kay had extended their study and included taste and smell as well as color lexicons in their survey, they would not have arrived at the conclusions they did. They would have been confronted with a multiplicity of historical trajectories, rather than the single (putatively) evolutionary trajectory that they believed they found.

Take the case of taste. English has four flavor categories, Japanese has five, the language of the Weyéwa of Sumba counts seven flavor terms, while that of the Sereer Ndut of Senegal has only three. When it comes to smell, however, the Sereer Ndut recognize five odor categories, the Weyéwa note three, the Japanese discriminate two, and English has no precise olfactory vocabulary.[2] The point here is that there is no single evolutionary pattern to be discerned behind these linguistic facts when categorization in various sensory fields is compared. What these facts reflect is rather the extent to which cultures differ in the intensity with which they attend to a given field of sense at a given moment in their history, some showing finer linguistic discrimination in the visual domain, others in the olfactory domain, and still others in the realm of taste. In this context the value of undertaking a *relational* study of the sensorium, rather than examining one sensory field in isolation, becomes evident. It also bears underlining that societies may communicate sensory values through other means than by language, so that Berlin and Kay's study would be entirely beside the point.

From Measuring Senses to Sensing Patterns

In the late nineteenth and early twentieth centuries anthropologists asked themselves whether the sensory differences they noted among different peoples were racial in origin (i.e., due to innate physiological differences) or environmental (i.e., due to different physical environments and the exigencies of physical survival). The more progressive anthropologists decided in favor of the latter view. Alfred Haddon wrote, for example, that "the differences in the mental characters and acuteness of the senses between the civilised and the uncivilised peoples are the result of differences in environment and in individual variability" (cited in Herle 1998: 99).

It was not until the 1930s that the question of how sensory differences may be social and cultural in nature started to receive much serious attention in anthropology. The handful of anthropologists who addressed this issue went against the contemporary trend to ignore the senses or to concentrate only on visual and auditory phenomena; instead they explored the associations between sensory practices and social values across a range of sensory fields. They therefore constitute the first true predecessors of the "anthropology of the senses," as this field would come to be known in the 1990s.

In 1935 Margaret Mead argued that the pronounced tactility of the Arapesh of Papua New Guinea was not a result of their "primitive" nature or their physical environment, but was directly related to their social values and practices (1956: 39–41). Mead was also responsible for developing the concept of "kinaesthetic learning" as distinct from verbal learning in the course of her research on Balinese character formation (Mead and Bateson 1942). The work that best exemplifies a sensuous turn of mind, however, is the 1953 book *The Study of Culture at a Distance*, which Mead edited together with Rhoda Métraux (see Yans-McLaughlin 1986 for an account of the political background to this study).

From a contemporary perspective, the Mead and Métraux anthology is remarkable for its insistence on the importance of studying the cultural patterning of sense experience. Mead and Métraux wrote:

> Just as linguistics requires a special ear [so cultural analysis requires a special honing of all the senses, since people] not only hear and speak and communicate through words, but also use all their senses in ways that are equally systematic . . . to taste and smell and to pattern their capacities to taste and smell, so that the traditional cuisine of a people can be as distinctive and as organized as a language. (1953: 16)

This methodological pronouncement, with its privileging of linguistics as a model for cultural analysis, contained the seeds of its own destruction. However, the stripping of the senses that the foregrounding of the language metaphor would eventually precipitate was held in check, at least for the time being, by the emphasis on developing *all* the senses.

Rhoda Métraux's chapter "Resonance in Imagery" presents a fine example of what could be called the sensualist approach to culture. She begins by asserting that the "images" (visual, aural, tactile, etc.) through which a people perceive the world form "a coherent whole." To grasp how a culture's sensory imagery forms such a whole, it is essential that one develop a "disciplined conscious awareness of the *two* systems within which one is working"—an awareness, that is, of the system of perception of the culture studied and of one's own perceptual system or style.

Regarding her personal perceptual style, Métraux remarked: "I myself can attend to and retain most precisely visual and kinaesthesic and tactile imagery, and I am likely to transpose imagery in other modalities into combinations of these" (1953: 361). The language of this quotation is unusual, coming from an anthropologist. It reads more like what a creative artist, such as a dancer or sculptor, might write. But Métraux was emphatic regarding the differences between her approach as a "research worker" and that of an artist.

The problem of the creative artist is to re-create and communicate an experience which is essentially personal and interior to himself. The research worker, on the contrary, is concerned with understanding in order to communicate to others systems which are external to himself—what he is attempting to communicate is not a generalized account of his own experience (which would be perhaps an *appreciation* of another culture) but rather an account of the way in which others experience the world. (360)

The explicit concern with producing an account of the way in which *others* experience the world explains the importance Métraux and her fellow research workers attached to disciplining their own perceptual styles. They did not want their personal sensory biases to interfere with the processing of sensations according to the alternative sensory patterns of the cultures they studied.

For all its apparent reflexivity, Métraux's approach cannot truly be categorized as "self-reflexive" in the sense in which that term is used today. It was not Métraux's concern merely to reflect upon how her own perceptual biases might affect her observations and share those reflections with the reader. Rather, she sought to *objectify* those biases through doubling her consciousness (i.e., creating a second self) and so transcend them. This approach to cultural analysis may be called the method of "being of two sensoria" (Howes 1990b: 60).

As an example of the kinds of insights such an approach could yield, consider the piece in *Culture at a Distance* entitled "Russian Sensory Images." The author, a Russian émigré, begins with a section on the sense of touch, followed by one on smells and another on hearing. Regarding touch, she writes:

The dictionary of the Russian language . . . defines the sense of touch as follows: "In reality all five senses can be reduced to one—the sense of touch. The tongue and palate sense the food; the ear, sound waves; the nose, emanations; the eyes, rays of light." That is why in all textbooks the sense of touch is always mentioned first. It means to ascertain, to perceive, by body, hand or fingers. (Anon. 1953: 163)

The reference to Russian textbooks treating touch first, in contrast to American psychology textbooks which always begin with sight, is confirmed by other observers (Simon 1957) and serves to highlight how the hierarchization of the senses can vary significantly even between cultures belonging to the same general tradition (here, that of "the West").

It is instructive to note how the author begins with a text (the dictionary definition of touch) but does not allow her analysis to rest there. The reason for this had to do with the prevailing methodological orthodoxy: texts and/or verbal utterances (the two had not yet been collapsed into one) were always to be supplemented by "*observation*" (Métraux 1953: 354–55; compare Clifford 1988: 31).

The term *observation* as used in the writing of Mead and Métraux and their circle did not have the same connotation of distantiation, nor imply the same exclusive emphasis on vision, as it does today (see Fabian 1983). For the sensualists (as they could be called) were committed to using *all* their senses in the study of culture, as we saw previously. Furthermore, much as they idealized objectivity, they also set great store in achieving empathy, or sensing along with their informants. This explains the acuteness of their "observations." By way of example, consider the following excerpt.

> Russians in general touch each other much less than Americans do. There is hardly any horseplay, slapping on the back, patting, fondling of children. The exception is when one is very happy or drunk. Then he hugs somebody. But that is not touching. (Anon. 1953: 163)

This passage nicely exemplifies the kind of awareness that results from being of two sensoria. The economy of touch is not the same in Russia as in the United States: what is regarded as normal in the latter culture (a slap on the back) the Russian would attribute to one or another altered state (drunkenness, excessive happiness).

In the section called "On the Sense of Smells," the author points out:

> In this country [referring to the United States], one can walk from one floor of a department store to another without being able to tell by smell what merchandise is being sold. In Russia

every store smelled of its wares, and smelled strongly. (Anon. 1953: 166)

The author goes on to give a wonderfully evocative list of smells that Russians know and enjoy: "the smell of the first snow," "the fleshy smell of plowed earth," "the damp cold smell of cats on back staircases," and so forth. The author also notes that Russian men "talk about the smell of the hands (palms) of the women they loved, or the smell of women's hair" (165). The sensuous focus of this essay, like that of others in the anthology, illustrates in a highly concrete way how cultural patterns are embodied through everyday sensory experience.

Questions about sensory difference would continue to be asked until well into the 1960s by research workers in the Culture and Personality School tradition inspired by Mead and Métraux. For instance, T. R. Williams, a student of Mead's, investigated the cultural structuring of tactile experience among the Dusun of Borneo (1966). A few other scholars working independently of Mead and Métraux also highlighted the importance of attending to cross-cultural variations in the patterning of sense experience. For example, Edward T. Hall proposed that "people from different cultures not only speak different languages but, what is possibly more important, *inhabit different sensory worlds*" (1966: 2).[3] He was led to this insight by his studies of proxemics, or how people experience and model the spatial world. These studies revealed that there is not one space, but many: thermal space, acoustic space, olfactory space, and so on, and that the overall mix, as well as how each of these spaces is experienced in its own right by the individual, depends on cultural norms. For example, according to Hall, the Japanese "screen visually in a variety of ways but are perfectly content with paper walls as acoustic screens" (1966: 43). This contrasts with the Dutch who depend on thick walls and double doors for screening purposes. Or again, Hall observes that "Arabs make more use of olfaction and touch than Americans" (1966: 3), which has implications for the regulation of interpersonal space during conversation and may pose problems for effective cross-cultural communication.

Some of Hall's notions were shared by Marshall McLuhan (1962, 1964), who was responsible for introducing the idea of media as "extensions of the senses" and cultures as consisting of contrasting "ratios of sense perception." As McLuhan's contribution was discussed in the Foretaste, no more will be said here beyond noting that McLuhan appears to have been a victim of his own media success. As a result, most of his theory has come down to us in the form of sound bites—"the medium is the massage," "the global village"—and has flitted in and out of fashion without receiving the sustained attention it deserves.[4] Fortunately, one of McLuhan's students, the cultural historian and media theorist Walter J. Ong, succeeded at taming his mentor's insights and working them into a comprehensive theory of the social, sensory, and psychological dynamics of oral, chirographic/typographic, and electronic communication (Ong 1967, 1977, 1982).

McLuhan and Ong did not put their theories to the test across cultures, but their work did inspire a number of others to do so. McLuhan's "sense ratio" definition of culture was operationalized by the cross-cultural psychologist Mallory Wober (1966, 1975). Wober developed a series of tests that revealed that West African subjects display significantly more "analytic ability" than North American subjects in tasks involving proprioceptive discrimination, while the reverse holds true in the case of tasks that depend on visual discrimination. Whereas the psychological anthropologists of another era would have attributed this differential performance to differences in racial character or environment, Wober, following McLuhan, attributed it to the contrasting aptitudes evoked by speech and dance as the most salient media of communication in Africa versus the printed word and (visual) image in America.

McLuhan's ideas were also field-tested after a fashion by Edmund Carpenter (1972, 1973).[5] Carpenter's writing contains many interesting observations on different modes of combining the senses, as in the following account of what is involved in tracking game in the Arctic.

> Reading tracks involves far more than just knowing where to look. Everything smelled, tasted, felt, heard can be as relevant as anything seen. I recall being out with trackers once and when I stooped to scrutinize the trail, they stepped back, taking in the whole. Interpenetration & interplay of the senses are the heart of this problem. (1973: 22)

Taking Leave of Our Senses

Both in his ethnography of the Aivilik and in his anthropology of media, Carpenter sought to document how the "sensory profile" of a culture, and alterations to that profile brought on by exposure to new media, can mold not only how people interact, but the very form in which they think. Thus, of the Aivilik he wrote:

> With them the binding power of the oral tradition is so strong as to make the eye subservient to the ear. They define space more by sound than by sight. Where we might say, "Let's see what we can hear," they would say "Let's hear what we can see." (1973: 33)

At the same time that McLuhan was developing his theory of sensory ratios, Claude Lévi-Strauss was elaborating the idea of a "science of the concrete" and the notion that "there is a kind of logic in tangible qualities" (1966; 1969: 1).[6] As with McLuhan, there is a strong emphasis on the relations within and between the senses in Lévi-Strauss's work (see, e.g., "Fugue of the Five Senses"). However, all of these relations turn out to be ones of contrast or homology, binary opposition or "correspondence." Lévi-Strauss makes no mention of hierarchization, domination, subversion, interplay, or any of the other intersensory relations that are suggested by McLuhan and Ong's and Carpenter's work. As noted in the Foretaste, Lévi-Strauss's stress on sensory contrasts derives from his subscription to a linguistic model of signification, while his emphasis on sensory harmony or "correspondence" probably reflects his Symbolist sympathies. It also reflects his abiding interest in tracing the operations of "mind" over and above those of the senses. Lévi-Strauss must thus be considered an intellectualist among the sensualists.

As a final example of sensualism in the anthropology of the 1960s, consider Victor Turner's work on the social, sensory, and (deep) psychological aspects of Ndembu ritual symbols (1967). The *mudyi* tree, for example, which secretes a milky white latex, symbolizes relationships and values ranging from the mother-child bond to matriliny, while the *nukula* tree, with its red gum analogous to blood, summons up a contrasting range of associations centered on huntsmanship and masculinity. While not as focused on the senses as the other work discussed here, Turner's notion of the "multivocality" of symbols may nevertheless be read as laying the foundation for a theory of the multisensoriality of symbols.

There are limitations to each of the approaches to the senses discussed in this section, such as Lévi-Strauss's manner of privileging the logical over the sensual, McLuhan and Ong's and Carpenter's technological determinism, Hall's spatialization of perception, and Mead and Métraux's obliviousness to the politics of representation. At the same time, by directing attention toward the interrelationships of the senses, all made a vital contribution. As will be recalled, Mead and Métraux promoted the study of the "systematic relationships between images within and among different modalities" (visual, auditory, kinaesthetic, tactile, olfactory, etc.). When the senses are ignored or when they are studied in isolation, all the interplay of sensory meaning—the associations between touch and taste, or hearing and smell—and all the ways in which sensory relations express social relations are lost.

From Sensing Patterns to Reading Texts

As we have seen, for the sensualists and some other leading figures in the anthropology of the 1950s and 1960s, doing ethnography involved sensing patterns. Their idea of "participant observation" was a sensationalist one. In the 1970s, however, there commenced a shift away from the participatory and sensual to more textual modes of understanding cultures. This shift involved the substitution of the idea of "reading cultures" for that of experiencing them. The "textual revolution," as this theoretical development could be called, was led by Clifford Geertz. Its origin may be traced to the publication of two seminal essays by Geertz that were later reprinted in *The Interpretation of Cultures*—namely, "Thick Description: Toward an Interpretive Theory of Culture" and "Deep Play: Notes on the Balinese Cockfight." It is in the latter article that that famous passage occurs where cultures are first spoken of as "texts": "The culture of a people is an ensemble of texts, themselves ensembles, which the anthropologist strains to read over the shoulders of those to whom they properly belong" (1973: 452).

Now, Geertz's artfulness as a writer is widely acknowledged.

Indeed, he is so artful that it is impossible to read "Deep Play" without getting caught up in the drama of the "metaphorical" status bloodbath that is the Balinese cockfight. However, aside from the textual gratification, or *jouissance du texte*, that Geertz's writing style evokes in us, what insights into Balinese culture does his method provide?

As is well known, Geertzian "interpretive anthropology" is grounded in hermeneutics. In its original form, hermeneutics was a doctrine that consisted of a body of rules for the interpretation of the written documents of Western culture—most notably, the Scriptures. A cockfight, however, is not a written document: it is a social activity, an *event.* Events do not possess the same stability as texts. This fact poses serious problems for the "circling" between exegesis and text that is so crucial to the proper conduct of hermeneutics: the action moves, the circle implodes. What conceivable justification is there, then, for Geertz's extension of the hermeneutic method from the study of texts to the study of action?

Taking his cue from the French philosopher Paul Ricoeur (1970), Geertz was able to cite various precedents in support of this extrapolation, such as the medieval Western *interpretatio naturae* tradition, which sought to read nature "as Scripture" (Geertz 1973: 449). It is telling that all of the examples Geertz adduces, following Ricoeur, stem from *within* the Western tradition. The chirocentric and culture-bound nature of these instances ought to have provoked suspicion.

No less suspect is the tenuousness of the reasoning involved in freeing events or actions from the flow of time so that they could figure as texts in the first place. Consider the following passage from Ricoeur's "The Model of the Text: Meaningful Action Considered as a Text" (the locus classicus of the extrapolation of hermeneutics from script to action).

What corresponds to writing in the field of action? . . . Certain metaphors may be helpful at this point. We say that such-and-such event *left its mark* on its time. We speak of marking events. Are not these "marks" on time, the kind of thing which calls for a reading, rather than for a hearing? (1970: 540–41)

While the wordplay in this scenario may have persuaded many of Ricoeur's readers—including Geertz—its rhetorical structure could hardly enjoy universal appeal. One has only to ask whether Ricoeur's play on words would make the same (or any) sense to one who is not of a literate culture to see the limitations of his argument. The following scenario from aboriginal Australia presents a case in point.

> Throughout North Queensland, the ear is believed to be the seat of intelligence, etc., through or by means of which the impressions of the outer world are conveyed to the inner. So, the natives of Tully River, when they first saw the whites communicate with each other by means of a letter, used, after looking at it, to put it up to their ears to see if they could understand anything by that method. (Chamberlain 1905: 126)

The Aborigines' response to the letter suggests that in North Queensland, "marks" on paper call for a hearing, rather than a reading. The Tully River people's epistemology is therefore the reverse of Paul Ricoeur's. The question they ask is: What corresponds to meaningful action in the field of writing?

The clash of epistemologies suggested by this juxtaposition of scenarios could be read as a reflection upon what it means to live on opposite sides of the "orality/literacy divide" (McLuhan 1962; Ong 1982; Goody 1986). As a member of a literate society, Ricoeur is inclined to equate intelligibility with legibility, and therefore tends to visualize as well as reify events—that is, to treat events as texts. As members of an oral society, the Tully River people are more inclined to equate intelligibility with audibility, and so attempt to listen to the letter—that is, treat the text as acoustically active.

It is instructive to reflect on the biases that the model of cultures "as texts" and the metaphor of "reading culture" smuggle into the interpretive process. Basically, the "reading culture" metaphor imparts both a visual and a verbal bias to any analysis. The visual bias stems from the ocularcentric character of the activity of reading. This bias means that the textual anthropologist (i.e., the anthropologist who relies on the metaphor of reading to order his or her experience of a culture) will tend to speculate, instead of participate. In addition to (unwittingly) positioning him- or herself as a voyeur, the textual anthropologist will have a strong tendency to reduce culture to spectacle.

Significantly, it is precisely on this latter point—the reduction of culture to spectacle—that Geertz's Balinese ethnography has been criticized most forcefully. In *Managing Turbulent Hearts*, for example, Unni Wikan argues that Geertz took the spectacle of Balinese social life at face value, that he failed to delve behind the mask of Balinese culture, and that this interpretive move prevented him from grasping the wealth of meaning and emotion that she herself claims to have discovered. Far from being a people lacking a self behind the mask, as portrayed by Geertz, the Balinese, on Wikan's account, have complex selves and never (or at best fleetingly) achieve the equipoise for which they are constantly striving.

As noted previously, the metaphor of reading also imparts a verbal bias to the interpretive process. The verbocentric character of the activity of reading means that the textual anthropologist will be predisposed to think of the people he or she studies as giving expression to the propositions of their "worldview" in their ritual and other activities. What the textual anthropologist fails to realize, however, is that not all knowledge need be verbalized (i.e., take the form of a proposition). Sometimes, especially in ritual contexts, understandings are deliberately left unsaid and instead communicated via the manipulation of multisensory objects, as Fredrik Barth found among the Baktaman of Papua New Guinea.

> When the Baktaman choose to cast their knowledge in a variety of simultaneous [sensory] channels and expressions, we should seek to understand its consequences and, if possible, its reason. A major explanation lies in the clear wish to *act* on the world and not just speak about it. (1975: 224)

Barth goes on to describe how the different sensory channels used in Baktaman rituals have "different potentials or strengths" with the result that the messages thereby communicated possess "different clarity and implications." It is obviously a matter of some importance not to gloss over such differences, but the textual anthropologist cannot help but offer glosses, and glosses of glosses, because of the verbocentrism of the hermeneutic method and the assumption that the business of anthropology is to keep on interpreting interpretations that are not our own.

The idea of "examining culture as an assemblage of texts" enjoyed a tremendous vogue in the 1970s, and still does. The older idea of cultures as "perceptual systems" nevertheless continued to exert some hold over the anthropological imagination. This resulted in the propagation of some very peculiar analytic metaphors, such as Alton Becker's (1979) notion of the "text-organ."

The notion of the text-organ combines the Geertzian idea of treating symbolic systems "as texts" with the German philosopher Ernst Cassirer's idea of symbolic systems as "organs of reality." According to Cassirer: "Symbolic forms are not imitations, but *organs of reality*, since it is solely by their agency that anything real becomes an object for intellectual apprehension, and as such is made visible to us" (quoted in Becker 1979: 2). Becker glosses this text as follows: "Here is another powerful metaphor, conceiving of symbolic systems as 'organs' of perception; not what we know and believe, but the means of knowing and believing."

Becker's invention of the text-organ may be seen as a quite logical solution to the epistemological conundrum created by the redefinition of the world as "the ensemble of references opened up by the texts" following in the tradition of Ricoeur (1970) and Geertz (1973). This redefinition paved the way for the imaginary text-organ to take over from the sense organs proper as the preferred (indeed, the only) means of knowing the world. The following passage from Becker's introduction to *The Imagination of Reality* illustrates how pervasive this substitution, or takeover, had become. Becker writes that to use the word *text* the way Geertz does when he writes "cultural forms can be treated as texts"

> is in form metaphoric, but perhaps *the idea goes beyond the metaphoric* in that a linguistic text, written or oral, may be *the same sort of thing* as a meal, a ritual dance, or a temple, to mention some of the non-linguistic texts described in these essays. And we can apply our ways of knowing about linguistic texts to these other sorts of symbolic constructions. (1979: 2; emphasis added)

Taking Leave of Our Senses

As this quotation attests, the idea of using language as a model for cultural analysis had made considerable progress since the 1950s when Mead and Métraux first suggested that the traditional cuisine of a people could be "*as* organized as a language." It never occurred to them that a meal should be considered "the same sort of thing" as a linguistic text. In the imagination of Becker and his contemporaries, by contrast, the image of the text had lost its status as metaphor. The menu had become reality, as it were.

From Reading Texts to Writing Culture

The passage from sensing to interpreting, which divided the anthropology of the 1950s and 1960s from that of the 1970s, led to a further transformation in the early 1980s: the passage from interpreting to dialoguing. Various terminological substitutions can be seen as marking this shift, such as the use of "storytelling" in place of "text" (Webster 1983), or the use of "negotiation" in place of "description," as in "ethnography [is located] in a process of dialogue where interlocutors actively negotiate a shared vision of reality" (Clifford 1988: 43). It was out of this substitution that "dialogical anthropology" was born.

The rise of dialogical anthropology should, in principle, have had the effect of calling anthropologists back to their senses, given the importance attached to "listening" instead of reading, "voices" instead of views, the "discursive situation," and so forth. In fact, however, the dialogical turn seems only to have further distanced many anthropologists from their senses and to have landed the discipline in the thoroughly postmodern predicament where, in the words of the foremost representative of postmodernism in anthropology, "perception has nothing to do with it" (Tyler 1986: 137). What Stephen Tyler means by "it" in this sentence is ethnographic writing. In other words, perception has nothing to do with writing culture.

Tyler could not have written this sentence lightly, for no scholar has plumbed the hegemony of vision more profoundly (on a linguistic level), nor come closer to evoking the spirit of orality (in writing), than he did in *The Unspeakable*. Tyler is truly a Nietzschean figure, a sensualist among the textualists. So what prompted him to write perception out of ethnography? Why, in the final analysis, did he feel compelled to banish the senses from anthropology?

Consider the following facts. The basic question with which any anthropologist writing now must grapple is, How am I to write with authority? Earlier generations of anthropologists had no problem with this question; they simply wrote. So did most anthropologists until the beginning of the 1980s. At that point a variety of texts appeared with titles like "Ethnographies as Texts" (Marcus and Cushman 1982), "On Ethnographic Authority" (Clifford [1983] 1988), and "Functionalists Write Too" (Boon 1983). While most anthropologists continued reading the old ethnographies for what they said (Malinowski as an authority *on* the Trobriand Islands), the authors of these new works started analyzing the older works (particularly Malinowski's) for the "rhetorical strategies" or "modes of authority" they deployed.

Thus did anthropology pass into a stage of "secondary textuality," as distinct from but continuous with the "primary textuality" of the 1970s.[7] That is, many ethnographers gave up the study of other cultures for that of other texts. As Marcus and Cushman put it in the manifesto that heralded the second textual revolution, "In this emergent situation, ethnographers read widely among new works for models, being interested as much, if not more, in styles of text construction as in their cultural analysis, both of which are difficult to separate in any case" (1982: 26). As this quotation attests, it no longer makes sense to try to distinguish between an author's theory of culture and that author's style of writing culture, for theory has become a question of style.

The styles of the new works have the appearance of being quite heterogeneous: some are written dialogically, others polyphonically; memoirs and confessions have become increasingly common, while the ethnographic monograph appears to be on its way out. Yet what above all distinguishes the new works or "experiments" (as they have been dubbed), and lends them unity relative to the so-called realist writings of the past, is that "in these experiments, reporting fieldwork experience is just one aspect of wide-ranging personal reflections" (Marcus and Cushman 1982: 26). This programmatic statement has a vaguely familiar ring; in fact, it sounds just like Rhoda Métraux's description of what an "appreciation" of a culture would look like. For Métraux, however, there was an important distinction to be drawn between offering an "appreciation" of another culture and an "understanding" of same, whereas for Marcus and Cushman there is no difference.

What is the reason for the heightened "self-reflexiveness" of the new works? The increased presence of "the I of the ethnographer" might seem to be inspired, or even necessitated, by the emphasis on dialogue, as opposed to "thick description." It takes two to dialogue: the "ethnographic I" and some "Other." Without discounting this suggestion, there are nevertheless two further explanations that merit consideration. First, the increased presence of the "I," and the greater importance attached to introspection, may be nothing more than an effect of the foregrounding of *writing* as a metaphor for ethnography, a metaphor that, to paraphrase Walter Ong, keeps throwing the practitioner's psyche back on itself (because writing and reading are fundamentally solitary activities) and thus fosters extreme forms of self-consciousness (Ong 1982: 69; see further Howes 1990b: 67–68).

Second, the heightened self-consciousness of the new works may be attributed to the general crisis in representation provoked by the overthrow of traditional canons of authority. As explained by James Clifford in "Partial Truths" (the introduction to *Writing Culture*):

> Many voices clamor for expression. Polyvocality was restrained and orchestrated in traditional ethnographies by giving to one voice a pervasive authorial function and to others the role of sources, "informants," to be quoted or paraphrased. [But once] dialogism and polyphony are recognized as modes of textual production, monophonic authority is questioned, revealed to be characteristic of a science that has claimed to *represent* cultures. (1986: 15)

Why is it so wrong to claim to "represent cultures" now? As far as can be told from "Partial Truths," the reasons are: first, that anthropologists are usually neither natives nor elected representatives; second, that to persist in such an endeavor would involve subscribing to "an ideology claiming transparency of representation and immediacy of experience" (i.e., a false ideology, presumably);

and, third, that "the proper referent of any account is not a represented 'world'; now it is specific instances of discourse" (Clifford 1986: 14).

It will be appreciated that the limiting of ethnography to reporting on "specific instances of discourse" involves a reduction in the scope of what once passed under this name—namely, supplementing interlocution with "participant *observation*," and always weighing which informant's version to "write up." Now, however, ethnographer and informant must be equally present in the text if a monograph is to conform to "the principle of dialogical textual production" (Clifford 1986: 14) or be consistent with the new emphasis on "the emergent and cooperative nature of textualization" (Tyler 1986: 127).

Just how "cooperative" or "dialogical" is the "process of textualization"? It is instructive to consider the famous cover illustration of *Writing Culture*. The caption to the photograph on the cover reads: "Stephen Tyler in the field." While Tyler might be in the field, he is certainly not of it. Rather, he is completely self-absorbed (hunched over his notepad, scribbling away, his informants—one of whom gazes over Tyler's shoulders—evidently quite bored). Is this what it means to be "self-reflexive"? Is this what subscribing to Clifford's principle of "dialogical textual production" entails? Whatever the case may be, the cover illustration certainly bears out another point made by Clifford (1986: 2): "No longer a marginal, or occulted dimension, writing has emerged as central to what anthropologists do both in the field and thereafter"—so central as to have displaced conversation!

It might seem that much ground had been covered in the period between the publication of the Balinese cockfight article and the appearance of *Writing Culture*. On the other hand, perhaps it is only the tablets that were turned. Was not the original idea, as Geertz put it, that "the culture of a people is an ensemble of texts, which the anthropologist strains to read over the shoulders of those to whom they properly belong"? Given that it is now the informant who gazes over the anthropologist's shoulders (as in the cover photograph of *Writing Culture*), it seems that the positions have indeed been reversed. Worryingly, the subjects of ethnography—or "informants" as they used to be called—appear to have been sidelined in the process. This in turn raises the issue of whether those original words of Geertz's should not be viewed as having sprung a trap, the "trap of the text," a trap that has effectively cut off anthropologists and anthropology from the world outside the text.

This is certainly the impression one is left with after reading Geertz's *Works and Lives: The Anthropologist as Author.* Contrary to its title, *Works and Lives* is not about the "lives" of Lévi-Strauss, Evans-Pritchard, Malinowski, or Ruth Benedict, all of whom it treats. Rather, it is about their literary styles, or as Geertz (1988: 21) puts it, the "theaters of language" they construct. The ethnographic realities these authors sought to recount, and the theories they sought to advance, have paled into *total* insignificance. *Works and Lives,* with its thesis that "the way of saying is the what of saying," is the most dramatic instance ever of literary involution in anthropology, or what could be called "the flight from theory to style" (Howes 1990b: 66). To accept its thesis is to fall into the same trap as Stephen Tyler, the trap of an all-encompasssing intertextuality.

Is there any way out of this trap? Perhaps, if we can but have the confidence to say "Wrong!" to the suggestion that ethnography "might be a kind of writing" (Geertz 1988: 1) and insist that our first task as anthropologists must be to keep "making sense" of cultures.

Antitext: Breaking Out of the Hermeneutic Circle

Let us take stock. We have seen how many early anthropologists were more interested in measuring the bodies and sensory capacities of their informants than in learning how the latter used their bodies and senses to create meaningful worlds. Then, in the anthropology of the 1950s and 1960s, the notion emerged that the world is the ensemble of images opened up by the interplay of the senses (as conditioned by culture). The sensualists and various of their contemporaries, such as Hall and Carpenter, believed that the best way to gain access to other cultural realities was through learning how to refine and recombine one's senses in new patterns. They emphasized the elaboration of techniques for the effacement of the self, such as Métraux's way of "being of two sensoria."

Then, in the early 1970s, the idea was introduced that "the world is the ensemble of references opened up by the texts," in Ricoeur's phrase. As this suggestion came to be practiced, the sense organs anthropologists had traditionally used to study cultures gradually atrophied and were replaced by the "text-organ." This development in turn paved the way for the literary involution of anthropology, or the flight from theory to style. Hence the situation in which we find ourselves today, a situation where it is no longer possible to separate an author's "style of text construction" from his or her "cultural analysis" (read: theoretical constructs), the latter having been completely absorbed into the former. In what Marcus and Cushman (1982) have called "the emergent situation," "the way of saying" is not only "the what of saying," it's all there is.

Is authority simply a question of style, as the secondary textualists argue so persuasively? Were the epistemological questions that the sensualists debated in their writings really nothing more than rhetorical strategies for convincing us that "what they say is a result of their having penetrated (or, if you prefer, been penetrated by) another form of life" (Geertz 1988: 4)? Whatever their limitations may have been—and there are many, such as their obliviousness to the politics of representation, their failure to problematize the internal sensory diversity of the cultures they studied, and their fantastic notions regarding their own abilities to assimilate other cultures whole (see below)—the sensualists *do* seem to have been better situated, or "sensitized," than ourselves for purposes of grasping other ways of life, and this for two reasons. First, writing before the textual revolution, their perceptions were not clouded by "the model of the text." Second, they were willing to let their interactions with informants take other directions than those dictated by the demands of textualization.

The much discussed "crisis" in anthropology is not just one of representation, as Marcus and Fischer (1986) claim, and the solution is not simply to adopt a more reflexive writing style. The crisis is still one of epistemology. Reflexivity always helps, of course, but perhaps we do not need to be more reflexive as anthropologists so much as we need to be more sensible. Being more sensible, we would be critical of the visual and verbal biases implicit in "the model of the text." For example, we would be conscious of the one factor Geertz overlooks in his discussions of how anthropologists get themselves "into print"—that factor being the *effects* of writing, print, and other such "extensions of the senses" (like tape recorders and video cameras) on consciousness itself.

Striving to be more sensible, we would also be more inclined to experiment with our bodies and senses, instead of simply toying with our writing styles. In "Resonance in Imagery," Rhoda Métraux gives some fascinating descriptions of how she and her contemporaries used their bodies and senses for cultural analysis:

> [One] anthropologist describes the process of assimilation [of another culture] as one in which he creates an "internal society" with "multiple voices" that carry on "multiple conversations" in his own mind. Another . . . seems in some way to ingest the culture so that, in effect, her own body becomes a living model of the culture on which she is working as well as the culture of which she is herself a member, and she continually tests out relationships in terms of her own bodily integration. And another describes the process as one of "receiving and sending kinesthetic sets, strengthened by auditory patterns—largely pitch, intonation and stress rather than words . . ." (1953: 361; see further Hall 1977: 175–87).

While cultivating the capacity of "being of two sensoria" had its problems, it was also often a source of profound insights.

Was the textual revolution a false turn? Do we need to go back to the anthropology of the mid–twentieth century to learn how to "make sense" of cultures again? In fact, there have been developments in the intervening years, stimulating developments. A number of anthropologists have seized on the importance of studying how the senses are socialized and how society and the cosmos are sensed. It is to their work that we shall turn next in an effort to break out of the hermeneutic circle and thus escape the trap of the text.

CHAPTER 2

Coming to Our Senses

The Sensual Turn in
Anthropological Understanding

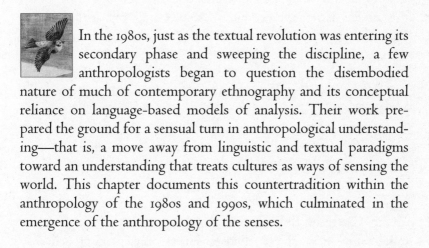In the 1980s, just as the textual revolution was entering its secondary phase and sweeping the discipline, a few anthropologists began to question the disembodied nature of much of contemporary ethnography and its conceptual reliance on language-based models of analysis. Their work prepared the ground for a sensual turn in anthropological understanding—that is, a move away from linguistic and textual paradigms toward an understanding that treats cultures as ways of sensing the world. This chapter documents this countertradition within the anthropology of the 1980s and 1990s, which culminated in the emergence of the anthropology of the senses.

The Body Relived and Revived

In the early 1980s, in a pair of seminal articles on the knowing body, Michael Jackson (1983a, 1983b) challenged the conventional manner in which the body had come to be understood within anthropology as, in his words, "simply the passive ground on which forms of social organization are inscribed" (1983b: 143). His main target was the work of Mary Douglas (1966, 1982). Douglas had elaborated her own decidedly Durkheimian paradigm for the study of body symbolism partly in conversation with certain analysts of a

Freudian persuasion. According to the latter, the problems that rituals involving bodily manipulation are intended to resolve are "personal" psychological problems, rooted in infantile sexual fantasies. For instance, rituals that center on the laceration of the penis may be seen as expressing male envy of female reproductive processes, such as menstruation (Bettelheim 1956).

In *Purity and Danger*, Douglas countered that insofar as such rites are public they demand a social explanation: "What is being carved in human flesh is an image of society." A little further on she states, "The rituals enact the form of social relations and in giving these relations visible expression they enable people to know their own society" (1966: 116, 128). Thus, according to Douglas, the body is a medium for the expression of the social; the social (including ritual) is not there simply to satisfy the impulses of the body. If, for example, a ritual expresses anxiety about the apertures of the body, this anxiety is not the product of some "oral" or "anal" fixation, but rather expresses the society's concern over the maintenance of its internal and external boundaries.

According to Jackson (1983a: 329), the way the body becomes an "it" in Douglas's scheme, a "sign" or "medium of communication" at the disposal of a "reified social rationality," is empirically untenable, for to construe bodies the way Douglas does contradicts our prior, individual experience of the body "as lived reality," or what Lawrence Kirmayer (1992) has called "the body's insistence on meaning." In classic Durkheimian fashion, Douglas has simply substituted "society" for "the mind" as knowing subject; while in classic Cartesian fashion, she continues to treat the body as unknowing inert object. Thus, while Douglas's approach may appear to be less superorganic than that of the textualists in light of her emphasis on the corporeal, when examined closely it turns out to be predicated on a denial of the somatic similar to that which results from privileging the linguistic.

In his own effort to overcome the mind/body dichotomy, Jackson elaborates what he calls a "non-dualistic" view of body metaphors. According to Jackson, body metaphors remain for the most part below the level of conscious awareness. In crisis situations, however, such metaphors are activated and reveal the "fundamental indivisibility" of word and action, mind and body. For instance, when our familiar environment is suddenly disrupted we feel "uprooted," "lose our footing," "fall," or are "thrown." The quotation marks here are misleading, in that the shock in such situations occurs simultaneously in body and in mind. That is, the "falling" is not something metaphorical derived from physical falling, for it goes to the "basic ontological structure of our Being-in-the-world":

> In this sense, uprightness of posture may be said to define a psychophysical relationship with the world, so that to lose this position, this "standing," is simultaneously a bodily and intellectual loss of balance ... Metaphors of falling and disequilibrium disclose the integral connexion of the psychic and the physical; they do not express a concept *in terms of* a bodily image. (1983a: 329)

As the preceding analysis suggests, it is possible to enrich our understanding of linguistic metaphors by examining how they are grounded in, or derive from, particular "experiential gestalts" (Lakoff and Johnson 1980). To achieve such an understanding, however, we must first abandon the notion of metaphor as a way of saying something "in terms of" something else, and recognize that metaphors in effect "disclose the identity of that which the intellect separates" (Jackson 1983b: 132).

Significantly, Jackson's approach foregrounds not "the" body, but relations *between* bodies. This shift of focus is given in his concept of the "unity of the body-mind-*habitus*" (after Bourdieu 1977; Jackson 1983a: 334). According to Jackson, patterns of body use cannot emerge but through *interaction* with other people and objects in an organized environment or *habitus,* and can only be understood in relation to that *habitus.* By way of illustration, he presents an analysis of how paths and pathway imagery figure in the *habitus* and discourse of the Songhay of Mali.

Jackson's account opens with a description of the physical structure of the Songhay village. The latter consists of a series of open spaces, each encircled by a cluster of thatched houses, which are interconnected by a labyrinth of lanes and narrow paths. He goes on to observe that, as in many African societies, the Songhay apply metaphors of pathways to social relationships. For example, the reason for giving a gift to an in-law may be expressed as: "So that the path between us does not die." The pathway metaphor is also applied to individual anatomy and physiology. Vital organs such as the heart and lungs are likened to crossroads where the "blood," "heat," and "breath" that move along the "pathways" of the body are concentrated and then diffused. Illness is signified as a blockage or reversal in the proper flow.

The tendency on the part of Douglas would be to regard the social body as projected onto or mirrored in the individual body by means of this imagery, so that the latter comes to serve as "a kind of linguistic analogue of social structure" (Jackson 1983b: 137). Jackson insists that it would be more accurate to regard this metaphorization of the body as a dialectical process of "reciprocal anthropomorphism." There is obviously an internalization of certain aspects of the social and material *habitus* taking place, in that the movement of goods along paths between people *becomes* the movement of vital substances along "pathways" internal to the body. However, this internalization would have no meaning, Jackson argues, were it not for "an externalization which has already occurred, in which the self through bodily movement in concrete situations [namely, social exchange] has discovered for itself an identity in relation to the immediate environment" (1983b: 137). What is more, there is a very real sense in which people's lives *depend* on the quality of the social relationships of exchange and cooperation "embodied" in the pathways that crisscross the village.

The principal way, therefore, in which Jackson's approach to the study of body symbolism differs from Douglas's has to do with his emphasis on the body in action and in relation to other bodies and the local environment (i.e., the emplacement of the body), rather than the structure and/or processes of the body as a model. This emphasis on the dynamic body follows from the premise that what is done with the body forms the ground of society "as lived."

How to Do Things without Words:
The Limits of Language

While Jackson's writing on the body goes further than most in its insistence on the unity of "body-mind-*habitus*,"[1] it goes even further in its emphasis on the autonomy of verbal and sensual (nonverbal) modes of thought and communication. According to Jackson, many things can be communicated through the body *without* having to make recourse to words. He illustrates this point through a discussion of the initiation rites of the Kuranko of Sierra Leone. Among the Kuranko, there is a marked tendency to "effect understanding" through bodily techniques rather than verbal elaboration.

> The value of moderation is inculcated through taboos on calling for food or referring to food whilst in the initiation lodge . . . Similarly, the importance placed on listening to elders during the period of sequestration is correlated with the virtue of respecting elders whose counsels guarantee social as well as physical life . . . Other senses are developed too, so that keenness of smell is correlated with the quality of discrimination (newly-initiated boys often quite literally "turn up their noses" at the sight of uninitiated kids, remarking on their crude smell), and control of the eyes is connected with sexual proprieties, most notably mindfulness of those domains and secret objects associated with the other sex which one may not see except on pain of death. (1983a: 337)

The purpose of Kuranko initiation rites is thus to teach the neophyte how to regulate perceptions in each of his senses. Through learning to use his senses in the approved manner, he develops a set of habitudes or dispositions that are consistent with the Kuranko moral order. It is through the cultivation of bodily awareness—the education of the senses—that ethical awareness is evolved. The ethical concepts do not come before the ways of sensing, however, they *are* the ways of sensing.

To elaborate on the last point, the meaning of the actions performed in Kuranko initiation rites is in their doing. These ritual acts do not "say something of something" the way Geertz, for example, makes the action of the Balinese cockfight *stand for* various abstract propositions about Balinese culture. According to Jackson, the Geertzian approach posits and seeks "truth at the level of disembodied concepts and decontextualized sayings" (1983a: 341). Such an approach is foreign to the way knowledge is constituted and communicated ritually in societies like that of the Kuranko, where bodily intelligence is privileged. Kuranko rituals are not texts to be read but rather *ways of sensing the world*, in which body and meaning, media and message, are intimately intertwined. According to Jackson, by taking what is done with the body as the touchstone of anthropological knowledge we can access that meaning in its integrity. By contrast, to deploy the model of the text would result in the meaning coming unhinged from the body (i.e., the message being divorced from the medium on which its meaning depends).

Complementing and at the same time nuancing Jackson's position on the relationship between the verbal and the sensual is Michael O'Hanlon's analysis of body adornment as a "system of communication" among the Wahgi of the Western Highlands of Papua New Guinea. There is no tradition of formal exegesis of the meaning of the individual elements of body adornment or overall structure of ceremonial display among the Wahgi. Indeed, there is a distinct "refusal to verbalize" on such matters, much as Anthony Forge (1970, 1979) found among the Abelam. However, while the Wahgi do not have much to say about the meaning of display, there *is* lots of "talk" about its sensory effects. In fact, it would appear on the basis of O'Hanlon's account that "talk" brackets display among the Wahgi: it both precedes and supersedes ritual events.

Let us begin by examining how talk precedes display. "Throwing talk into the open" is the Wahgi expression for the ritual confession of all the "hidden" acts of betrayal, theft, or adultery, and emotions of anger, that must take place before a display is mounted. If there is any holding back, if any moral breaches remain unexposed, the men's "skin" will not manifest the glistening, fiery, glowing appearance that is desired in display, but instead appear lustreless, dry, and flaky. A spectator may remark: "Go back again and talk and then we will see" (O'Hanlon 1989: 126–30).

What Wahgi display communicates is the state of moral relationships within and between clans. As a direct reflection of the state of these relations, display performs an "authentificatory role" vis-à-vis the exaggerated verbal claims made by the performing clan about its strength, numbers, solidarity, and so forth, and the rival accounts of other clans, which the Wahgi regard as equally dubious. The proof of adherence to moral codes is in the dazzling quality of the men's "skin," their appearance in performance. "A man whose skin glows has not transgressed," Wahgi say, and it is this quality that enables them to decide between conflicting verbal reports of a clan's unity and strength (O'Hanlon 1989: 138).

A Wahgi elder gives the following account of the effects of display.

> People dance *gol*. They begin inside the *geru* house fence. Then shouting *"Oooooo!"* they emerge. Neighbouring groups, hearing this, say "Let's go and see the *gol*." Sometimes the dancers appear ashy and dark. People say: "Their drums don't really thunder. The *gol* is a bad one and the dancers' skin poor." But sometimes the dancers' appearance is bright, like the sun at dawn when everything glitters, it's bright like that. When it's like that their singing is good, the thunder of their drums makes the ground tremble just like a plane does, and spectators say: "Their *gol* is really good. *Aiyao! Aiyao!* Look at them!" and cheer in approval. (O'Hanlon 1989: 111)

This description brings out nicely the sequence in which the senses of the audience are summoned to register the moral virtue and integrity of the performers: first hearing, then sight, then cheering/hearing/trembling (see further Nihill 2000).

For all the emphasis on the effects of display on the audience as proof of intragroup integrity in Wahgi culture, an element of indeterminacy remains. This brings us to the way "talk" not only precedes but also supersedes display.

> People may remain uncertain of their judgment [of whether a display is good or bad] until they hear it confirmed by others . . . I myself have been asked by participants, who seemed genuinely anxious to know what I thought, whether or not particular festive or martial displays were impressive. There seems to be a significant tendency here to devalue firsthand observation. Extra weight is given to others' evaluations precisely because their assessments have already proven their substantiality through being reported. (O'Hanlon 1989: 135)

Thus, final judgment is always deferred. There is, significantly, no institutional mechanism for reaching a consensus. Given the absence of a jury system, or anything like it, there is just "talk."

The work of Jackson and O'Hanlon is helpful with respect to clarifying the relationship between the verbal and the sensual, but neither theorist takes the further step of analyzing the culturally specific ways in which the senses are combined in performance—the interrelationships of the senses. Before turning to consider some examples of theorists who have taken this next step, I would like to signal how O'Hanlon's account of Wahgi discourse or "talk" differs from what the textualists have led us to expect. Contrary to the view that treats culture as the product of a dialogue between ethnographer and informant, Wahgi culture cannot be reduced to what people say. As is very clear from O'Hanlon's account, Wahgi discourse is embedded in a complex structure of mutually limiting and informing sensory registers of communication—visual, acoustic, kinaesthetic, and, yes, verbal. Were it not for O'Hanlon's description of this structure (the very structure that the dialogical anthropologist's "discursive model" would screen out), we would not be able to grasp the *sense*, the situatedness, of Wahgi "talk."

It is a curious fact that textual anthropologists, for all their concern with language and "discourse," rarely pay much attention to the *medium* of speech—namely, *sound*. "We take the sound of language for granted," writes Paul Stoller (1984: 569). This state of affairs is not surprising, given the way the "text-organ" takes the place of the sense organs proper within the textualist worldview, as discussed in the last chapter. (Words might as well be silent as far as the text-organ is concerned.) Steven Feld, in his work on the ear-minded culture of the Kaluli of the Southern Highlands of Papua New Guinea, provides a valuable exception to this tendency.

Coming from the discipline of ethnomusicology and being an accomplished musician himself (see Keil and Feld 1994: 1–50 for an account of Feld's intellectual biography), it might be expected that Feld would be particularly interested in sound and sound-making. His work is indeed about the play of sound among the Kaluli, but it is also about the interplay of the senses, or "iconity of style" as Feld puts it. As such, his work transcends the traditional sensory limitations of ethnomusicology.

In *Sound and Sentiment*, Feld describes how the Kaluli structure their perception of, and participation in, the natural and social world in terms of sound. Living in a dense tropical rainforest environment, views are few and far between. The Kaluli have, accordingly, developed acute spatial skills for audition, and they use these to advantage over vision to orient themselves in the forest. Indeed, the Kaluli have a sophisticated vocabulary for sounds. For instance, they distinguish verbally between sounds (mostly of birds) that are at ground level or above, near or far, and so forth (1982: 62, 144–50).

Feld discovered evidence of auditory imagery taking precedence over visual imagery in the Kaluli imaginary: "When presented with pictures [of birds] or specimens out of context, Kaluli tend to think of and imitate the sound, then to say the name of the bird" (1982: 72). Similarly, when asked direct questions including the name of a bird, Kaluli are inclined to say "It sounds like X" before they will offer "It looks like X." This is largely because the Kaluli hear birds much more often than they see them. But this practical detail should not deflect attention from the fact that the Kaluli are a society of birdlisteners, not birdwatchers.

The multiple levels of meaning the Kaluli project onto and detect in the sounds of their environment reflect the extent to which hearing is a field of productive specialization for them. Thus, at one level, bird sounds provide an index of the physical environment. For example, in addition to using them to reckon space or distance, the Kaluli employ them to reckon time and the weather (1984: 394). At a second level, the Kaluli differentiate and classify the various species of birds in their environment by reference to their calls. At a third level, bird sounds are perceived as the "voices" of the spirits of the dead. The spirit voice is referred to as the "inside" of the bird call (1991: 89). By tripling the meaning of what are for them the most salient sounds in their environment, the Kaluli have developed threefold hearing, as it were.[2]

The Kaluli privilege the aural over the visual in their ceremonial as well as everyday life, as appears from Feld's account of the *gisalo* ceremony. The *gisalo* is sung and danced by brilliantly attired men only at night, in the darkness of the longhouse. This staging is meant to evoke the melancholy image of a bird at a waterfall in the darkness of the forest.

In the dark house, as in the forest, it is hearing, not vision that is the dominant sensory mode. While the audience is aware of the motion, color and demeanor of the dancer, the nuances of meaning lie in the texts of the songs and the sounds of the voice, the instrumental pulse and the bodily motion. (1982: 180)

Ideally, this orchestration of the senses will have the effect of moving the whole audience to tears (see further Schieffelin 1976).

While they may be hierarchized in Kaluli culture, however, the senses are not segregated. Hearing is intimately related with sight and also with smell. Feld describes how the Kaluli experience of "the dense sensuality of evening darkness, with voices overlapping the misting light rains and insects and frogs of the nearby bush [is] sensually continuous with the smoky aromas that fires or resin torches release into the longhouse and diffuse out into the ever-moist night air" (1996: 99). Hearing and smell, indeed, share the same verb in the language of the Kaluli. Such intermingling of sensory experience informs not only the aesthetic appreciation of the environment, but also the organization of Kaluli society.

The spatial-acoustic metaphor of "lift-up-over-sounding" (*dulugu ganalan*), for example, is key to both sensory and social domains of Kaluli expression and experience. This sonic form is evoked by Feld as creating "a feeling of continuous layers, sequential but not linear . . . a spiraling, arching motion tumbling slightly forward, thinning, then thickening again" (Keil and Feld 1994: 115). It is the sound of a waterfall, or the ideal pulse of a drum; it is the sound of human voices over against a waterfall, or the sound of one performer's drum rising up over the others' and being overlapped in turn. "Lift-up-over-sounding" is also the pattern Kaluli adopt in their collective work: the tendency is for people to join in the work in "anarchistic synchrony," and never to pull together in unison, for that would not be consistent with the Kaluli ethos of egalitarianism and "cooperative and collaborative *autonomy*" (Feld 1988: 83–84). Among the Kaluli, therefore, musical style and social style correspond. Sound structure and social structure are intimately intertwined.

Interestingly, Kaluli body decoration and dance style may also be seen as informed by the sonic image of "lift-up-over-sounding." The latter motif is visually mirrored in the layers of possum fur, feathers, and palm streamers, as well as the alternating shiny/dull pattern of face paint, which the Kaluli wear on ceremonial occasions. "Lift-up-over-sounding" is kinaesthetically echoed in the bobbing movements of the dancers, which set the various layers of the costume into motion. "There is thus a visual/bodily/sonic textural densification in costume, dance, and sound that merges with a visual/bodily/sonic in-synch and out-of-phase sensation" (1988: 89–92). It is by means of the production and reproduction of this "in-synch and out-of-phase sensation" that Kaluli culture achieves its "groove," which is to say its feel, its integration.

Another ethnomusicologist who has transcended the conventional sensory bounds of her discipline is Marina Roseman (1991). *Healing Sounds from the Malaysian Rainforest* also makes a major contribution to the study of ethnomedicine, since among the Temiar, music and medicine are intrinsically connected: the prevailing form of medical practice is best characterized as "singing to heal."

Roseman describes how the Temiar conceive of persons as endowed with a set of four potentially detachable souls. These include an odor soul and a shadow soul, which create a kind of bubble around the person. This bubble must be respected by others on pain of illness in the event of boundaries being crossed or confused. Each person, like each animal, plant, and landform, is also thought to possess a head soul and a heart soul, or upper and lower soul as they are also called. During dreams, the head soul of the dreamer is believed to go out and meet with the unbound upper or lower soul of these other entities. The soul of the animal or plant may express a desire to become the dreamer's spirit guide. The spirit/medium relationship is confirmed by the spirit guide bestowing a "song" (a term also meaning "path, way") on the dreamer. When the latter sings this "song" in the context of a ceremonial performance, he or she becomes imbued with the spirit guide's voice, vision, and knowledge, and hence with the power to diagnose and treat illness.

"Soul loss" is the most commonly recognized form of illness among the Temiar. It is held to be caused by an excess of longing for communion with a given spirit entity. Treatment involves remodeling the patient's desires by intensifying and releasing them under the controlled conditions of a trance-dance. Such dances are constructed so as both to focus human longing on the spirits and to entice the spirits to descend and briefly take part in human affairs. The means used to attract the spirits include the sweet-scented flowers that are woven together to form an altar, the intensely seductive swaying motions of the dancers, and the sound of the bamboo tube stampers.

The beat of the bamboo stampers echoes and amplifies the rhythm of the cicada's call. This beat also corresponds to the rhythm of the human heart. The pulsating sound of the stampers, the cicada, and the human heart are all associated with states of longing in the Temiar imaginary. The rhythmic pulse of the stampers is intended to intensify and modulate the patient's heartbeat and by so doing bring the latter back within the fold of society. The whole of Temiar medicine is thus constructed on the notion that the emotions can be modulated through humanly controlled sound, and wayward souls recovered by spirit mediums literally beating and singing a path out of the forest for their patients.

As do Michael Jackson and Michael O'Hanlon, therefore, Steven Feld and Marina Roseman provide forceful ethnographic examples of how meanings are transmitted and experienced through sensual modes of communication and of how perceptual relations are also social relations, making culture a lived, multisensory experience. Where Feld and Roseman depart from Jackson and O'Hanlon is in their close attention to the specific dynamics of the relationships between the senses in both mundane and ritual contexts.

What Perception Has to Do with It:
The Anthropology of the Senses

In the previous chapter I referred to Stephen Tyler's 1986 declaration that "perception has nothing to do with it." In the late 1980s and early 1990s, a number of anthropologists—myself included—became increasingly convinced that perception has everything to do with it, the "it" being good ethnography. It is during this time that a theoretical justification and framework for elaborating a sensuous anthropology begins to be developed. In this project the anthropologists' own experience in the field, along with the writings of scholars such as Jackson and Feld and older works on perception, culture, and cognition from the 1960s, provide inspiration and conceptual tools.

In outlining the sensuous turn that occurred at this time I will first look at the writings of Paul Stoller and Nadia Seremetakis and then discuss my own approach to the anthropologial study of the senses, developed in collaboration with Constance Classen.

In his early studies of spirit possession among the Songhay of Niger, Paul Stoller became aware of the importance of hearing in Songhay cultural experience. One might say, indeed, that this awareness was thrust upon him when a Songhay sorcerer told him: "You *must* learn how to hear, or you will learn little about our ways" (1984: 560). Stoller's awakening to the significance of hearing among the Songhay led him to reflect, in a McLuhanesque fashion, on the importance of exploring the roles of different sensory *modes* of perception and not just focusing on the objects of perception. Stoller writes, in terms of sound:

> Most anthropologists use the sound of language or music as a means to gather information with which they "construct" the culture of the Other. We take the sound of language for granted. The Other, however, may consider language . . . as an embodiment of [the power of] sound. (1984: 569)

Stoller's initial insights regarding the role of sound and hearing in Songhay culture led him on to explore the symbolism of taste for the Songhay and thence to extrapolate on the ethnographic importance of attention to a wide range of sensory nuances. Stoller, together with Cheryl Olkes, notes, for example, that while food has long been a subject of anthropological study, taste has received comparatively little attention. In Songhay culture, social structures may be conveyed, manipulated, and embodied through the taste of food. The thickness and spiciness of the sauce with which food is served constitutes a measure of the closeness of the relationship between host and guest. In effect, the closer the connection, the blander and thinner the sauce. "Sauce makers, however, often scramble these expectations (serving thin sauces to guests and thick sauces to relatives) to express socially significant themes" (Stoller and Olkes 1990: 76). Playing on Geertz's notion of "thick description," Stoller and Olkes argue that to make their ethnographic descriptions truly thick, anthropologists should spice them with the sauce of sensuous observations (see also Stoller and Olkes 1987; Stoller 1989).

In his 1997 book *Sensuous Scholarship*, Stoller aims to "reawaken profoundly the scholar's body by demonstrating how the fusion of the intelligible and the sensible can be applied to scholarly practices and representations" (xv). The basic point of the book is that indigenous sensory modalities and models of understanding can provide a critique of abstract, Western systematizing epistemologies through confronting us with how knowledge and memory are embodied—experienced through the senses and the emotions.

Stoller describes, for example, how "cultural memories are embedded in the smells, sounds and sights of Songhay spirit possession ceremonies" (1997: 65). In these ceremonies the spirits of Songhay ancestors and of culturally significant others, such as neighboring Hausa and Europeans, are embodied by mediums. In order to interpret these ceremonies Stoller turns to Michael Taussig's theory of mimesis, according to which the capacity to mimic or copy allows one to embody, and to a certain degree master, the Other (Taussig 1993). By "possessing" the spirits of others in their own bodies, the Songhay attempt to take charge of their histories and memories of cultural contact and render them sensorially immediate and malleable.

A potential criticism of Stoller's work is that, while he speaks of the importance of fusing the intelligible and the sensible, or reason and the sensuous, he nonetheless tends to conceptualize them in terms of classic Western dualisms. Thus the concepts of "reason," "text," and "Western" are grouped together and opposed to those of "emotion," "body and senses," and "non-Western." These dualisms are further classified as "high" and "low": "histories 'from above' that are read, re-read, interpreted, and re-interpreted" and "histories 'from below' that are embodied in song, movement and the body" (Stoller 1997: xvi). It is difficult to ascertain to what extent Stoller is making critical use of these European dualisms and to what extent he is simply exporting them across cultures.

The fact that texts and writing have traditionally been associated with reason in Western culture, while the body is associated with the emotions, for example, does not mean that the text is intrinsically rational in nature or the body intrinsically irrational. These associations developed within the particular context of European history and therefore may not be valid in other cultural contexts. It is useful to consider here Constance Classen's study of "literacy as anti-culture" in the Andes (1991). Classen examines how, in indigenous Andean culture, writing (and, by extension, European historical accounts) is associated with savagery, sorcery, and the destruction of the earth by forces from the underworld. The dynamic sensory exchange deemed to be characteristic of Andean culture, by contrast, represents reason, civilization, and the integration of the earth with the upper world. Here Western textuality furnishes the history "from below," while Andean "embodiment" offers a history "from above."

In Stoller's ethnographic approach, reason and rationalism are, temporarily at least, bypassed or minimized in order to focus on the sensuous experience of his apprenticeship as a sorcerer. Yet, as Stoller himself learned through his examination of Songhay gustatory symbolism, sensuous experience is not opposed to reason, rather it is replete with logic and meaning, both personal and communal. Consequently, sensuous evocation is not just a way of enlivening ethnographic description, or of infusing scholarship with sensuality. It is an essential basis for exploring how peoples make sense of the world through perception.

Nadia Seremetakis's writing on the senses is also informed by a preoccupation with sensuous memory. Seremetakis's association of the senses with memory is apparently inspired by nostalgia for a pre–European Economic Community realm of sensory significance and integrity in Greece. She writes that "the vanishing of tastes, aromas, and textures [is] being writ large in contemporary European margins with the joint expansion and centralizations of EEC market rationalities" (1994: 3). She evokes, by way of contrast, the rich sensuality of her childhood visits with her rural Greek grandmother.

> The child, now living in the city, returns to visit the grandma in the country. The trip to the village to visit grandma was by train. ... Every station was identified with specific foods, their particular tastes and smells. ... The child travelled through substances

to reach grandma. . . . The child greets the grandma who has been surveying the road like a gatepost, and passes into her world through the smells and texture of her dress. (1994: 29)

While Seremetakis is eloquent on the subject of how sensory experiences bring people together and make life memorable within unique cultural contexts, she is less forthcoming about the particular social values they embody. What traditional morals, expectations, or roles are being conveyed through all the evocative smells, tastes, and textures Seremetakis remembers so vividly?

Seremetakis uses her own memories as a basis for reflecting on how personal and collective memories are encoded through sensuous artifacts in Greece. She argues, in fact, in favor of "an anthropology of the senses [that] is concerned with how intrinsic perceptual qualities of objects express their sensory history, and how this salience can motivate and animate their exchange and shared consumption" (1994: 134; see also Carp 1997). Her habit of describing artifacts as "express[ing] their sensory history" or "bear[ing] within them emotional and historical sedimentation" (1994: 7) creates a curious illusion of material culture as a realm of multisensory recording devices, with each artifact registering and relaying memories and histories. This illusion gives sensory history the static, reified qualitiy of the objects within which it is said to be contained. In fact, the "intrinsic perceptual qualities of objects" do *not* "express their sensory history." Objects may well be multisensory mnemonic devices. But the memories and meanings they evoke are always embodied within *persons* and are therefore always part of dynamic living processes.

Seremetakis's emphasis on memory locates the construction of sensory meaning only in the past. However, what gives objects their sensory meaning—and what may give them new meanings—is not just the memories we associate with them, but how we are experiencing them right now. Sensory signification is a continuing development, not a simple reliving of once-learned associations.

The major flaws in Seremetakis's approach are hence that she neglects to consider how sensory phenomena may function as social symbols apart from, or in association with, specific individual or collective memories (just as the color red, for example, may serve as a general symbol for danger), she tends to disembody sensory history by placing it within artifacts rather than within the people who interact with the artifacts, and she detracts from the importance of ongoing sensory experience by emphasizing perceptual recall. These flaws seem to be due in part to her desire to elaborate a particular writing style, an ethnographic poetics of the senses, that fosters an emphasis on image over content and on an evocative turn of phrase over conceptual clarity. Nonetheless, Seremetakis is to be credited with theorizing how an anthropology of the senses may be extended to material culture by linking perception, memory, and materiality in order to explore how we remember and relive our personal and shared histories through our sensuous experience of the material world. Indeed, any criticism of her or Stoller's pioneering works in the anthropology of the senses must be tempered by a profound appreciation of their groundbreaking efforts in the field.

I will conclude by discussing my own understanding of the anthropology of the senses with reference to work that is currently being undertaken in the field. Much attention has been paid in recent years to the hegemony of vision in Western culture and various twentieth-century counterreactions to visual domination, particularly among French intellectuals (Jay 1993; Levin 1993). Within anthropology, such works as Anna Grimshaw's *The Ethnographer's Eye,* Lucien Taylor's (ed.) *Visualizing Theory,* and David Tomas's *Transcultural Space and Transcultural Beings* have extended this tradition of reflection and critically interrogate the visual emphases of the anthropological endeavor. Grimshaw's work is particularly interesting for the reading it offers of various schools of thought in modern anthropology as "ways of seeing" that parallel moments in the development of modern cinema. However, anthropology should not be reduced to the eye of the beholder; more needs to be said about the alternatives to the Western gaze, the multisensory modes of constructing and experiencing the world that all cultures possess.[3]

Recent ethnographic work, much of it inspired by the call for a more sensible and at the same time sensuous anthropology, increasingly demonstrates the extent to which the so-called lower senses of smell, taste, and touch may participate in highly significant symbolic systems. Ethnographers such as Susan Rasmussen and Vishvajit Pandya, for example, have revealed the centrality of olfactory codes among the Tuareg of Niger and the Ongee of the Andaman Islands, respectively. Rasmussen writes:

> Social and ritual uses of scent in Tuareg culture reveal that aroma has referents transcending its physical qualities. Smelling is not simply a pleasurable or painful chemical experience, which may trigger memories and alter moods or behaviors; it is also a symbolic and moral phenomenon. (1999: 69)

Wary perhaps of the earlier racist implications of the Western interest in non-Western uses of smell, taste, and touch, scholars worry that any attempt to explore these sensory domains across cultures constitutes a marginalization or stereotyping of the Other (i.e., Marks 2000: 208; Ingold 2000: 252). Yet, when we divest ourselves of the Western prejudice against smell, taste, and touch as "animalistic" or "exotic," the fact that certain societies have complex olfactory or tactile codes no longer marks them as "primitive" or "exotic," but instead signals their "sophisticated cultural elaboration of a particular sensory domain" (Classen 1997: 405).

Perhaps the most powerful example of a society that codes every sensory quality with social meaning and transforms every flower, every animal, every artifact into a multisensory moral emblem and mnemonic device is the Desana of the Amazonian rain forest.

> The Desana believe . . . that sensory properties are not only, or even primarily, manifest in the world, but exist within the human brain. According to the Desana, the brain is made up of compartments which contain a variety of colors, odors, flavors, sounds, textures and other qualities, all of which have related moral concepts and which together produce a state of consciousness. The purpose of the material world, in fact, is thought by the Desana to be to serve as a reminder of these ideal sensory and social values stored within the brain. (Classen, Howes, and Synnott 1994: 122; see further Reichel-Dolmatoff 1981)

With the Desana, the whole environment becomes a field of sensory signs.

The Desana continuously see, hear, taste, touch, and smell their social and cosmic order all around them. Though rarely as explicitly elaborated as among the Desana, this is true in different ways and to different degrees of all peoples. Hence, it is only by attending to the ways in which *all* sensory phenomena may be culturally coded that one can have, and relate, a full-bodied experience of culture.

Even scholars working within such seemingly unisensorial fields as ethnomusicology or visual anthropology may benefit from broadening their sensory bounds. Among the Desana, the sounds of each musical instrument "will be associated with a color, temperature and odor, and be thought to convey a particular message to the brain by [their] vibrations" (Reichel-Dolmatoff cited in Classen 1993b: 133). At times, nonauditory aspects of music may even take precedence over the auditory. When undertaking a study of African music, Robert Kaufmann discovered that certain musical instruments were valued more for the ways in which they engaged the sense of touch than for the sounds they produced. Kaufmann concluded that the concept of music as exclusively auditory in nature "has been one of the principal stumbling blocks in Western attempts to understand African music" (1979: 252).

Kaufmann was alerted to the tactile aspects of African music only by the disconcerting fact that certain musical performances were scarcely audible, even to the performer. (The *mbira*, a musical mouth bow, for instance, produces intense vibrations within the mouth but only very soft external sounds.) With a background in the anthropology of the senses, ethnomusicologists would come to the field prepared to explore the potentially multisensory dimensions and associations of music.

However, it is not easy to cultivate such cross-sensory awareness, because one of the defining characteristics of modernity is the cultural separation of the senses into self-contained fields (chap. 1).[4] Susan Rasmussen tellingly notes that her initial fieldwork was compromised by her "tendency toward the compartmentalization of visual and oral from elements of taste and smell" (1999: 58).

The first lesson of the anthropology of the senses is that the senses operate in relation to each other in a continuous interplay of impressions and values. They are ordered in hierarchies of social importance and reordered according to changing circumstance. Thus, while sight was generally deemed to be the highest and most important of the senses in premodern Europe, within a religious context hearing—attending to the word of God—was often given primacy (Classen 2001: 356). The senses may be perceived as being in conflict with each other. Among the Tuareg, olfactory messages may contradict oral communications (Rasmussen 1999: 56). They may be perceived as working together. David Smith writes of the Canadian Dene that their "bush sensibility emphasizes paying attention to as many of the senses as one can, and, even more cogently, to all the senses as they interact to produce a unique level of awareness" (1998: 413). The dynamics of intersensory relationships are what make the sensory models employed by societies and individuals vital, interactive, and versatile.

Just as it has been customary in the West to compartmentalize the senses, it has also been customary to associate the senses and sensuality with only certain social domains, most notably aesthetics and sexuality. However, all domains of life—from social organization to exchange relations to ritual communication—are permeated with sensory practices and values, and all may be better understood by including these practices and values. This will be brought out in Part 2 of this book, which is dedicated to the study of social exchange as sensory exchange and the crossing of the senses in ritual communication in two Melanesian culture areas.

A good example of a field that has been greatly enhanced by a closer attention to sensory experience and meaning is the anthropology of medicine (Howes 1995; Classen and Howes 1998).[5] The importance of placing the body and the senses at the center of the social study of medicine has been emphasized by Robert Desjarlais, who grounds his investigation of the aesthetics of illness and healing in Nepal in the visceral experiences of the patient's body (1992). Two other particularly rich accounts in this context include Marina Roseman's moving book on the Temiar (1991) discussed earlier and Carol Laderman's breathtaking analysis of Malay shamanistic performance in *Taming the Wind of Desire*. Both Roseman and Laderman are critical of the tendency to treat the sensory dimensions of medical practice as purely aesthetic or ornamental and describe how music, odors, and dance are vital—indeed, integral—to the healing process in the Malay Peninsula (see further Laderman and Roseman 1996). Also noteworthy in this connection are Judith Farquhar's evocative account of the effectiveness of tastes as symbols in Chinese medicine (2002) and Adeline Masquelier's probing analysis of how "the unifying principle of sweetness" interrelates the contexts of alimentation, obstetrics, possession, and the excesses of consumerism among the Mawri of Niger (2001).

The emphasis placed on sensory experience by Desjarlais, Farquhar, Roseman, Laderman, and Masquelier is crucial, but it needs to be accompanied, as it is in their work, by an exploration of sensory meanings. The anthropology of the senses requires not just surface impressions of the sensuous features of a society—the savors of the local cuisine, the sounds of the marketplace—but an in-depth examination of their social significance (Howes 1991: 3–21). As Desjarlais notes in *Body and Emotion*, impressionistic descriptions do not explain "how cultural categories shape the form, tenor, or meaning of bodily experience" (1992: 37; see further Masquelier 2001: 227).

Indeed there are grave possibilities for misperceptions to arise when anthropologists rely solely on their own senses for an understanding of the sensory world of another people. Misgivings about this approach have been expressed by a number of contemporary anthropologists (see Hollan 2001: 57–58). Seremetakis wonders how it is possible for "desensitized" Western anthropologists to "perceive the senses of the cultural other" (1994: 125). Indeed, it is not possible without considerable sensory and cultural reorientation (Laderman 1994). If one has grown up in a society in which the sense of smell is little valued or trained, one cannot hope to suddenly be able to perceive all the complex olfactory nuances of another society simply because one has entered into another sensory and social environment. Even with the best of efforts, a Westerner may never be able to perceive all the olfactory signifiers distinguished by the Desana, for example, which include odors associated with age, diet, and emotional state (Reichel-Dolmatoff 1985). In these circumstances, anthropologists must elicit the sensory models of the people they are studying, and not just rely on their own bodily experiences—or worse, think they can derive grounding from the asocial, contextless models of "perceptual systems" proposed by Western philosophers (e.g., Merleau-Ponty 1962, 1964) and psychologists (e.g., Gibson 1966, 1979).[6]

An influential example from the turn of the twentieth century of this practice of trying to directly embody other life-styles involves the German explorer K. E. Ranke. Ranke attempted to duplicate in his own body the experience of life among the Bakaïri, an indigenous people of Brazil, by living and sensing the world as they did. The notion was that "if [an] anthropologist faithfully followed his subjects' way of life, he would serve as a one-person research instrument because he would literally think and feel as they did" (Kuklick 1998: 175; see also Richards 1998: 147–50). Ranke, however, found his attention to be so absorbed by the exigencies of daily life that he was no longer capable of aesthetic enjoyment or serious reflection. The apparent conclusion from this was that the Bakaïri similarly were so caught up with the sensory side of life that they had no opportunity to develop their mental capacities (Kuklick 1998: 175).

Ranke's practices of imitation had not been sufficient for him to penetrate how the intense sensuality of daily life, which seemed to his European frame of mind to exclude the possibility of meaningful thought, might itself be full of aesthetic and conceptual significance for the Bakaïri themselves.[7] Ranke's experience (which would seem to have involved a more corporeal immersion into the local life-style than that experienced by most anthropologists) indicates the importance of investigating the particular meanings and values diverse sensory phenomena hold for people. It is necessary, indeed, to reconceptualize the senses as *ways* of thinking and knowing before one can understand how a people like the Desana (about whom Ranke would probably have drawn similar conclusions to those he reached regarding the Bakaïri) can invest their sensory universe with complex theories concerning the nature of life and the functions of the human mind.

Though one speaks of "investing" the senses with meaning, in fact, perception and meaning become inseparable in cultural context. In *Inca Cosmology and the Human Body*, Constance Classen describes how the cosmology of the Incas was based on and experienced through the structure and functions of the human body. The Incas lived their cosmology—and ensured the continuing vitality of the cosmos—through a regime of sensory practices, from the harvest ritual of embodying the celestial passage of the sun through song, to the everyday practice of enacting the cosmic principle of integration through fluidity by sharing a drink (1993a). Such corporeal cosmologies remind us that the word *sense* in English contains the dual connotations of perception and meaning: to sense and to make sense may be one and the same.

As we have seen, anthropologists and other scholars have developed a range of theories concerning how people order their sensory perceptions. Perhaps the most prevalent notion in recent decades is that the visual domain will always be dominant across cultures. In support of this, it is customary to point to various neuropsychological evidence (e.g., nerve fiber counts) that appears to suggest that sight is the most informative of the senses (Jay 1993: 5–7) and to dismiss any suggestion that any other sense might rival vision in cultural importance as "exoticization" (Keesing 1997). In contrast to this view, one of the chief arguments of the anthropology of the senses has been that to focus on the visual is to ignore other vital sensory fields of cultural elaboration. Even when visual culture is at its most striking, more may be going on than meets the eye. Sally Ann Ness writes of public dance performances in the Philippines, for example, that while some aspects of dance are meant to be "nice to look at," others are meant to be felt by the performers (1992). The importance of these kinaesthetic experiences cannot be captured by the ethnographic eye. Similarly, analyzing the visual features of body decoration among the Ongee of the Andaman Islands will not reveal the crucial fact that the decorative clays are used by the Ongee to modulate the release of smell from their bodies and thus transmit personal olfactory messages to the spirits (Pandya 1993: 123).

In contrast to the visualist paradigm, there is another model that holds that anthropologists should turn their attention to nonvisual culture in non-Western societies. This model has several origins. One is the old notion that "primitive" cultures will make more use of the "lower" senses than they will of the "elevated" (read: civilized and civilizing) sense of sight (chap. 1). In the mid–twentieth century, McLuhan and his followers proposed that oral cultures would be less visually oriented than literate cultures because their dominant mode of communication, speech, depended on the sense of hearing. More recently, the reaction against the visualist emphasis of Western epistemology has led a number of anthropologists to turn their back on sight, as it were, and search for other sensuous ways of knowing.

While an "antivisualist" approach may well be useful for correcting the Western visual bias and discovering previously overlooked sensory codes, it nonetheless prejudices the results of the researcher by introducing a bias *against* sight. While non-Western cultures may not share the same visual worldview as the West, they still will have their own culturally significant elaborations of the sense of sight. Indeed, as Constance Classen has pointed out, even oral cultures may deem sight to be the most important avenue for knowledge, though their notions of the role and nature of sight may differ significantly from those prevalent in the West (1993b: 135–38).

A third Western model for the study of the senses is the "synaesthetic" one. This model has been put forward by Lawrence Sullivan in "Sound and Senses" as a multisensory alternative to the model of the text- and sight-based paradigms of analysis (1986; see also Isbell 1985). What attracts Sullivan about the model of synaesthesia—literally "the joining of the senses"—is its encompassing nature: "The symbolic experience of the unity of the senses enables a culture to entertain itself with the idea of the unity of meaning" (1986: 6).

Sullivan's synaesthetic model has similarities to Merleau-Ponty's philosophy of perception, according to which "the senses translate into each other without any need of an interpreter" (Merleau-Ponty 1962: 209). It is, however, more from information theory, and the way that theory has been received into anthropology through the work of Edmund Leach (1976) and others, that Sullivan derives his notion of the "unity of [sensory] meaning." According to information theory, a unique transmission of a single message through a single sensory channel might not be sufficient to get the message across. Communicating the same message through all the senses increases the likelihood of its reception, hence the multisensoriality of much ritual communication. "Although the receiver of a ritual message is picking up information through a variety of different sensory channels simultaneously, all these different sensations add up to just one message" (Leach 1976: 41; see likewise Lévi-Strauss 1969: 164).

However, what if there is more than one "message"? What if the messages are in conflict with each other, or the sensory channels are weighted differently? These questions do not interest the information theorist because of the latter's preoccupation with the unity of meaning. They do, nevertheless, concern the sensory anthropologist, who must attend to the divergences and hierarchies of sensory symbols in the culture under study, and not only to their integration.

The fourth, and perhaps most entrenched, paradigm for studying the senses holds that the senses have inherent, phenomenal properties that will determine how they will be understood and how they will structure information across cultures. Thus, for example, it is said that sight is intrinsically objectifying or linear or hegemonic, or that touch is inherently synthetic, proxemic, or nurturing, or that smell has a special connection with intuition or memory. Sometimes these associations are taken for granted, as when Stoller, for example, describes smells as "the strongest catalysts of memory" (1997: 85). Sometimes they are explicitly elaborated, as in the work of Walter Ong (1967, 1977).

It cannot be denied that the senses have certain inherent physical characteristics and that these characteristics will influence the ways in which they are used and understood by different peoples. The problem arises when certain sensory characteristics are identified as paramount and construed as *determining* the social role of the senses across cultures. Each sense has a broad range of characteristics that will be emphasized differently across cultures. Thus as Classen has noted, among the Tzotzil, who emphasize temperature, touch may be a distance sense, while among the Desana, who emphasize color, vision may be a synthetic sense (Classen 1993b: 121–38).

Furthermore, societies will have different theories concerning how the senses work and how they are divided or integrated. In premodern Europe, for example, sight was conceptualized as a "contact" sense, as it was believed that the eyes sent out rays that brought back seminal images from the objects with which they came into contact. The Cashinahua of Peru apparently distinguish three different forms of vision: "monomodal" sight, which is employed in everyday social life; "intermodal" sight, which interacts with smell and hearing and is activated through extrasocietal contact with spirits or on a hunt; and "synaesthetic" sight, which mingles the different senses and characterizes hallucinogenic visions. From the Cashinahua perspective, "each mode of vision constitutes a different relation to reality" (Keifenheim 1999: 32). To give an example from another sensory register, the Desana extend the sense of smell to the entire body. Among the Desana:

> The concept of odor is not limited to a purely sensorial experience, but includes what we might call an "air," or an ill-defined sensation of attraction, repulsion, or fear. The Desana state this quite clearly when they say that odors are perceived not only by the nose, but that they constitute an element of communication which somehow involves the whole body. (Reichel-Dolmatoff 1978: 271)

No Western theory of the senses, whether one uses Merleau-Ponty or Marshall McLuhan or Walter Benjamin or anyone else as one's guide, can substitute for or comprehend such culturally specific indigenous epistemologies.[8]

Along with being theorized differently, the senses also have different metaphorical associations across cultures. The sense or sensory phenomena that one society associates with reason, another may associate with sorcery, the sense that one society links with emotion, another will associate with cognition, and so on. These associations are actualized in the ways in which people employ their senses to think about and live in the world (Howes and Classen 1991; Classen 1997).

If we wish to understand the cultural formation of the senses in non-Western societies, therefore, it is not to Western theories and practices of the senses that we should turn, but to the theories and practices developed within the society under study. It may be unreasonable to hope that Western scholars in general will become more attentive to such alternative anatomies of the senses and epistemologies of perception as we shall be considering in this book, but anthropologists should at least make the attempt.

No matter how small and homogenous a society, there will be divergences from the dominant sensory model by individuals or groups within the society. Some of these differences may be institutionalized. For example, women may be understood to have different ways of sensing than men. In *The Color of Angels* Constance Classen examines how in the West women have traditionally been associated with the more "corporeal," "proximity" senses of taste, touch, and smell, and men with the more "rational," "distance" senses of sight and hearing. In terms of everyday practices, women were expected to concern themselves with sewing, cooking, cleaning, and child care at home, while men went out to hear and discourse, to see and "oversee" the world.[9]

Often, however, the differences are not institutionalized but arise from the different situations and experiences of members and groups within a society. While everyone belonging to a culture will be influenced by the dominant sensory model—or ensemble of sensory values and practices—not everyone will adhere to it. Alternative models may be elaborated that correspond to the particular experiences of the persons in question and challenge the dominant order (Howes and Classen 1991: 272–74). This is particularly true of large, heterogenous societies in which people with many different backgrounds and interests live together. Lisa Law, for example, has examined how Filipino domestic workers living in Hong Kong take over the heart of the city on Sundays and recover from the subtle forms of sensory acculturation that occur in Chinese homes by recreating the tastes, smells, and sounds of their homeland (2001).

These examples bring out another important point about the cultural formation of the senses. Sensory models not only affect how people perceive the world, they affect how they relate to each other: sensory relations are social relations. In his study of the Suyà of Brazil, Anthony Seeger describes how women and men are grouped by the Suyà into olfactory classes that reflect their social status.

> Odor characterizes the natural and the social worlds . . . Human beings are not all equally social. Men are socialized through initiation and lose their strong-smelling odor. Women, on the other hand, by their very sexuality are strong smelling. Old people are neither as fully social as adult men nor as sexually marked as young women, and old males and females are both pungent. (1981: 119)

Susan Rasmussen describes a similar use of odor symbolism to distinguish social groups among the Tuareg and also records how scents are exchanged among the Tuareg to promote social alliances (1999: 62–64; see also the analysis of "the odor of the other" in Classen 1993b). In her book on food and sex in postsocialist China, Judith Farquhar offers a stimulating exposition of how social relations are constructed through sensory relations in the context of the banquets that have become so important to the creation and maintenance of social relationships under the new entrepreneurial order (2002: 144–53).

The continual interplay between sensuality and sociality that one finds across cultures makes it essential for a sensuous anthropology to explore the social, as well as the conceptual, dimensions of perception. As anthropologists have traditionally concentrated on the study of non-Western societies, and as the anthropology of the senses wishes to free itself from Western textual or visual epistemes, it may seem logical that anthropologists interested in the senses should concern themselves with non-Western cultures. While, from a Western perspective, other societies may have the attraction of possessing radically different modes of perception that challenge, and seemingly fill the "gaps" in, the Western sensorium, Western societies themselves have complex sensory orders that also merit study. A great deal has been written on the role of sight in Western culture. Many other sensory domains, however, remain scarcely investigated. Yet, as Classen, Synnott, and myself demonstrated in our cultural history of smell, even the denigrated "lower" senses are elaborated into extensive symbolic systems in the West (Classen, Howes, and Synnott 1994). Much of this non-audiovisual sensory history has been suppressed or ignored in modernity. In his examination of the "cultural anaesthesia" produced by modern institutions and mass media, Allen Feldman speaks of "a vast secret museum of historical and sensory absence" that awaits exploration and analysis (1994: 104). Even aside from such "hidden histories," however, the very plurality of what we call the "West" ensures that there are a plethora of alternative sensory models flourishing within the intellectual home of anthropology. Anthropologists, therefore, do not have to go abroad to "come to their senses."

The purpose of this discussion has been to evoke something of the breadth and depth of the anthropology of the senses and to alert scholars interested in employing an anthropological approach to the study of the senses to the extraordinary potential for research in this area, as well as the most common theoretical and methodological traps in the field—some of which I myself have experienced and no doubt may be said not to have wholly extricated myself from.

What now of the end product of all this sensuous ethnographic investigation: the ethnographic text? Is this not an anticlimax, a pitiful reduction of multisensory experience to disembodied script, a final surrender to the vilified model of the text? Without doubt it is, to a large extent. Are there any alternatives? The primary one that has been proposed is film. The argument is that film is a more evocative medium than writing and better able to convey sensory impressions (Stoller 1997; Marks 2000: 210–23). I can see how this might be true in certain cases, for example, when trying to convey the dynamics of a dance. Yet it seems to me that, in a cinematic presentation of an olfactory ritual, the visual images would have a strong tendency to "overshadow" the aromatic evocations. Writing here has the advantage that no sensory data are directly presented by the medium itself (except, of course, for the visual nature of the printed word itself). This creates a kind of equality among the senses and makes it possible, for example, to describe an olfactory ritual primarily in terms of its aromatic elements.

In some cases, therefore, I feel that writing is more effective than film in conveying sensory imagery and experiences. Writing also allows readers to realize that they are at a distance from the culture being described, that they are learning about it secondhand. Film, by contrast, because of the immediacy of its visual and acoustic representations, may give viewers the mistaken impression that they are acquiring firsthand knowledge about the society depicted.

May we not go beyond graphic and audiovisual modes of representation and spray our audiences with perfumes (as Rasmussen [1999: 70] has suggested), or invite our colleagues to an ethnographic meal? This has a certain appeal (especially for anyone who has sat, suppressing yawns, through a long, dry slide presentation). We may even learn how this might be done from recent multisensorial projects in theater and art.[10]

This approach, however, has two evident drawbacks. The first is that to experience "proximity" sensations we need to be proxemic, and most of the dissemination of anthropological information takes place at a distance. This drawback may eventually be partially overcome by new technologies that will enable us to transmit sensations of smell and touch electronically (Geary 2002; Howes 2001). More serious, however, is the fact that anthropologists don't know how to communicate the kinds of things we want to communicate through smells and tastes and textures. We lack the necessary codes not to mention techniques. Any spraying of perfumes or sampling of foods, therefore, would still have to be accompanied by a more customary written or verbal exposition.

Perhaps this is not so bad. After all, one of the central tasks of the anthropologist has always been one of translation, translation into a means of communication that can be shared with other members of the academic community (and ideally also with the people one studies). This translation is inevitably imperfect, at times gravely so. Yet rather than try to change our modes of thought and media of communication and attempt to conceptualize the world through smell or touch, let us admit that there are dimensions of sensory knowledge that we (given our particular cultural backgrounds) cannot hope to dominate, which must remain foreign to us. Anthropologists are not masters of the sensory universe, we are travelers and guests.

PART 2

Melanesian Sensory Formations

CHAPTER 3

On the Pleasures of Fasting,
Appearing, and Being Heard
in the Massim World

 The Massim region of Papua New Guinea is known for the natural beauty of its volcanic islands, coral reefs, and emerald lagoons. It also has a reputation for being the site of the "Isles of Love"—a reputation based on Bronislaw Malinowski's depiction of the erotic beliefs and practices of the Trobriand Islanders in *The Sexual Life of Savages* and the reprise of this motif in Paul Theroux's *The Happy Isles of Oceania*.

Malinowski's enforced stay in the Trobriands, where he was interned as an enemy alien by the Australians during World War I, started the tradition of anthropological fieldwork. His immediate successors included Reo Fortune and Géza Róheim who conducted research on Dobu and Duau (southeast Normanby Island) respectively in the 1920s. Many generations of anthropologists have followed suit, making the Massim one of the most richly documented ethnographic areas in Melanesia. One thinks of the work of Michael Young on Goodenough Island, Debbora Battaglia on Sabarl, Martha Macintyre on Tubetube, Nancy Munn on Gawa, and Annette Weiner—along with numerous others—on the Trobriands. I myself was able to visit Dobu and Bwaiowa (southeastern Fergusson Island) briefly in 1990 and will be drawing on some of my own experiences in what follows.

The principal aim of this chapter and the next is to give a sensory analysis of the ceremonial exchange system known as the

"Kula Ring" from Malinowski's description of it in *Argonauts of the Western Pacific*. The kula embraces most, though not all, of the inhabited islands of the Massim (fig. 1).[1] Two sorts of valuables move against each other around the Ring: necklaces (*soulava* or *bagi*) and armshells (*mwali*). The former circulate clockwise, the latter counterclockwise. Every man of the kula (women do not generally participate) must therefore have at least two partners, one to his geographical right, from whom he receives necklaces in exchange for armshells, and one to his left—his "*mwali* man," as they say— from whom he gets armshells in return for necklaces.

The reason for concentrating on the Kula is that it is the most distinctive and the most widespread, hence representative, institution of Massim society. Ideas and practices, as well as valuables and other material resources, have diffused along its paths over the years. One effect of this is that the area of the Massim covered by the Kula possesses a degree of cultural unity that is not met with elsewhere in Papua New Guinea. The Kula may therefore be said to constitute an "encompassing framework" of Massim culture.

Of course, there is no such thing as Massim culture per se. The Trobriands, for example, traditionally formed "a cultural isolate—*hierarchical, non-cannibal,* and, surprisingly, '*ignorant of paternity,*'—in an ocean of largely egalitarian and, from the Trobriand view, dangerous neighbours"—*cannibals,* who, moreover, took delight in "proselytising of their *knowledge of paternity* to the Trobrianders, much to the latter's disgust" (Glass 1988: 57).[2] These differences should be borne in mind when reference is made to "the Massim" or "Massim culture" in the following discussion. As we shall see, however, the differences between the culture of the Trobriands and the other islands are not random, but form a system. The system to the differences permits us to analyze the area in terms of its unity. At the same time, it should be emphasized that the present analysis is based mainly on accounts pertaining to the island societies of Duau, Dobu, Bwaiowa, Gawa, and the Trobriands and can only be said to hold for these societies.

Throughout the area covered by this study, there is found the same organization into small, matrilineal exogamous landholding groups called *dala* in the north and east, *susu* in the west and south.

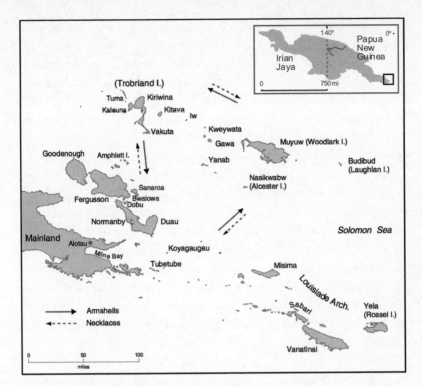

Fig. 1. Map of the Massim Region, Milne Bay Province. (Map by Derek Parent, based on Leach and Leach 1983, map 1, ix–xi.)

One key characteristic of this Massim form of social organization is the tension that exists between the individualization of the person or "expansion outward" of the self and the conservation of the resources of the group. Expansion outward, or "penetrating the matrilineal boundary that sets off the self from others," as Annette Weiner (1988: 159–61) defines this process, is accomplished through bestowing gifts on others and receiving gifts in turn. This giving represents a strain on the resources of the *dala* or *susu*. Nevertheless, the "fame" that the individual achieves through exchange reflects back on the matrilineage and makes the group's own fame "climb higher" too. As a result, it is generally the case that the individual is perceived as an extension of the group in the Massim world, rather than as standing in opposition to the group.

In Malinowski's posthumously published *Diary,* a recurrent theme is that of "the open, joyous, bright mood of the sea" and how this atmosphere contrasts with that of the jungle. The jungle is dark, "sultry, and saturated with a specific smell"—the smell of rotting vegetation—"which penetrates and drenches you like music" (1967: 95). Malinowski was attempting, by means of these lines, to "sketch a synthesis" of life in the Tropics. He found that land and sea are constitutive of two radically opposed modes of being. Being at sea is purifying and uplifting; being on land, one can never completely shake off the feeling of heaviness in the head and body, or escape the smell of things fermenting. While Malinowski never quite put it this way, one could say that the land/sea opposition is "good to feel," as well as to think. It is the fundamental axis of Massim existence. The experience of this axis is one of the most lasting impressions I retain of my 1990 voyage to Bwaiowa and Dobu.

At Budoya, Bwaiowa, the hills are alive with the sound of music, or once were. Maria von Trapp of *The Sound of Music* fame spent five years here attached to the Catholic mission in the late 1950s and early 1960s, together with her brother Johannes and sister Rosemary. She taught the Catholic converts of the area to sing hymns in various European languages. The words and melodies of these hymns are remembered, but the general opinion is that they no longer have the power to "awake" people the way they once did. In Maria's time, the Budoya choir always won the singing competitions against the Protestant choir from down the coast at Sala'mo. The Sala'mo choir was coached by Tongan missionaries, reputed to have the best voices in the Pacific, but they were no match for Maria and her choristers.

The way some people reminisced about Maria gave me the impression that they regarded the time of her being here as a kind of golden age of orality, now in process of disappearing. Words were becoming emptier, though of what it was difficult to say. Words were also becoming fewer. I once pointed to some plaited coconut leaves on an areca palm and asked what they were for. The leaves make the tree taboo, I was told, but they are "just a sign now . . . Our fathers used to speak into them." When bespelled, the twisted leaves had the power to inflict deadly diseases on anyone foolish enough to interfere with them. But the spells had fallen out of use and been forgotten.

Other spells are remembered, but no longer produce effects. Julia, a woman in her mid-thirties, apologized to me for not being able to raise the spirit of the hot spring at Dei'dei (half an hour's walk from Budoya) when we visited it one day: she knew the words for doing so, and we watched expectantly as she uttered them, but the water only bubbled instead of shooting skyward. The problem, apparently, had to do with her delivery, the way she pronounced the spell. In effect, her words were emptier of sound than the words of the previous generation.

My conversation with Julia recalled the talks I had had with other members of her age-group about the dwindling power of the songs they had been taught by Maria. It was as if a whole generation—the first to be taught to read and write, significantly—were undergoing some kind of "crisis of intonation." Yet this is to paint too somber a picture of a place where orality is surely thriving. Every night in Budoya one could hear people practicing songs and dances in preparation—six months ahead of time—for the inauguration of a new mission hospital on Goodenough. Everywhere I went I was asked to tell "stories" and was given things (a fresh coconut, a basket) in payment, as if stories were some kind of currency.

My talks with the men of Budoya and surrounding villages ranged over many subjects, most notably making *mona* (a men's dish, as it were, on which more in the next chapter) and kula exchange. The rules governing the exchange and classification of kula shells were explained to me with the aid of diagrams drawn in the sand and valuables produced for my admiring inspection. Knowledge of the kula appears to be stored visually, given the way the men spoke of "looking around" and "seeing" how the "roads" or "paths" (*keda*) of their partners connect with those of other men who were known to be in possession of shells of note, before "playing" their own *mwali* or *bagi*.

As the expression "playing a *mwali*," which is drawn from the language of playing cards, suggests, to kula is to gamble. There is always the danger of a shell being converted from its proper "path" onto some other track, for while there is a rule to the effect that a partner should receive a valuable of equivalent rank to the one he gave on an earlier occasion, there is no mechanism to enforce this rule. The field is therefore open for each of the men who goes out on a kula expedition to attempt to persuade his hosts to divert shells from their "rightful" path into his own hands. That is where the competition, passion, and intrigue of the kula come in.

The image that occurred to me from listening to my Bwaiowan friends talk was one of the kula as a highly intricate interisland switchboard, or electronic circuitry.[3] However, it is customary, following Malinowski, to picture the Kula as a Ring:

> Not even the most intelligent native has any clear idea of the Kula as a big, organised social construction . . . For the integral picture does not exist in his mind; he is in it, and cannot see the whole from the outside . . . [The] Ethnographer has to construct the picture of the big institution, very much as the physicist constructs his theory from the experimental data, which always have been within reach of everybody but which needed a consistent interpretation. (Malinowski 1961: 83–84)

There are some rather serious discrepancies, however, between the "big picture" that "the Ethnographer" managed to construct and the history of the institution that various anthropologists, most notably Martha Macintyre, have managed to reconstruct, based on oral histories and archival materials (these discrepancies will be dealt with in chap. 4). In the interim, kula with a small *k* will be used to signal that it is the indigenous conception and practice of kulaing as opposed to Malinowski's Kula that is being discussed.

One of Malinowski's aims in describing the Kula was to explode the myth of "Economic Man"—that is, the standard economistic view of human beings as acquisitive and rational or calculating by nature. If this view were correct, Malinowski (1961: 89, 167) asked, then why do we find people like the Trobrianders, living in tropical conditions where "there is a plenty of utilities," going to such lengths (and expense) to exchange these "long, thin red strings, and big, white worn-out objects, clumsy to sight and greasy to touch," which are of no utilitarian value whatsoever? The Trobriand custom of filling one's in-laws' storehouse with the better part of one's *own* yam harvest was another practice Malinowsi liked to cite to undermine the notion of "Economic Man."

Malinowski himself rationalized these practices by positing the existence of a "fundamental human impulse to display, to share, to bestow" (1961: 175). The "impulse to display" is manifest in the way yams, for example, are arranged in conical heaps in the gardens after they have been dug up, and again in front of the in-law's storehouse, before being put away. In like manner, a man typically loans his kula valuables to female relatives to wear on ceremonial occasions, rather than wear them himself.

Malinowski's discovery of a social system in which the motive for production is exchange rather than consumption, and capital accumulation is all but negated as a result of the stress on circulation, was a major find. Indeed, Western economists have yet to absorb all of the lessons to be learned from Massim economics. At the same time, few students of Massim society would any longer agree with Malinowski that "the love of give and take for its own sake" is what animates the kula, or any of the other spheres of Massim exchange. As Annette Weiner notes, what the kula is about is "not giving for the sake of giving, but creating own individual fame through the circulation of objects that accumulate the histories of their travels and the names of those who have possessed them" (1988: 9).

"Fame" in the language of the Trobriands, as in other Massim languages, is signified by the word *butu*, which also means "noise, sound." The circulation of kula objects is thus understood by Massim people themselves to be geared to the production and circulation of sound. This suggests that if we wish to understand the kula "from within," it is imperative that we train our ears on the analysis of this institution. Most studies to date have focused on the objects of kula exchange, not its sounds. These studies have yielded many important insights into the economic and social dimensions of kula exchange (for a review see Leach and Leach 1983), but they remain incomplete. As we shall see, the kula is a "total sensory phenomenon" in addition to being a "total social phenomenon" (Mauss 1966).

One point that should be noted before proceeding is that the kula is a predominantly masculine sphere of action. Women cook food for kula visitors, wear some of the valuables their men bring back on ceremonial occasions, and also compose and perform chants that celebrate the men's exploits. However, while women thus have an essential role to play in producing the social and sensory order of the kula, they remain in most cases excluded from exchanging valuables themselves.[4] This is a serious social and sensory handicap, for it is only by exchanging kula shells, and thus becoming the subject of speech, that a person acquires the lasting fame so valued in the Massim.

Eating and Being Seen

Food is not counted among the necessities of life in the cultures of the Massim, nor is it appreciated for its nutritional value: one eats because one wants to, not because one needs to (Malinowski 1929: 441; Macintyre 1987: 55.) If eating well has little to do with nutrition, it has even less to do with quality or taste. A good feast is one at which people eat "till we vomit," as they say—a case of quantity *over* quality (Malinowski 1961: 171; 1965 I: 216). An even better feast, from the perspective of a host, is one at which guests not only have their fill of yam, but also see how full the host's storehouse of yams remains *after* the feast is over. *The* image of abundance in the Massim is that of a village that gives off a rotten stench as a result of all the food that is permitted to rot in its storehouses (see Kahn 1986: 36; Munn 1986: 88; Weiner 1978: 179; Malinowski 1961: 169). It is not the food cooked for a feast but the food that rots despite a feast—the conspicuous decay over and above the conspicuous consumption—that hosts pride themselves on, and that is commemorated in song.

Hospitality in food is one of the mainstays of a man's reputation in the kula, and eating well is one of the main reasons for going on a kula expedition. At the same time, the activity of eating ranks lowest in the hierarchy of kula activities. The ordinary members of an expedition must subsist on their own provisions until the first kula gifts have been received, and the leaders (canoe owners) will not touch the local food until they have received their fill of valuables (Malinowski 1961: 230, 360; Munn 1986: 52). The agonism of exchange takes precedence over the pleasures of eating.

One of the synonyms for "feasting" in Western parlance is "breaking bread together." This phrase has many intimate emotional associations (e.g., of communion). In the Massim, these associations are inverted: the accent is on "breaking" rather than "togetherness." Feasting and commensalism are poles apart. In short, *food is for dividing, not consuming.* This point was brought home to me night after night during the time I spent on Dobu as the guest of a prominent family. Each night that I sat down at the table laid out for me by my hosts, I found myself stranded, facing away from everyone else, and having to strain over my shoulder to take part in a conversation where I had no place. The table could have been positioned another way, so that I faced my hosts (who took their meal seated on a low platform beneath their raised house), but they obviously did not want that. On Dobu, "eating is a single family affair. Visitors . . . may be given food, but if so they eat it apart with their backs turned to the givers" (Fortune 1963: 74–75).

Division takes even greater precedence over ingestion at a public gathering. Memorial and other feasts are "occasions for the *distribution* of food rather than the collective consumption of it," in that the guests customarily take their allotted portions home with them to eat (Macintyre 1987: 57; Malinowski 1961: 153; Bromilow 1929: 148). Similarly, the members of a kula party traditionally receive their food at their canoe (Malinowski 1929: 260).

The divisiveness of food in the Massim, which is another aspect of its being "for dividing," has impressed many Western observers. Annette Weiner (1988) describes how food taboos divide noble lineages from commoner lineages in the Trobriands and how jealously these taboos are guarded. Susan Montague (1983) was struck by how emphatically her Trobriand informants insisted that it is not the capacity to speak, but rather dietary differences, that divide animals from humans. Michael Young called his book on competitive food exchanges between clans and villages on Goodenough Island *Fighting with Food*. Géza Róheim, who carried out psychoanalytic research on Normanby, was impressed by how food appeared to divide parents from children. "Preventing shortage of food by spoiling children's appetites is a peculiar feature of Duau magic" (1950: 223). This magic involves slipping the children bespelled mushrooms, the effect of which is to make them never want to eat more than a little, however much food they may be offered. Similar kinds of appetite-suppressing magic are found throughout the Massim (Malinowski 1961: 169; Young 1983: 46, 56–58; Munn 1986: 85).

Malinowski records that "abstention from food is to them [the Trobrianders] a virtue and to be hungry, or even to have a sound appetite, is shameful" (1965 I: 227). Anecdotes from other islands such as Normanby (Róheim 1950: 181) suggest that this attitude toward hunger is widespread and deeply entrenched (compare Kahn 1986). There would appear to be three reasons why having a good appetite is cause for shame, and eating ranks lowest in what Nancy Munn (1986: 105) has called "the scale of self-constitution." All three have to do with the importance attached to "the work of expanding outward" in the Massim world (Weiner 1988: 161).

The first pertains to the way eating interferes with one's capacity for giving. The least productive way to dispose of one's food resources is to consume them oneself. It is considered better, in the sense of more "productive of value," as Nancy Munn (1986) would say, to use appetite-dulling magic on oneself and one's children so that the food remains available for distribution to overseas kula visitors. The advantage of this course of action, as a Gawa man explained to Munn, is that the visitors "will take away its noise . . . its fame . . . If we ourselves eat, there will be no noise, no fame, it will disappear . . . Gawa would have no kula shells" (1986: 49).

The second reason pertains to the kinaesthetic effects of eating. Eating makes the body heavy and slow. As the Gawa man quoted previously also pointed out, when people eat too much, all they want to do is crawl home, lie down, and go to sleep (Munn 1986: 49–50). The ideal bodily state is quite the opposite: it is one of lightweightness (buoyancy) and speed of motion, as exemplified in the dance, or better, the "precarious but delightful sensation" of lifting over the crest of the waves in an outrigger canoe as it flies over the surface of the sea (Malinowski 1961: 106–7; Scoditti 1983: 26). The bright, open space of the sea represents the dynamic pole of Massim modes of being in the world, and the dark, enclosed space of the house, the static pole (after Munn 1986: 105; Battaglia 1990: 30–32).[5] The preference is for the former because it contains the most possibilities for bodily surpassment—or expansion *outward*—as opposed to the contraction of bodily activity in sleep— and in particular, the sleep of surfeit. It bears remarking in this connection that Massim women are commonly supposed to dislike traveling by sea. As a result, women are associated with the "heaviness" of being on land. This association is reflected in the belief that a woman should not touch or even glance at a canoe before it is launched, or she will cause it to be heavy and slow (Bromilow 1929: 145; Chowning 1960).

The third reason eating ranks lowest in the hierarchy of kula activities has to do with the visual effects of food consumption. There is an antithetical relationship between eating fully and appearing beautifully, but this does not have anything to do with being overweight, as might be supposed. It is not the bulk but the surface of the body that is of primary concern. Consider the following discourse on body aesthetics, recorded by Malinowski in the Trobriands.

> Here [in the Trobriands] we are ugly; we eat bad fish, bad food; our faces remain ugly. We want to sail to Dobu [to kula]; we keep taboos, we don't eat bad food. We go to Sarubwoyna [beach]; we wash; we charm the leaves of *silasila;* we charm the coconut; we *putuma* (anoint ourselves); we make our red paint and black paint; we put in our fine-smelling *vana* (herb ornament in armlets); we arrive in Dobu beautiful looking. Our partner looks at us, sees our faces are beautiful; he throws the *vaygu'a* [valuables] at us. (1961: 336)

Note how observing the food taboos is mentioned before any of the acts of self-decoration, such as washing the body or applying face paint. The combined effect of these acts is supposed to be that the Dobuan host "sees our faces are beautiful" and "throws" the desired armshells or necklaces at the visitors. The implication is that were the Trobrianders not to keep the food taboos, their faces would "remain ugly," that the ablutions and so on would make no difference to their appearance.

The washing and scrubbing is to remove the "hiding darkness" or dirt from the body; this act is sometimes followed by stroking the skin with mother-of-pearl shell to "smooth out, improve, whiten" in the words of a Trobriand beauty spell (Malinowski 1929: 219–20, 354–55; Weiner 1988: 69). The oiling and painting are meant to give a further, "expansive quality of sharp brilliance to the body that intensifies visibility and presence" (Munn 1986: 98). This complex of ideas is nicely expressed in the words of a Dobuan kula spell, uttered while the ritualist stands in the sea, alone, striking himself with the fine-scented leaves of a plant that is also used in love magic.

> Dawn over Woodlark Island, the sun casting off its
>   coating of night
> your breaking forth from covering as the sun breaking
>   forth from darkness
> my breaking forth from covering as the sun breaking
>   forth from darkness
> your fine skin breaking forth from the evil peeling
>   from your body
> my fine skin breaking forth from the evil peeling
>   from my body.

(Fortune 1963: 230)

By means of this spell, the ritualist seeks to identify himself with Kasabwaibwaileta, whence the references to "your breaking forth." Kasabwaibwaileta is a mythical figure who attracted prodigious amounts of wealth and women as a result of being able to slough off his old, wrinkled, peeling, ulcer-ridden skin and appear as a radiant youth (Fortune 1963: 230; Róheim 1950: 184–86; Malinowski 1961: 322–26; 1929: 290–91; Young 1987). This rite invoking the complicity of Kasabwaibwaileta is the last magic the Dobuan performs before going to meet his Trobriand kula partner.

The notion of beautification as involving an expansion of the surface of the body, or its extension in light, also finds expression in the following love magic spell from the Trobriands, uttered while the ritualist scrubs himself with leaves:

> Beautiful will my face remain,
> Flashing will my face remain,
> Buoyant will my face remain!
> No more it is my face,
> My face is as the full moon.

(Malinowski 1929: 366)

The implication of this and the preceding spell is that ugliness is only skin-deep. It can always be rubbed off to expose the light from the inside, which radiates like the sun at dawn, or the moon when it is full—an effect that is further enhanced by the application of brightening substances like coconut oil and paint. For the decorative process to yield this effect, however, those doing the decorating, as well as those decorated, must not eat. In some cases it is prohibited to eat anything at all for a prescribed period, in others it is only necessary to avoid eating certain foods (Munn 1986: 97–98, 101–3; Malinowski 1961: 360). In either case, consumption is *limited*. If these taboos are broken, the decorated person (or object, such as a prowboard) will present a "blunt" and "dull" appearance, instead of the "piercing" and "shiny" one that is desired (see Munn 1986: 97–98; 1977: 48; Scoditti 1982: 82–84).

The reason food consumption is thought to dull body decoration is that eating is an act of *interiorization*, associated with sluggishness and the darkness of the inside of the house. Kula, beauty, and love magic are aimed at the *exteriorization* of the person, which is accomplished by peeling or scrubbing off the body's coating of "hiding darkness" and extending the body in light, making it "buoyant" (Munn 1986: 89–94, 99–101). Seeing the flashing body and face of the kula visitor is supposed to make the host's senses swim, or "move his mind," as the expression throughout the Massim goes, and "loosen" his grip on the valuables he holds, so that he relinquishes them (Munn 1983: 278, 284–86; Macintyre 1983: 25). It is for this reason that the act of appearing or "being seen" ranks higher than the act of eating in the hierarchy of kula activities, and no self-respecting leader of a kula expedition will touch the local food until he has attained his fill of valuables.

Fragrant Sight

There is more to body decoration in the Massim than meets the eye. Virtually every act of self-decoration extends the body through the medium of smell as well as light, since all of the local cosmetic substances (the native pigments and oils) are either naturally fragrant or are made aromatic (Malinowski 1929: 296–97; Weiner

1988: 69). What is the role of odorizing (and deodorizing) practices in the hierarchy of kula activities, and of smell in the scale of sensing?

Massim attitudes toward smell are complex and deserve a chapter unto themselves (chap. 7). For purposes of sorting out where being in good odor fits within the hierarchy of kula activities, however, we can proceed by studying the corpus of Trobriand love-magic rites. This apparent detour is justified by the fact that the structure of love magic is identical to that of kula magic, and its study will therefore assist us in the larger task of this chapter. In essence, there is an order of progression to the corpus of love-magic rites, which in turn sheds light on the sensory order. The following account of Trobriand love magic is presented from a masculine standpoint, since that is the only one Malinowski bothered to describe. It should be emphasized, however, that women and men are equally versed in the spells and draw on the same corpus of rites.

The most common (and least potent) rite for purposes of ensnaring another's affections involves the ritualist washing himself in the sea and scrubbing himself with leaves. In this way, he deodorizes and at the same time lightens his skin. As he throws the leaves away, he chants: "Dream-spell of my charm, go and effectively influence the eye of So-and-so." Ideally, the desired one will come to dream of the magic-maker, with his "flashing," "full-moon" face (Malinowski 1929: 366–67).

The next rite in the corpus involves offering the loved one a charmed betel nut or token piece of food. Such gifts are never refused. Betel, in particular, is enjoyed for the way it freshens the breath and reddens the mouth, not to mention its mildly intoxicating effects. The spell that goes along with this gesture refers to "the faces of my companions and rivals" being "cast off," while the image of the ritualist's own face takes their place in the woman's "belly" (seat of the emotions) (Malinowski 1929: 368; Weiner 1988: 70–71).

If neither of these rites should work, or even if they do, the magic maker proceeds to the final solution. This rite, the most potent of the lot, involves uttering a spell over a mint plant (*sulumwoya*) boiled in coconut oil, stealing into the woman's house at night, and spilling the oil of mint under her nostrils. Alternatively, the ritualist may use the occasion of a dance to flick or rub some oil on her breasts. Either way, *sulumwoya* gives "a full and undivided sway" over the loved one's eye, her mind, and her emotions, which is why this rite is the culminating act of love magic (Malinowski 1929: 371).

One of Malinowski's informants boasted to him that "I am ugly, my face is not good-looking. But I have magic and therefore all women like me" (1929: 375). There is an apparent contradiction here: if the magic does not change the ritualist's features, then how can the desired one come to perceive him as beautiful and be attracted to him? How is the effectiveness of love magic to be explained?

Malinowski himself suggested that love magic works as a confidence-booster. He also pointed to the apparent progression from reliance on the "ethereal medium" of dreams in the first spell to rites involving increasingly direct physical contact (proffering the betel nut, spilling the oil), so that the suitor's intentions actually become known to the desired one, which would obviously have helped to communicate them (1929: 368, 374–76).

Malinowski's ostensibly practical, commonsense explanation does not do justice to the intricacy of Trobriand sensory symbolism. When the sequence of rites is examined from an indigenous standpoint, it emerges that the progression is not simply from dream to physical contact, but from practices centering on the elimination of dirt and body odor in the first rite, through the mastication of some substance in the second, to impregnation with odor in the third. Moreover, each rite involves a progressively deeper penetration of the desired one's consciousness.

Thus, the first rite clears the way for the extension of the ritualist's face in light—his face becomes "as the full moon" or "as a bud of the white lily," to quote from the spell—and takes possession of the woman's eye. The reason this rite is considered the least potent of the three seems connected to the fact that it does not make the ritualist's face a fragrant sight. The leaves used in washing magic are selected for their smoothness and sponginess, not their odoriferousness (Malinowski 1929: 365–66). The washing ritual (unlike the next two rites) thus helps smooth the magician's image, but does not odorize it. At the same time, it is better to be in no odor than to be in bad odor (i.e., to smell of perspiration), so the ritual is deemed to have some positive effect on the desired one's image of the magic-maker.

The second rite uses the medium of food, while the third rite works through the medium of smell. The former takes control of the woman's belly, while the latter takes possession of *all* her faculties. This may be interpreted as evidence of the primacy of olfaction over gustation (i.e., smell is considered a more effective medium than food for working magic).[6] At the same time, vision would appear to be considered superior to olfaction insofar as it is the loved one's *eye* or visual imagination, not her olfactory imagination, that is the ultimate target of the rites.

Summing up, it appears that while love magic no doubt boosts confidence, and physically confronting the desired one probably helps make amorous intentions known, it is not for these reasons that it is presumed to be effective by the Trobrianders. Love magic works primarily on the principle of smell. Each rite in the sequence results in the suitor being *imagined or seen in a different odor* by the desired one, and each new odor is better than the last. The result of the first rite, for example, is that the image the suitor projects has a clean odor, which is better than the filthy smell that might otherwise coat his body. The result of the second rite is that the desired one comes to associate the sight of the suitor with a fresh, invigorating scent—the scent of the betel nut he has given her, which she chews while gazing upon him. The result of the third rite is that the suitor's image comes to be imbued with the odor of mint in the desired one's consciousness, in wakefulness as in sleep, and *nothing* carries so many erotic associations as the scent of mint (on which more in chapter 7).[7]

It will be noted that in each of these rites, smell both complements sight and is transposed or transmuted into sight, for the smell provokes a "vision." This observation helps clear up the mystery of how Malinowski's ugly-faced informant was yet able to attract so many women: he knew how to smell beautifully, and thus appear visually handsome.

The translation of one sense into another—a scrubbing into a smell (or absence of smell), a scent into a sight—appears to follow a pattern. Studying this pattern of sensory transposition gives us access to the conventional structure of intersensory relations in the

Massim world. We saw earlier how not eating certain foods is supposed to translate into greater bodily mobility and brighter body decorations—that is, increased visibility and presence, or the "expansion outward" of the individual. Cleansing and odorizing the body also contributes to the intensification and expansion of a person's presence through diffusing a pleasing aroma. What is more, we find the same tendency to "visualize" the effects of such practices as in the case of fasting: on Kitawa (eastern Trobriands), for example, to be in good odor is to have a "shiny aroma" (Scoditti 1983: 269).

The preceding analysis suggests that being seen and being in good odor are very close in the hierarchy of kula activities as in the Massim scale of sensing. Nevertheless, vision takes pride of place, insofar as it is normally in the visual field that the effects of odorizing or deodorizing the body are described as registering, rather than the reverse.

Being the Talk of the Kula: Attaining Thunderdom

A "man of influence" (big man, chief) will pride himself on the fact that there are islands where people have "never seen my face, but they know my name" (Weiner 1988: 143; Munn 1986: 106). Such renown stems from the circulation of the man's name in connection with the shells of note, also distinguished by name, that have passed through his possession. This brings us to the aural dimension of kula exchange, a dimension that is regarded by Massim people themselves as more extensive than the olfactory or visual dimensions, and that has been the subject of greater symbolic elaboration. The reason for this greater elaboration seems to be that there are no geographic limits to the distance at which a person's name can be spoken, whereas there are limits to the distance at which a person can be seen, or scented.

The acoustics of kulaing are best broached by examining the steps involved in attaining kula stardom—or perhaps "thunderdom" would be a better word, since the process is actually one of becoming a name with no face, quite different from "stardom" as we know it in the West. This metaphor is suggested by the closing lines of a Trobriand kula spell: "my fame is like thunder / my treading is like earthquake" (Malinowski 1961: 199). These words encapsulate the aspiration of *every* man of the kula.

The handsome young man of the kula, who is just starting out, pays much attention to his body decoration. He goes places to be seen, but more importantly to "listen." "Listening" is a more productive activity than being seen in two ways. First, by appearing to "listen" and lending assistance to his sponsor (father or mother's brother), the youth becomes known to the latter's partners as trustworthy and dependable, and therefore stands in better stead of inheriting the older man's kula paths. Second, it is only by "listening" to the discourses of more senior men that the youth can acquire the knowledge of the names, transaction histories, and current locations of shells, as well as the speaking skills necessary to obtain shells. As Munn (1986: 51) states: "kula activities proper are centered in speech."

"Kula speech" includes discourse about the identities and locations of shells, and the rhetorical skills necessary for persuading partners to relinquish shells. A "man of influence," or "big man," is one who has mastered this speech and thereby established himself as a "name"—that is, one "to whom others should 'listen' . . . or to whose requests they may be influenced to 'agree'" (Munn 1983: 277; Montague 1983: 42). A man's name, in this sense, condenses all of the acts of persuasion he has accomplished in the course of his kula career. Junior men feel themselves to be lacking a name. Indeed, the problem for the junior man is precisely that he is a face with no name. His aspiration is to become a name with no face. He wants to grow out of being seen and into being talked about or heard. That is the trajectory of thunderdom.

The successful kula career involves a progression from the realm of sight to that of sound. This hierarchization of the sensory qualities of the person is manifest in other ways as well. Consider, for example, the names of the categories into which shells are classified, as recorded by Shirley Campbell (1983) on Vakuta, southern Trobriands.

On Vakuta, the highest standard or class of necklaces is called Bagiriku: *riku* means "earthquake" or "to shake." It is said that when a man hears the name of a valuable belonging to this category, his body will "shake with desire." The second highest class is called Bagidou: *dou* means "to call, to beckon." Necklaces of this category are said to "call" armshells to them. The name of the highest class of armshells, Mwarikau, contains a reference to "blindness" (*kau*), which Campbell interprets as connoting age, in that failing sight is culturally associated with advanced age. The second highest category of armshells is called Mwaributu: *butu* means "noise, sound," and "news, rumor"—hence "fame."

All valuables belonging to the previously mentioned classes are distinguished by the fact that they possess individual names and individual histories, in addition to the requisite tactile and visual qualities (diameter or length, smoothness, color, etc.). It is striking that the names of these categories make no reference to the latter qualities: rather, the references in the names are all to the sonorous and motile qualities, or acoustic and kinetic *effects* that the valuables are deemed to produce. The aural bias of this classificatory schema is also manifest in the way the name of the highest class of armshells (Mwarikau) contains a reference to blindness—that is, it encodes the progression from the visual to the aural that comes with age. This non- or antivisual reference is also consistent with the way such valuables would be heard about more than they would ever be seen, because they move so slowly around the kula circuit.

Bwibwi is the term used to denote the range of shell appendages or attachments, such as trade beads, seeds, other types of shells, and bits of plastic or tin (fig. 2). These attachments indicate the status and classification of a shell; for example, five cowrie shells attached to the lip of an armshell signify that it belongs to the Mwarikau category. According to Campbell (1983: 234), the attachments indicate status but do not add to it: they are "mere decorations." This is an unfortunate choice of words. Things that look to be merely decorative are typically packed with symbolic significance in the Massim. For example, the sensory qualities of the media used to decorate or "extend" a person's body are not only indicative but *constitutive* of the value of that person. That the same goes for shell decor becomes apparent when we examine the sensory effects produced by the attachments. Basically, the appendages serve to extend the boundaries of the valuable by virtue of their mobility and the way they make a chiming or tinkling noise. It is fitting that the attachments enlarge the body of the shell, extending it outward in space, given the connection between beautification and exteriorization that was noted earlier. It is also fitting that they impart motion

Fig. 2.   Kula valuables. (Drawing by George Classen.)

(specifically a trembling motion) to the shell, since the essence of a valuable lies in its mobility—its being for transmission. The main function of the attachments, however, is to "signify success in kula exchange through sound" (Campbell 1983: 234; Munn 1986: 114), hence the significance of the tinkling sound they make. This function is particularly evident on Vakuta, where kula exchange takes place mostly at night. The man who has just won a valuable has a friend carry it off to the beach. "In response to the [chiming] sound of *bwibwi,* villagers will call from the dark to inquire for whom the carrier walks" (Campbell 1983: 236). News spreads quickly, and soon the man's name and that of the valuable are on everybody's lips.

The sound of the *bwibwi* chiming is the first ramification of the success of the man who has just won a valuable on the kula exchange. The news is relayed by various creatures, such as the Monitor Lizard, who trumpets on the island of Tewara (off Dobu). "The women staying at home [on Dobu] hear the sound and send round word that their men folk have secured valuables" (Fortune 1963: 221). It is much the same in the Trobriands: returning home from Dobu, the kula voyagers' waiting kin "profess to hear thunder roar and feel the ground shake—nature's witness to the success of the voyage and the spreading fame of the men" (Weiner 1988: 139). Upon the men's safe arrival home, songs are composed and performed by the women to commemorate the successful expedition. In the context of these performances, women, rather than men, are

> the others who transform the selves of the male actors by converting the latter's particular acts and material acquisitions into a verbal discourse that circulates apart from them, the artifacts, and the relevant momentary events. At the same time that [these] chants are about fame and its processes, they also make famous what they chant about. (Munn 1986: 112–13)

The Scale of Self-Constitution and the Structure of Intersensory Relations

There is a hierarchy or scale of kula activities (fig. 3). The scale discriminates five modes of being in the world, or categories of sensuous action. Each category is ranked relative to the others in terms of its capacity to "extend" the person of the kula voyager, and his control over motion—the movement of minds, the movement of shells—*outward* from the actor's immediate locus in time and space. A negatively valued act is understood to yield no return, either in the form of shells, or in terms of the "extension" of a person's name. A positively valued act, in addition to yielding things (kula valuables), precipitates a transformation in the perceptual qualities of the performer. The effect of the transformation registers on the next level up in the scale of self-constitution. It may also resonate further, up to the highest level, which is that of thunderdom (Level 5). The categories are thus articulated to each other in accordance with a very specific pattern of transposition, which for ease of reference may called the Massim rule of sensory transmutation.

Some examples will help illustrate how this rule works. Starting at Level 1: to refrain from eating is thought to make an actor feel more active or mobile and "buoyant" than he otherwise would. The effect of not eating registers at Level 2. Not eating is also believed to intensify the visibility of an actor's body decorations, and thus contributes to his "being seen," an effect that registers at Level 3. Furthermore, not eating makes food available for display and distribution to overseas kula visitors, and so contributes to the provider being "talked about" (Level 4).

Starting the series of transmutations again, this time at Level 3, the olfactory and visual brilliance of the kula visitor's body decor is supposed to augment the persuasive power of his speech (Level 4a). As a result, the host immediately consents to his request for shells. This fact in turn contributes to the kula voyager being "spoken of" by others (Level 4b), with the result that his *butu* (fame, noise) goes up (Level 5).

The acoustic dimension of body and shell decor merits further scrutiny. According to Munn, shell decor "extends the body [of the shell] in space and the mobile decor makes a sound that ramifies the space—as if putting it into motion—so that what may be out of sight may nevertheless be heard" (1986: 114). To pursue Munn's point, the most important thing about a kula valuable is not that it should be seen, but that it should sound. It is the attachments that give the shell its sound and, in this way, may be said to *complete* the valuable. As we know from Campbell, the attachments do not add to the value of the shell. At a deeper level, however, they *are* the value, in that their sensory properties symbolize the value of trembling motion and "noise" (*butu*) in the cultures of the Massim. This interpretation of where value resides fits with the fact that it is not the intrinsic properties of a valuable that make it really valuable, but its human-added ones; namely, its mobility and "noise."

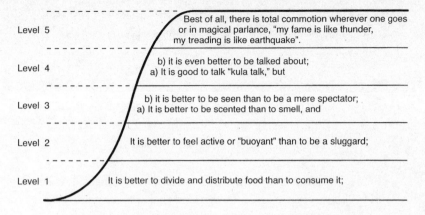

Level 5	Best of all, there is total commotion wherever one goes or in magical parlance, "my fame is like thunder, my treading is like earthquake".
Level 4	b) it is even better to be talked about; a) It is good to talk "kula talk," but
Level 3	b) it is better to be seen than to be a mere spectator; a) It is better to be scented than to smell, and
Level 2	It is better to feel active or "buoyant" than to be a sluggard;
Level 1	It is better to divide and distribute food than to consume it;

Fig. 3.   Model of the Massim scale of self-constitution

Noise and mobility are the source of the shell's "history" (literally, its being talked about), as it circulates through different hands, and in time acquires its own individual path, and its own personal name. Most shells, however, like most men, never attain status in the upper ranks of kula exchange. They are adjudged too small to warrant a name in the first place, so there is no way of keeping track of them. They arrive in numbers on an island, and leave in numbers, or as it is put in Gawan parlance, "disappear" (Munn 1983: 303). In effect, they pass unseen, even though their number makes them empirically more visible than the larger, older, slower-moving *mwali* and *bagi*. This point brings out nicely how being an object, or a face, with no name is "not to be" in the Massim. Existence, like beauty, is in the ear of the beholder.

While it is easy to appreciate how there may be some sort of connection between ornamentation and noise production in the case of shell decor, this is more difficult to see in the case of body decor: there is nothing obviously sonorous about coconut oil, face paint, or the feathers with which people adorn themselves. However, while these things may look like "visual symbols" to the Western eye and are typically analyzed as such by anthropologists, in the Massim they have a different, more extensive resonance.

The desired resonance is evident in the following spell aimed at spreading the renown of a Gawan *guyaw* or "man of influence."

Whose feathers? the feathers of the *guyaw*
They hear echoing sound, the Raramani people take
    it away . . .

This spell, which is spoken by the *guyaw* himself, refers to the feathers that decorate his head. These feathers, typical masculine decoration for dancing, serve as a metaphor for his kula necklace. According to Munn's interpretation of this spell:

> The decoration . . . that the *guyaw* has put on, his head-feathers and necklace, creates an echoing sound that spreads south and is heard by the Raramani people, who in this way know of him. One may suggest that fame is metaphorical body decor that ramifies as sound beyond the body. (1986: 111)

To elaborate on Munn's last point: the spell effects a conversion of the sight of the *guyaw*'s feathers into an echoing sound that is heard far away. This transformation in the perceptual qualities of the feathers—their coming to emit sound rather than color and light—is a product of the value-creating activity of putting them on and being seen. This perceptual transformation follows from the rule of sensory transmutation, according to which the effects of a positively valued action always register at successively higher levels in the hierarchy of sensing. In the present case, the result of the *guyaw*'s act of appearing is an act of hearing on the part of the Raramani people.

The Gawan spell can also be analyzed as an example of the selectivity of perception, the preceding analysis notwithstanding. Thus, a feather headdress is an impressive sight. However, it also has other sensory characteristics. Among these is the rustling sound it makes when its wearer moves with it on. It is this characteristic that has been seized upon in the spell. The reason that the sound of the feathers, which is actually less noticeable than their visual splendor, becomes their defining characteristic in the spell has to do with the purpose of the incantation. Its aim is to spread the *guyaw*'s renown. This purpose is best achieved through sound because, according to the Massim scale of sensing, sound is a more extensive medium than color or light (or odor), and being heard ranks higher than being seen. The spell therefore deflects attention from the visual qualities of the feathers onto their acoustic qualities. In this way, the ritualist makes a bigger impression on the minds of those to whom the spell is addressed.

Significantly, the spell also exaggerates or amplifies the sound of the feathers: it imagines their rustle to be audible as far away as Raramani. This amplification may be effected by means of some onomatopoeic expression or other, which the quotation unfortunately omits. However, an example of such an expression can be found in the spell with which a Trobriand garden magician "anchors" the season's yam harvest in the storehouses of the chief and other villagers. It should be noted that a yam-house is "a media for display" as much as it is "a receptacle for food" (Malinowski 1965 I: 257). The spell in question begins by naming each of the parts of the chief's yam-house in an extremely vivid and detailed fashion. The spell concludes with the following formula:

Tudududu . . .
The magical portent of my yam-house rumbles over
    the north-east.

(221)

Tudududu is an onomatopoeic expression that stands for the roll of thunder. As noted earlier, thunder is *the* symbol of renown. The spell therefore both anticipates this renown, *and brings it about,* by effectively transforming the sight of the yam-house into a sound. Otherwise put, by means of this spell, a medium for visual display (the yam-house) is extended beyond the realm of sight and ramifies as sound. The senses of sight and hearing interact with and play off each other within a structured order of value.

The Magico-Acoustical Power of Words

Massim magic has been subjected to many different interpretations, from the functionalist analysis of Malinowski (1923, 1961) through the structuralist analysis of Stanley Tambiah (1968) to the materialist analysis of Annette Weiner (1983). In this section, after briefly reviewing Malinowski's and Tambiah's accounts, we shall see what a sensory analysis (complementing Weiner's analysis) can contribute to the understanding of Massim thaumaturgy.

According to Tambiah (1968: 188), Malinowski held that "magical language was an emotive use of language, that magic was born of the emotional tension of particular situations and that the spells, ritual acts and gestures expressed a spontaneous flow of emotions," or "contagion of ideas" (see Malinowski 1961: 394–96, 432). Tambiah himself rejects this theory and argues that Trobriand magic is better understood as a rational, metaphorical use of language. The main points of difference between these two theories are best illustrated by considering the last lines of the Trobriand love spell quoted earlier: "No longer it is my face / My face is as the full moon." Following Malinowski, what this spell reveals is lots of emotion. Following Tambiah, it is possible to see that the spell establishes a metaphorical relation between the full moon and the speaker's face, while the (verbal) substitution of the moon for the face transfers the abstract qualities of the former (light, roundness) onto the latter—if only verbally and in thought.

Trobriand magic also has a "practical side," according to Tambiah. This consists in "clothing" its linguistic procedures in select material symbols and actions, as appears from the following quotation, which concerns one of the central rites of garden magic.

What then is the garden magician up to when he scrapes some soil from a bush hen's nest, brings it into contact with an adze, and recites "The belly of my garden grows to the size of a bush hen's nest"? Is this a case of mystical contagion between bush hen mound and the size of the yam, or is it simply a metaphorical equivalence set up verbally between the property of size displayed by the bush hen's nest with the desired same property in the yam, and lending the mental comparison an air of operational reality by using the soil of the bush hen's nest as a medium of transfer? (Tambiah 1968: 194)

Tambiah immediately responds to his own question: "The rite of transfer portrays a metaphorical use of language (verbal substitution) whereby an attribute is transferred to the recipient via a material symbol which is used metonymically as a transformer." In other words, the "practical" side of Massim magic is more apparent than real: the whole procedure is actually "symbolic" from beginning to end.

Massim magic definitely exploits the "expressive potential" of language, as Tambiah suggests. However, there is more to the magical power of words than the metaphorical use of language, just as the magician's manipulation of objects does more than lend an "air of operational reality" to some mental comparison. To elaborate on the last point, Tambiah's view of objects and gestures as the mere "clothing" of some concept or word is contradicted by Annette Weiner.

> These objects [leaves, stones, betel, etc.] are as important as the spell, because without the appropriate object, the action of the spell would be ineffective. Words must be spoken into a material form that will transfer knowledge [or "abstract qualities" in Tambiah's terminology] from one domain to another. Appropriate objects and words are perceived to be necessary to mobilise the specificity of thought into actual events. (1983: 702)

Nancy Munn is even more explicit. She states that the medium (object, gesture) "both contains and models" the message or thought of the spell (1986: 85).

Just as objects matter more to the conceptualization and actualization of a spell than Tambiah's treatment of them as mere "clothing" would allow, so too is there more to the magical power of words than the mere metaphorical use of language. The principal function of magical speech in the Massim world consists in the acoustic amplification of its referent, as we saw in the case of the *guyaw* chanting over the feather headdress and the garden magician chanting over the yam-house. Onomatopoeia is the paradigmatic device for effecting such amplification—that is, for extending a visual object beyond itself in space. *All* speech does this, however, since according to the "native view" of language, the connection between words and the objects they stand for is intrinsic: "The words by which a [Trobriand] magician exercises his power over a thing or a process, are believed to be co-existent with them. The magical formula and its subject matter were born together" (Malinowski 1961: 398; see further 1923: 322–23; 1965 II: 54–62).

This nonrelational, nonrepresentational, but rather *presentational* conception of the meaning of words stands in bold contrast to the view of language that comes out of Saussurean linguistics. The Saussurean view is, of course, the favored view of scholars of a structuralist persuasion, such as Tambiah. Onomatopoeia is of interest to the structuralist only insofar as it can be used to illustrate the doctrine of "the arbitrariness of the linguistic sign": in French roosters go "cocorico!" but in English "cock-a-doodle-doo!" As this variation attests, the relationship between words and their referents is arbitrary, rather than intrinsic. Onomatopoeia is, therefore, nothing more than a special use, or instantiation, of "language" (*la langue*).

Tambiah dismisses the "native view" of language as unscientific and goes on to trace for us the play of metaphor and metonymy in the design of Trobriand spells. But this dismissal is too quick. Tambiah's blind acceptance of the Saussurean explanation of onomatopoeia prevents him from seeing how onomatopoeia is transcendent of language (and the categories structuralists use to talk about language) rather than a special instance thereof. However, this alternative understanding of onomatopoeia is only possible if one goes over to the "native view" of language and develops an ear for its actual sound.

Consider the question, Is onomatopoeia a case of metaphor or metonymy? The answer is that it is both and neither at once. Indeed, not only is onomatopoeia unclassifiable as a case of *either* one or the other linguistic procedure but, as an extension of the actual sound emitted by the object, it is also, of course, *extra*-linguistic. The point here is that to understand the magical power of words in places like the Massim one has to open one's ears. To trace the interplay of metaphor and metonymy in a magical text, and to show how these linguistic procedures appear to be carried over to (or out *in*) action, the way Tambiah does, is an interesting and instructive methodological procedure. But this procedure yields a false picture, insofar as one assumes that such an analysis also exhausts the meaning of a spell. The meaning of a spell is precisely in its performance, which, in the Massim, means above all in its *sound*, not its verbal structure alone.

Sound Magic

Consider the Trobriand kula rite that derives its name from the mint plant, *sulumwoya*. There are two stages to the *sulumwoya* rite: the first involves the ritual plucking of the mint; the second, boiling the mint in coconut oil to preserve it. In the first stage, the ritualist goes to his garden, finds a *sulumwoya* plant, takes a piece of it in his hands, and waves it to and fro. "It roars," "it quakes," "it boils, foams up," the ritualist chants as he shakes the plant. He proceeds to charm his kula accoutrements (lime spatula, comb, mat, etc.) and headparts (nose, occiput, "speaking organ," etc.) by naming each object or anatomical part and proclaiming "it boils." The spell concludes with the formula:

> My fame is like thunder,
> my treading is like the roar of the flying witches,
> tudududu.
>
> (Malinowski 1961: 200–202)

Malinowski was uncertain as to which of two possible readings should be given to the words of the *sulumwoya* spell: "as the oil of *sulumwoya* boils, so may the eagerness of my partner foam up," or "as the oil of *sulumwoya* boils, so may my renown foam up." He attributed this lack of clarity and consistency to the fact that in magical speech words hang together emotionally rather than logically, and were it not for the context there would be no telling what they meant at all (1961: 338, 442).

Malinowski's difficulty in making sense of this spell was actually self-inflicted. What he should have recognized is that both readings are correct; they simply pertain to different levels in the Trobriand sensory order. It should be explained that while the magic of *sulumwoya* is practiced on the ritualist's own person (in that he sets his own kula objects and his own headparts "boiling") the effect of the magic is to produce a *co*-motion, a corresponding state of agitated motion, in the partner. This co-motion is supposed to influence the partner to agree to the Trobriander's request for valuables with exceptional haste, whence the latter's mounting fame. Thus, at one level, the boiling oil symbolizes the co-motion in the partner's mind at the *sight* of the Trobriander's face and kula objects. At another level, the quaking oil (along with thunder) symbolizes the Trobriander's influential *speech* and *fame*, or "noise-force" (Montague 1983: 41; see further Munn 1983: 286; Fortune 1963: 224). The visual-kinetic image of the oil as "quaking" is invoked to accomplish the first purpose, but this image is eclipsed by the acoustic image of the oil as "roaring"—a sound that in turn ramifies as thunder. The *sulumwoya* spell may thus be said to encode a progression from appearing to being heard. This progression is consistent with sensory norms and relations that have emerged as characteristic of Massim culture in the course of this chapter.

All Malinowski could see in this spell, however, was the expression of some "exceedingly obscure and confused *concatenation* of ideas" (1961: 338). Such a condescending "explanation" makes one agree with Tambiah's rebuke of Malinowski: "explanations in terms of irrational mystical associations seem to me to be the refuge of the literal-minded" (Tambiah 1968: 200). The alternative, Tambiah suggests, is to be more metaphorically minded. However, there are pitfalls to this extreme as well. Indeed, Tambiah appears to entertain an even more exalted view of the magical (read: metaphorical) power of language than the Massim magician whose mentality he purports to be explaining. For example, according to Tambiah, "Language is an artificial construct and its strength is that its form owes nothing to external reality; it thus enjoys the power to invoke images and comparisons, refer to time past and time future, and relate events which cannot be represented in action" (1968: 202). It would be more accurate to say that language *is* action for the Massim magician, that its form owes *everything* to external reality, and that its strength lies in its power to elicit "a sudden awareness of the very textures and surfaces of the world and of language" (Jameson quoted in Weiner 1983: 703).

By way of experiencing the kind of awareness magic provokes, consider Malinowski's discussion of the expression *papapa*, as used in a spell that removes the heaviness and imparts speed to an overseas kula canoe.

> The word *papapa*, "flutter," stands for a phrase: "let the canoe speed so that the pandanus leaves flutter." Of course the word expresses much more than this sentence, because it is intelligible only to those acquainted with the part played by the pandanus leaves in the decoration of the canoes, with the native ideas about magical association between flutter and speed, and with the ritual use of pandanus streamers. (1961: 435)

To grasp the meaning of *papapa* it is thus necessary to examine some of the uses to which pandanus leaves are put in Massim culture. As Malinowski notes in the preceding quotation, it is customary to use such leaves to adorn the mast, rigging, and sail of a canoe. As he states elsewhere:

> The decorative effect of the floating strips of pale glittering yellow is indeed wonderful, when the speed of the canoe makes them flutter in the wind. Like small banners of some stiff, golden fabric they envelope the sail and rigging with light, colour and movement. (1961: 216)

Bespelled pandanus streamers are also used in some dances, either tucked in the armbands or held in the hands, and there is a special art to holding them so that they quiver in the approved manner. A Trobriand chief will send a bespelled pandanus leaf to a distant partner before paying the latter a visit. This gift is supposed to "make the partner eager to bestow valuables on the sender" (Malinowski 1961: 216–17).

The use of pandanus leaves for "decorative" purposes is clearly motivated by their capacity to extend the surface, and emulate (or accentuate) the motion, of the sailing canoe as of the dancing body. At the same time, the leaves "magically" impart their own visual and kinetic qualities to the canoe as to the dancer. The use of pandanus leaves for communicative purposes, such as between distant chiefs, exploits the sensory properties of the streamers in a similar fashion: the aim of the sender is to envelop the receiver's mind in the same buoyant, trembling motion as his own, and by creating this "synthetic image of mobility," to use Munn's phrase, to get the partner to relinquish shells quickly.

Having acquired the requisite knowledge of the sensory logic behind the ritual use of pandanus leaves, we can readily appreciate what Malinowski meant when he wrote, "To the native, who knows all this and in whose mind the whole context rises, when he hears or repeats '*papapa*,' the word quivers with magical force" (1961: 435). The structural anthropologist (Tambiah) would interpret this passage as meaning that it is on account of the visual and kinetic images the word *papapa* summons *to mind* that this word can be said, metaphorically speaking, to "quiver with magical force," and that it is able to *stand for* the attribute or concept of speed. The sensory anthropologist would object that, on the contrary, the word actually does quiver with magical force—*when one repeats it to oneself and listens to it in its spokenness.* The word derives its form from the fluttering sound made by the leaves: *papapa, papapa, papapa . . .* It is an extension of that sound, and because this sound only arises when there is movement, the word is experientially associated with motion and speed.

The main problem with Tambiah's "symbolic" analysis of Massim magic is that it presumes that a thought comes first, and that media are secondary, albeit necessary to "express" or "symbolize" the thought. What I have argued here, in company with Munn and Weiner, is that the mediating substances and gestures of Massim magic do more than transport thoughts—they *model* them. The ritualist's thought derives its specificity, its form, *from* the medium in which it is embedded at the same time that the medium *exteriorizes* the ritualist's thought. I would further argue that the acoustic properties of language matter at least as much to the power of magical speech as the "figurative" or "expressive potential" of language so emphasized by Tambiah. Indeed, as Weiner points out, "Repetition of the spell, accompanied by changes in rhythm, is believed to be *the effective force* in causing the words to enter the appropriate object" (1983: 703).

Repetition

Not surprisingly, Tambiah adopts a different, less forceful view of the meaning of repetition. According to Tambiah, repetition is redundant. Taking his cue from information theory, he regards redundancy as "a device used in ritual to transmit its message," as well as a kind of "'memory bank' in the absence of written language" (1968: 201). As an example of how spells store knowledge, Tambiah refers to the chant that the garden magician uses to "anchor" the yams in the storehouse of the chief. He sees it as significant that each part of the storehouse is named, followed by the expression "shall be anchored." Tambiah evidently subscribes to an extremely verbocentric theory of knowledge. He thinks that all knowledge must be verbalized to be retained. It is not enough that knowledge of how to build the yam-house is already embedded in the physical structure of the yam-house, which is before the magician's very eyes as he performs the chant.

The source of Tambiah's mistake is apparent: focusing on the informational content of the spell leads him to ignore how the chant is designed to act on the world, not simply speak about it. Specifically, the aim of the spell is to transform the sight of the yam-house into the sound of thunder, so that it may resonate in the minds of others.

The meaning of repetition, according to Annette Weiner, is that it effects an expansion of the magician's own personal space, and a concomitant penetration of the personal space and minds of others.

> The force of magic stretches the boundaries of one's own mind as it penetrates and may diminish or destroy the boundaries of someone else's mind [by means of the object that] absorbs the words and becomes the material extension of all the powers brought to bear in the supreme ego-centered moments of the repetitious chanting of the spell. (1983: 705)

When one compares this understanding of repetition (i.e., repetition as carving out a space in the real world, as extending the person in space) with Tambiah's understanding of repetition (repetition as redundant, as mnemonic device) what stands out most about the structuralist theory of magic is its mentalism and lack of sensuality. Tambiah assumes (quite rationally, it is true) that magic has no effect, that it is "symbolic action," so its effects must be "symbolic" too. But as the preceding discussion has revealed, what actually holds true is just the opposite. Massim magic is sensual rather than "strictly metaphorical," and presentational rather than representational. The magical power of words consists principally in the energetic expenditure of sound, not simply the expressive potential of language.

CHAPTER 4

On Being in Good Taste

Gustatory Cannibalism and
Exchange Psychology

 In the Massim way of sensing the world, the sense that is subject to the most restrictions is that of taste. In this chapter, we first examine how the repression (or constant deferral) of gustation is related to the centrality of exchange in Massim society, with the result that foods are classified and valued by reference to their presentability rather than their delectability. It also shows how Massim food preferences are ordered by a principle of likeness to humanity, as in the case of pork, which is reputed to be the next best thing to human flesh—at least in those areas where cannibalism was formerly practiced.

The ensuing exploration of "gustatory cannibalism" in turn brings out the surprising fact that kula valuables were traditionally exchanged not only for other valuables but also for body parts. This fact shatters the "big picture" of the kula as a "force for peace" bequeathed to us by Malinowski. There are various explanations for the failure of Malinowski's vision, and following a consideration of these explanations, a sensous interpretation of kula exchange is advanced that relates it to sensory exchange.

The second half of the chapter is devoted to tracing the lineaments of the Massim anatomy of the senses and the intellect, and exploring some of the challenges that this indigenous model poses both to the theory of oral mentality espoused by the communications theorists Marshall McLuhan and Walter Ong and to Western psychology of perception generally.

A Taste for Exchange

In the Massim world, people derive their identities from restricting their tastes. For example, Trobriand noble lineages maintain their identity by observing the food taboos that their ancestors brought with them when they first emerged from the ground (Weiner 1988: 99–101). In point of fact, every social position in the Massim world, be it temporary like that of the pregnant woman or mourner, or permanent like that of the sorcerer or carver, is hedged in and defined by taboos on the consumption of particular foods.[1] In a similar way, the hosts and sponsors of a canoe-launching, marriage, or mortuary feast do not eat any of the food they have prepared themselves, but rather distribute it to their guests (Munn 1986: 73; Thune 1980; Róheim 1932; Weiner 1976). By so doing they affirm both their own and their alter's identities. It is through giving, rather than consuming, that identities are constructed and maintained (McDowell 1980).

Reputations are also built on giving. To be a big man on Duau, for example, is to be "one who distributes and is not stingy" (Róheim 1950: 241, 227; see also Munn 1986: 49–53, 62–63; Austen 1945: 19–21). The big man's biggest fear is that guests on their way home from a *sagari* (food distribution) may remark, "Look at this piece of pork! It is nothing! Wait till we give a *sagari*. That will be something" (Róheim 1950: 239; see also Thune 1980: 233; Austen 1945: 21; Silas 1926). The big man is thus primarily concerned with providing a more than sufficient *quantity* of food. This does not mean that quality is ignored but simply that delectability is not the foremost quality that makes food good to present at a Massim feast.

What makes a food presentable and therefore valued? The value of a foodstuff is partly determined by its durability. Taro, for example, is more perishable than yam, and for this reason it ranks lower than yam in the hierarchy of foodstuffs (Malinowski 1965 I: 296; Róheim 1950: 235). Unusual shape is another much-esteemed quality. For instance, long yams are less palatable than short yams, but their fantastic forms make them highly suitable for display. Long yams thus frequently figure as the centerpiece of a prestation (Róheim 1950: 235; Malinowski 1965 II; 89–91). Density, however, would appear to be the single most important quality. The densest, most "solid" foods, yam and pork, are also the ones that rank highest in the hierarchy of food. Without them, a feast is not a feast; when they are present in abundance, people remember the subsequent repast as an occasion when they were able to eat to the point of being so gorged they had to vomit.

The case of yam brings out well just how unelaborated the field of taste is in the Massim world. This starch is both the staple food and, as noted earlier, the food of choice in most parts of the region. It comes in many varieties. Given that yams are the food of choice, one would expect the varieties to be distinguished by flavor, but in fact it is only by reference to their color, size, and odor that they are discriminated (Róheim 1950: 233–35). Why not their taste? Because yams, like virtually everything else in the Massim, are for display and distribution before they are for consumption. They are classified accordingly—that is, in terms of their most *presentable* characteristics. Taste as such is devalued because to taste something is to make it *disappear*. There is no pleasure in making something disappear for any self-respecting Massim person, much less a Massim big man: only in giving it away.

Disappearing Taste

We have seen that Massim peoples distinguish and rank foods primarily on the basis of their density, shape, and durability, rather than their flavor. This does not mean that they do not make use of flavor categories in their everyday discourse. They do, but these categories are relatively restricted in number, and not even primarily gustatory in nature.

In Kilivila, the language of the Trobriands, for instance, there is a word for "sweet" (*sumakenia*), a word for "sour" (*pupuya*), and a word for "bitter" (*yayana*), but no word for "salty"; rather, this sensation is included under *yayana*, "bitter."[2] In the language of Dobu, the corresponding terms are *dibidibi* (sweet), *maiyuyu* (sour), and *dalele* (salty, bitter).

According to Senft's dictionary of Kilivila, *sumakenia* means "rich, tasty" as well as "sweet." *Yayana* signifies "hot-tasting, harsh" in addition to "bitter." Pork, yam, and *mona* (a viscous, sweet, coconut cream soup, which mainly men prepare) would be the prototypical tastes belonging to the *sumakenia* category. Ginger, salt water, and betel nut would be the prototypical tastes of the *yayana* category.

The fact that *sumakenia* means both "tasty" and "sweet" could be interpreted as further evidence of the allegedly universal human gustatory preference for sweetness (see Mintz 1986: 17–18). Such an interpretation smacks of reductionism, however, and should be guarded against, particularly given that *sumakenia* also means "rich," and the primary substances belonging to this category are, in fact, distinguished from other foods more by their density than by their sweetness. Rather than a flavor category per se, *sumakenia* is best regarded as a category of sensuous action, or mode of being in the world, and defined in terms of its effects. As regards its effects, the *sumakenia* category groups together substances that are "good to feast on" because they are filling, and sometimes also sweet.

The substances classified as *yayana* have a contrary function: betel nut, salt water, and ginger are "good to fast on" because they are not food. The main reason betel nut is not counted as food is that it "wakes people up," making them more active instead of less active (like food proper). In addition to stimulating sociability, betel nut is regarded as an aid to productive activities, such as carving. On Kitawa, for example, both the "clarity" (delineation or sharpness) of the image in the carver's mind and the actual execution of the design are supposed to be enhanced by chewing betel (Scoditti 1982: 81). The idea here seems to be that the harsh, biting taste of betel nut produces sharpness of consciousness.

Salt water and ginger play a prominent role in sorcery. Róheim records, "If a father knows the art of *barau* (sorcery) he will always take his boy to the sea water. He must drink a lot of salt water to get his intestines purged before he can become a *barau*" (1950: 205). The reason for this practice is that the belly is thought to be the seat of memory: it must be purged in order for the boy to be able to remember the spells he is taught by his mentor.

Sorcery is seen as a productive or "value-creating" activity, in Nancy Munn's (1986) terms. It involves an *exteriorization* of the self, just like carving or gardening. In order for this outering to be effective, though, various proscriptions and prescriptions regarding food in-take must be observed. Fortune describes how

> the sorcerer engaged in sorcery believes that he must keep his body hot and parched; hence the drinking of salt water, the chewing of the hot ginger, and abstention from food for a while . . . The sight of a magician chewing ginger, spitting it on to the object charmed at intervals, and muttering his spell at the same time is a common one in Dobu. (1963: 295)

The sorcerer's abstention from food proper follows from the emphasis on exteriorization. Eating is an act of interiorization; to eat would be to nullify the process the sorcerer wishes to set in motion. The sorcerer also purges his insides with salt water. In this way, his digestive tract becomes a conduit for the "noise-force" (the magical words that he retains in his belly) to burst forth (Montague 1983: 41).

The sorcerer also heats up his mouth and breath by chewing ginger. The result is that the words he speaks acquire additional sensory properties (heat, pungency, bite) that augment the expansive, penetrating power of their sound. The atmosphere around the sorcerer becomes charged with all these qualities in "the supreme ego-centered moments of the repetitious chanting of the spell"—moments that literally "stretch the boundaries" of the sorcerer's mind (Weiner 1983: 705). The effect of all the chanting, spitting, sweating is that *the sorcerer's senses come to give off impressions* instead of receiving them. He "goes out through his senses," as it were, just as the spell is supposed to go out, invade the personal space of the victim, and undermine the latter's autonomy.

Edibility and Humanity

In the Massim, edibility is *intimately* related to humanity, in contrast to Western consumer society, for example, where, as Marshall Sahlins has shown, edibility tends to be inversely related to humanity (1976: 174–75). Consider yams, the foremost dietary staple in the Massim. One of Reo Fortune's informants remarked, "Yams are persons, with ears. If we charm they hear" (1963: 107). Yams are also credited with the power of sight, thought to be sensitive to smells, believed to come out of the earth and roam about at night, and "like women . . . give birth to children" (i.e., seedlings) (Fortune 1963: 107–9; see further Malinowski 1965 I: 232; Brindley 1984: 76–80; Kahn 1986: 101). Thus, yams participate in Dobu society as fully sentient subjects. Their likeness to humanity makes them the most edible of vegetables.

The principle that edibility is intimately related to humanity also explains other Massim food values, such as the preference for garden crops over wild roots and berries, and the ranking of domestic pigs over wild pigs as sources of protein (Róheim 1950: 233; Malinowski 1965 I: 164; 1929: 190; Weiner 1988: 101). In both these cases, the preferred food is physically closer to humanity (see further Battaglia 1990: 45–50). An additional contributing factor in the case of pork is that domestic pigs, if they are kept in pens, are fed cooked tubers; hence, they share the same diet as human beings.

There are also two other factors that commend pork (generally) to the Massim palate. One is the perceived resemblance between the smell of pig cooking and the smell of human flesh cooking.[3] The other factor has to do with the symbolic association of greasy, oily substances, like pig meat and coconut cream, with human substance—specifically, men's semen—as has been pointed out by Miriam Kahn (1986: 118–19). This identification is the basis for pork as well as *mona* (coconut cream soup) figuring so prominently in the hierarchy of foodstuffs: their substance is more "compatible" (being symbolically identical) with human bodily substances than, for example, dog meat or greens.

The complementary opposite of the association of greasy, oily substances with semen is the association of substances that retain a pungent, salty odor, such as fish from the sea and crustaceans, with female menstrual blood (Kahn 1986: 119). This association explains why fish is considered fit for human consumption (being humanlike in essence), but is not valued as highly as pork, on the analogy of things feminine generally being ranked subordinate to things masculine.

To sum up, Massim food preferences appear to be governed by a principle of *likeness to humanity* whereby delectability (in the Western sense) is subsumed under assimilability, the latter being a function of the compatibility of the food substance with human bodily substance, as defined culturally (see Battaglia 1990: 45–50). Given all this emphasis on likeness, how is difference expressed? In Massim societies, difference is expressed through giving—that is, through *not eating* the food one produces or prepares oneself. This is the reverse of Western consumer society where, according to Sahlins (1976), social standing is expressed in terms of the *consumption* of differently valued cuts and kinds of meat (steak versus liver, beef versus pork, etc.) by different classes of people.

A Taste for Human Flesh?

If edibility is so intimately related to humanity, it follows that the most desirable and edible substance in the Massim world must be human flesh. Malinowski's Trobrianders denied the logic of this argument, for reasons that probably had much to do with the emphasis on maintaining social and bodily boundaries in their relatively stratified society. The thought of being "assimilated" (or cannibalized) was terrifying and repulsive to them (Malinowski 1961: 346).

In the more egalitarian (less rank-conscious) societies of the western and southern Massim, cannibalism was practiced, and human flesh appears to have been considered thoroughly delectable, if the following text recorded by Róheim on Duau is any indication.

> [The members of a Duau war party] bring back into the village the man they have killed. They do not eat him themselves but they exchange parts of his body for *kune* [kula] goods. "The *bagi* is the *pokara* (initial gift) for human flesh. For a *mwari* they give a breast, for a *dona* an arm, for a *bagi* a leg. A nose bone [decoration] will purchase a head, a stone axe a neck. If somebody has no *kune* objects he will say, "Please chop off a little bit for me." "Pig is bad, man tastes better." "It is our own smell, therefore it is good," they would say. (1950: 220)

Note how "man" or human flesh is said to "taste better" than, for example, pig, because "it is our own smell," not simply "like" our own smell. Indeed, "man" was so good to eat that people paid for human flesh with kula valuables—an armshell for a chest, a necklace for a leg, a *dona* (breastplate of mother-of-pearl shell) for an arm.

What is so good about an arm (as opposed to a foot or knee joint, for example) that it could only be purchased with such a comparatively rare object as a *dona?* It was explained to Róheim by a man of Dobu that "the arm is good because people oil it and put sweet smelling leaves on it" (1954: 488). This explanation is a consummate expression of "gustatory cannibalism," but to the Trobriand, or for that matter, the Western ear it is a disturbing manifestation of depravity, of "structureless confusion" (Visser 1991: 6). This Western horror at the very thought of cannibalism is conditioned by the image of the cannibal as a homicidal maniac, slavering over his victim, eager to tear into the corpse's flesh.

But perhaps this image is largely a phantasm of Western consumer society (Root 1996). The image of the flesh-craving cannibal does not really fit the Massim world, where gustation is so restricted. In point of fact, as Martha Macintyre (1983) has documented, it was taboo for the man on a cannibal raid who killed the victim to partake of the latter's flesh himself. In motivational terms, therefore, eating was the last thing on the cannibal raider's mind. What was first on his mind, particularly if he was the leader of the expedition, was that he had already received a kula necklace as a *pokara* or "initial gift" from his "sponsors" (typically a kin group wanting the death of some relative avenged), and that he would have to produce some body from the enemy village responsible for the death if he wanted to requite the *pokara* and come into the other valuables promised him.

If the raid proved a success, the war leader's sponsors would be delighted. The "payback killing" put an immediate end to the restricted sensory regime of mourning for their deceased relative, meaning they could wash and decorate themselves again. What is more, they had a body that they could carve up and distribute in exchange for kula valuables! In the alternative, if the leader was able to bring back a live captive, he could ransom the prisoner from his sponsors and go on to ransom the person back to the enemy village. The currency in all these transactions consisted of more pigs and kula valuables. These items the war leader was free to dispose of as he saw fit; that is, he could use the kula shells in internal (local) exchanges for land, to purchase a canoe, as a mortuary payment, or in the (extralocal) interisland kula. Moreover, the fact that the valuables had been exchanged for a life, or a death, added both to their own renown and to that of the transactor.

This account of the intricate rules surrounding the circulation of human parts in the Massim world undermines all of our most deeply held assumptions about what motivates cannibal behavior. Every time we would expect an act of consumption to occur, we find it being deferred to enable yet another exchange to take place, which yields more valuables, which go on to figure in other exchange transactions, so that no one ends up richer (or any less hungry), only more famous. This experience of having our expectations frustrated is telling. It underlines the psychological difference between being a member of a consumer-oriented society (Root 1996) and belonging to an exchange-oriented one.

Refiguring the Kula

Malinowski's idea of the Kula (with a capital K) as a force for peace—or "encompassing framework" that created a context conducive to trade and regional integration—was fundamental to his "big picture" of the institution (1961: 92, 99–102). This idea of the Kula as a substitute for war was in turn popularized by Marcel Mauss in his well-known essay *The Gift*.

However, as Martha Macintyre's historical research has now firmly established, the preeminence of the kula in Malinowski's day was largely attributable to pacification. Furthermore, the kula actually *alternated* with war in the period prior to pacification. Patterns of alliance were not permanent, as Malinowski claimed ("once in the Kula always in the Kula" [1961: 83]), but cyclical, "with *kune* [kula or trade] partnerships severed by war, reconstituted by appeasement, and then liable to disruption by war at a subsequent time" (Macintyre 1983: 33). It was the same with the objects of kula exchange, as we have just seen: the shells could be regarded as peace-bonds, but they were just as often used as war bonds (i.e., to procure a killing).

Significantly, the protocol for the reception of a peacemaking expedition was the same as that for a kula expedition. What is more, the dress and magic used for kulaing and peacemaking were the same as those for warring and going courting. Macintyre describes how this magic is supposed to function.

> War magic for the body, like *kune* magic, and courting magic, is aimed at the beholder. The sight of the anointed body strikes terror, admiration or love into the heart of the person confronted, rendering him or her submissive. Just as *kune* men with strong body magic can "turn the minds" of their partners, so the warriors thus adorned could take captives easily—the enemy was overwhelmed by the sight of the warrior and could not even flee. (1983: 25)

It follows that *as in war so in appeasement, as in appeasement so in the kula, and as in the kula so in love (courtship)*. There is no rupture to this sequence; for example, there is no reason for analyzing the kula any differently from war.

This finding shatters Malinowski's "big picture" of the Kula Ring. His vision of the Kula as a closed circle of ceremonial exchange and a force for regional integration now appears to have been a visual abstraction with little or no resonance in terms of local perceptions and realities. As we now know, the kula was not a "ring," since the shells were constantly passing in and out of it (to be exchanged for land, a canoe, a spouse, a body part, etc.), then as now. Furthermore, there was nothing special about the kula as a form of social activity, since people comported themselves the same way when they went kulaing as when they went warring or courting or suing for peace.

Malinowski's invocation of the circle or "ring" may be read as an early example of the practice of representing social structures in terms of elementary plane figures. Such figures have the advantage of giving the anthropologist's constructions a definiteness and a reality they might not otherwise possess, the classic example being Evans-Pritchard's use of an equilateral triangle to depict lineage relations among the Nuer (Karp and Maynard 1983; Jackson 1989).[4] In the Massim case, it is apparent now that the metaphor of the ring introduced an artificial separation: it suggested that kula exchange was bounded, a realm apart, when in point of fact it was continuous with all the other sorts of exchange and forms of activity in place. It would take anthropologists more than fifty years to see through Malinowski's "big picture" and begin to perceive the kula for what it is, and was (Weiner 1976; Leach and Leach 1983; Lepowsky 1993: 208–14).

If the image of a circle is not appropriate to the description of the kula, is there some other motif that is more apt for making sense of this institution and the culture of which it is an expression? The primary criterion in the selection of any such motif is that it be an image with "resonance" (after Métraux 1953). A resonant image would be one that has meaning across a variety of sensory modalities (instead of registering exclusively in the eye's mind) and at the same time makes sense of the symbolic equivalency between kulaing, warring, courting, and peacemaking that has emerged as a crucial point of convergence in the preceding analysis.

Perhaps the best motif for "making sense" of Massim culture is the image-experience of a wave or succession of waves. At one level, the continuous-wave motif may be seen as describing the shape of social experience on the intervillage and interisland plane. It represents the *alternation* of kula (or trade) with war in the relations between any given set of island or village communities in the situation that obtained prior to pacification.[5]

At another level, this time more concrete, the wave motif may be seen as describing the *actual* routes along which kula objects traveled prior to pacification and continue to travel today, constantly cycling in and out of the supposedly "closed circle" of the Ring. Thus, the peaks of the undulating line of a succession of waves signify the path of a valuable when it is being used for purposes of kula exchange, the troughs its conversion for use as a war bond, or in exchange for body parts, for land, for a pig, for a canoe, as a mortuary gift, and so on. The normal scenario would be for a valuable to reenter the kula after figuring in one or more of the latter transactions, hence the resumption of the cycle. The only scenario in which such a reconversion could not be realized would be in the event of a shell being "killed," as sometimes happens, in order to be sold to a foreigner.

At a third level, which is still more concrete, the wave motif may be seen and *felt* to condense the ideal shape of sensory experience in

On Being in Good Taste

the Massim. For the motif is directly connected to the "precarious but delightful sensation," as Malinowski put it, of riding over the waves in an outrigger canoe. As discussed previously, the most valued kinaesthetic sensation in Massim experience is this feeling of buoyancy that comes from being at sea. The wave motif is the visual correlate of that sensation, a sensation that reverberates throughout Massim culture. For example, it recurs in the style of most dances, which involve the performers staging graceful bobbing and rolling or swooping motions with their arms. It also appears in the form of the elongated curlicues that are such a pervasive design element in the carved wooden prowboards of the Massim region (Scoditti 1977).

At the most fundamental level, which is also the most sensuous (or multisensory), the wave motif *embodies* the Massim sensory order, or way of being in the world in each sense. It does so by encapsulating the *pattern of relations between the senses* in which the four major forms of activity we have been considering (i.e., kulaing and courting, warring and peacemaking) are grounded. To elaborate, there is a sequence to the way in which the senses are mobilized in the course of each of these forms of action. This sequence is consonant with the hierarchy of sensing that informs the Massim scale of self-constitution (chap. 3). Put another way, the sequencing of the senses in ritual action meshes with the ideal sensory attributes of selfhood, and the two together manifest the elementary structure of the Massim sensory order, or way of sensing the world.

The sequencing of the senses in Massim ritual action, with its threefold phasic structure, is show in figure 4.

Phase 1: Each of the four forms of activity considered here involves a preliminary period consecrated to the purification of the senses: drinking seawater to cleanse the insides of the body, washing magic to cleanse the body surface. The senses primarily affected by these initial rites are taste and the various modalities of touch.

Phase 2: There follows an intermediary period that endures up to the moment the actors or parties to the exchange make contact. During this period, there is an ongoing repression of the senses of taste and touch in that certain kinds of food and sex are prohibited. This is in order to produce the desired effects in and through the other senses: smell, sight, and hearing.

Phase 3: It is on the exteriorization of the latter senses, and the connection or "co-motion" so established between the parties to the exchange, that the success of the undertaking depends. This success in turn leads to the affirmation and fulfillment of all the senses, including taste, in the context of the feast that marks the termination of the transaction. As a result of the feast, people feel full for a change. This leads to a contraction of sensory activity (the sleep of surfeit) and the return to "normal times."

However, the normal relations among individuals will no longer be the same. For while everyone involved in the undertaking will have participated in the ascension of the scale of sensing, some individuals will have succeeded in extending their persons through the media of smell, light, and sound, *further* than other individuals. The effects of their success in this regard will continue to inform social and sensory interaction after the descent—that is, after the feast. However, this only lasts until the next major event in the life of the community or individual. Then the triumphant ones will have to prove themselves masters of the sensory discipline necessary to produce the desired olfactory, visual, and acoustic effects that undergird their new social status all over again.

In figure 4, the line that leads from tasting (bottom) to hearing (top) represents the ascension of the senses. This ascension unfolds in accordance with the rule of sensory transmutation, whereby the effects of action in one sensory domain manifest themselves in the next, hierarchically superior domain. The line that descends from the apex is meant to suggest the contraction of sensory activity in the aftermath of the feast. The horizontal lines of the graph plot the continuing influence of the individual's demonstrated mastery of the hierarchy of sensing on social interaction during the intermediary period leading up to the next major event.

To concretize this discussion, take the example of the kula. The members of a kula expedition abstain from eating certain foods in preparation for the voyage. Upon arrival at their destination, they compete to outscent, outshine, and outtalk each other so as to win

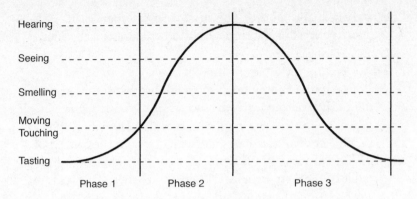

Fig. 4. *Model of the Massim way of sensing the world*

the coveted valuables from their hosts. When they return home, there is a feast, and songs are composed to celebrate their successes. The songs linking the names of particular local men to the names of the high-ranking kula valuables they have just won play an important role in perpetuating, or often upsetting, local power relations.

The activity of kulaing is easily assimilable to the model in figure 4. The next section will show how the same pattern of relations between the senses structures social interaction in the context of the collective courting ritual known as the *butia* festival.

The Kula Set to Flowers

The *butia*-flower competition (*kayasa*) is one of the high points of the Trobriand ritual calendar. This festival takes place during, or as an extension of, the *milamala* period (the annual postharvest feast of the returning spirits) when the *butia*-tree is in bloom. The sweet-scented white flowers of the *butia*-tree

> are collected in the jungle, made into wreaths and garlands, and exchanged with a blowing of conch-shells. As the natives put it: "We make *kula* (ceremonial exchange) with *butia* wreaths." In fact, . . . the exact terminology of the kula is followed in these transactions . . . The competitive element in the *butia* festival lies

in the quality and quantity of the presents received and given, and, as in all forms of such exchange, to give or to receive a magnificent gift contributes to the glory of either side. (Malinowski 1929: 254–55)

The similarities between the *butia* festival and kula exchange are quite striking. Like the kula, the *butia* festival is a corporate undertaking, organized by the big man or chief of a village. Other correspondences include the way fellow villagers treat each other as rivals, while persons of other villages are sought out as partners; the way the parties to an exchange indulge each other's vanity; and the way the protocol of kula exchange is followed down to the last detail—the dress is the same, the sequence of prestations and counterprestations is the same, the terminology for the gifts is the same. The only difference is that the exchange is along cross-sex lines rather than same-sex ones.

The symbolic equation that Malinowski's informants pointed out between their favorite time for courting—the *butia* festival—and the occasion of a kula visit shows that they *did* have an idea of what the kula was all about, and Malinowski was just being arrogant when he wrote, "Not even the most intelligent native has any clear idea of the Kula as a big, organised social construction." Had Malinowski but listened a bit more carefully to what his informants were saying, he might have recognized that kula exchange does not constitute a sphere unto itself. Rather, as we now know, it is continuous with all the other forms of Massim exchange—including the exchange of such transient (perishable) things as floral wreaths.

The fact that floral wreaths can stand in for kula objects is a point of considerable significance, for it means that kula exchange is not defined by the objects through which it is transacted so much as the relations it entrains. But this point is a difficult one to grasp, because it flies in the face of numerous deep-seated assumptions concerning the essentialness of things in the Western episteme (Tyler 1984; Descombes 1986). Specifically, it obliges us to start conceiving of kula objects as bundles of relations rather than as entities and to start approaching them through their effects, their qualia, rather than as things. In short, it obliges us to develop a less "objective" or reificatory understanding of the objects of kula exchange, if we want to to bring our theoretical approaches to the kula into line with indigenous understandings.

What would a "nonobjective" understanding of kula objects entail? When we attempted to focus in on kula valuables qua objects (chap. 3), we found our attention being directed *beyond* the shells themselves to their attachments, as if the shells had no value in themselves. Moreover, it was through studying the sensory properties of these attachments (how they extend the boundaries of a shell, how they tremble, how they flash, how they chime) that we caught our first comprehensive glimpse of the ranking of the senses in Massim experience. This suggests that the function of shell decor is not simply to attract attention to the shell itself (i.e., the shell as object); rather, the decor's prime function is to refer the shell to its place in the sensory and symbolic order of Massim culture. If this analysis is correct, then it is true that the shells and their attachments ought *not* to be regarded as isolated things; rather they should be treated as extensions or icons of the Massim model of the relations between the senses that gives them their meaning.

We shall come back to this idea of kula shells as icons of sensory interaction presently. But first let us explore some of the ways in which kula shells can be seen as icons of human interaction, an idea originally suggested by Nancy Munn (1983: 284, 302–4).

The shells are icons of human interaction first in the sense that there is a history of human interaction condensed in the acquired properties of each valuable. These acquired properties include the shell's personal name, its smoothness, and its patina or "glow"— the result of constant handling and polishing. The shell's history, as reflected in its acquired properties, is what determines its status in the hierarchy of shell standards. Shells have no intrinsic value, or, put another way, no existence as things in themselves.

A second way in which the shells function as icons of social relations involves the manner in which each shell gives expression to the relationship in which its particular holder stands to others. That is, each shell's history and grandeur correlates with the seniority and reputation for successful kula transactions of its possessor. The shell standards thus provide a material framework in terms of which men sense their own relative worth and can express their estimation of the worth of others.

Kula shells are replaced by floral wreaths in the context of the *butia* festival. Like the shells, the wreaths are ranked in terms of their size and quality, and as in the kula, to give or to receive a magnificent wreath contributes to the glory, the "fame" (*butu*) of either party to the transaction. The homology between these two forms of exchange appears to be spoiled by the fact that *butia* wreaths are perishables whereas kula shells are durables. From another angle, however, which is perhaps what Malinowski's informants were trying to communicate, the shells are no more permanent than the flowers, for their value too lies in their being *for transmission*, in their *passing on*. Indeed, the only lasting thing about a shell is the "noise" (*butu*) it generates in passing. Thus, kula exchange is not defined by the objects through which it is transacted (flowers can serve just as well as shells), so much as *by the effects it produces*. And the most important effect it generates is the outering of "sound" (*butu*).

Munn expands on the meaning of *butu*:

> [*Butu*] is an icon of the action which produced it. Just as a man moves or "turns around" the mind of his partner to obtain shells . . . so also his own name moves or "turns around" . . . because he has received a shell . . . *Butu* generalizes the immediate control exerted in a transaction: as a product sedimented from this control (and an icon of it) it is also detachable from the fixed locus of the act—an acquired aspect of social identity that can operate as a component of a man's influence in later transactions. (1983: 288)

Munn is here interested in how influence is built up through successive acts of shell acquisition. The preceding analysis has shown that this influence can be analyzed further into the specific sensuous actions that need to be performed by an actor in order to acquire the shell valuables he desires and to maximize his fame in the process. As we have seen, these actions consist of not eating, emanating buoyancy, having a good odor, appearing brilliant, and employing kula speech so artfully that one's host immediately consents to one's request for valuables. In short, *butu* is the icon of an individual's demonstrated mastery of the Massim scale of sensing. It is the extent to which an actor proves (and has previously proven) himself capable of *extending* his person through the media of smell, light, and sound that is reflected in the "extension"—the grandeur and history—of the shell that he succeeds in prying loose from his hosts. However, the shell is not the prize (any more than the garlands are the prize in the context of the *butia* festival): the prize is the *butu* of it all, which is destined to yield even more shells or garlands in future.

The Sensory Life of Things

This brings us to a key juncture in our sensory analysis of Massim culture. We began by examining the hierarchy of sensory activity in the context of kula exchange. We went on to extend our analysis to those domains of Massim culture, such as courting and warmaking, that promised to shed additional light on the former. What we have now discovered is that kula exchange is informed by the same sensory model as these other domains: it is not a sphere unto itself, nor does it provide any sort of "encompassing framework." Rather, kula exchange is an occasion, alongside courting, warring, and peacemaking, for *the production of effects* according to the Massim way of sensing the world. Our understanding has thus come full circle, and we now find ourselves studying the position of kula valuables among other "things" (such as body decor, food, and flowers) *in the Massim hierarchy of sensing.*

The reason "things" must be placed in quotation marks is that they do not have the same objecthood in Massim culture that they do in Western culture. Yams, for instance, are regarded as sentient subjects rather than mere vegetables. This is in fact true of all potential "objects" of exchange, and especially true of kula shells. In Massim terms, kula objects are bundles of sensory powers and relations.

The sensory powers of kula shells include the capacity to smell, to hear, and to see. For example, kula shells are said to sniff each other out and "play nose-to-nose" like dogs (Malinowski 1961: 348); depending on the standard, kula shells are also said to be attracted by each other's redness, or to respond to each other's calls (Campbell 1983). The range of sensory powers and appetites attributed to the shells suggests that they are no mere "objects" of exchange. It is rather as if they were the *agents of their own circulation,* given the sensory desires projected onto them.

In addition to being credited with different sensory powers, different standards of shell appeal to the senses in differing "ratios of sense" (after McLuhan 1962). Thus, older shells tend to be adorned with numerous attachments. These attachments extend the boundaries of the shells, giving the impression of continual motion, and also emit a chiming sound. Older shells also have personal names. This is in contrast to low-ranking or new shells, which, besides lacking names, are coarse instead of smooth and "glowing," and tend not to be adorned very much.

The ratios of sense embodied in the different shell standards may be said to provide a sensory profile of their respective owners, who, as we have seen, are ranked on a scale ranging from those with a face but no name to those with a name but no face. It is significant that the one quality and the one power the shells are lacking is taste: there is not one reference to the valuables as having gustatory appetites in the ethnographic record. Like the culture of which they are an icon, it is their lack of taste that keeps them on the move. Their mobility is dependent on the negation of gustation.

The Theory of Oral Mentality

The importance attached to *butu* ("noise") and the primacy of hearing in Massim society is precisely what one would expect of an "oral society," according to the theory of oral mentality. We owe the latter theory to the communications theorists Marshall McLuhan (1962), Edmund Carpenter (1973), and Walter Ong (1982), who devised it to account for what they took to be certain characteristic features of the social and cognitive organization of preliterate societies. Aspects of the theory of oral mentality can be found reiterated in the works of numerous anthropologists, such as Goody (1977, 1986), Stoller (1984), Tyler (1987), and Jackson (1989), and other cultural theorists, such as Lowe (1982), Illich and Sanders (1989), and de Kerckhove (1995).

On Being in Good Taste

This section briefly summarizes the main tenets of the theory of oral mentality, then examines them in light of our emergent understanding of the indigenous anatomy of the senses and the intellect. It will be shown that the theory overlaps with aspects of the indigenous model, but rarely for the correct reasons, because orality theory rests on some peculiarly Western assumptions about the nature of the senses, the centrality of language, and the representational powers of mind.

According to the theory of oral mentality, in the absence of writing, speech is necessarily the dominant mode of communication. This has the following consequences: (1) primacy is accorded to sound; (2) hearing is the dominant sense; (3) the intellect is associated with hearing; (4) knowledge has to be cast in verbal formulas, such as rhymes or commonplaces, to be memorable; and (5) the individuation (or rational structuring) of ideas, as of people, is comparatively slight.

Primacy is accorded to sound.   Primacy *is* accorded to sound or "noise" as opposed to light in the Massim world. However, this follows from the importance attached to "expansion outward" and other such cultural values, not simply from the absence of writing (Feld 1986). Sound is valued because of its power to intensify a person's presence. This is apparent in the case of the sorcerer who, through energetic and repetitious chanting, extends or "stretches" the boundaries of his own personal space and brings about a corresponding diminution of the personal space and autonomy of his victim. Sound is also credited with greater expansive potential than sight because a person's name can be spoken at a greater remove than he or she can be seen.

Hearing is the dominant sense.   It *is* possible to construe hearing as the dominant sense in the Massim world. Hearing is associated with both socialization and sanity, as appears from the Duau child-rearing maxim that holds that "if a child runs about too much to other villages and does not listen to father and mother, when his parents die he will be like *uwauwa* (mad), not knowing how to do things properly" (Róheim 1950: 198). It is of related interest to note that the chief god of the Trobriand underworld is supposed to have large ears, which flap continually (Glass 1986: 56). The exaggerated ears of this deity may be seen as iconic of the extended role of hearing in Massim culture.

However, this interpretation of the cultural salience of hearing is misleading to the extent that it deflects attention from the fact that even greater value and importance is attached to "being heard." It is the same with the other senses: being seen is valued over seeing, being smelled is valued over smelling, and not eating (so there can be more food to distribute to others) is valued over eating. The way sensing the world is conceptualized in Massim psychology is, in an interesting sense, exactly the reverse of the way perception is conceptualized in Western psychology. In the Massim, perception has to do with the *production* of effects in others, as opposed to the *reception* of in-coming stimuli. This ex-centric conception of the perceptual process is consistent with the cultural emphasis on "expansion outward." The self-outered, as opposed to self-centered, directionality of Massim sensory psychology may also be seen to go along with the exchange-oriented, as opposed to consumer-oriented, character of Massim society.

The intellect is associated with hearing.   There is support for the proposition that intelligence is associated with hearing rather than, say, sight in the Duau child-rearing maxim quoted previously. Further support derives from the fact that in the language of the Trobriands "insanity" is denoted by a word that also means "deaf" (Senft 1986). Thus, mental disorder is conceptualized as a kind of hearing disorder.

However, the intellect is not actually thought to be situated in the ear or head. Malinowski records, "The seat of *nanola*, 'mind' is located in the throat, in the larynx, as they say," this being the place from which a person speaks (1961: 408–9; 1965 I: 445). The same association is found on Dobu (Fortune 1963: 168) and in a weakened form on Gawa (Munn 1986: 68). It follows that hearing is not yet knowing in the Massim, at least not in the same way "hearing is understanding" for such ear-minded peoples as the Suyà of Brazil (see Seeger 1981; Howes 1991: 175–78), or "seeing is believing" in the West (Dundes 1980; Tyler 1987). In the Massim, for something to be known it must first be voiced.[6]

In the Massim world, then, thinking seems to involve speaking and hearing oneself talk at the same time, either inwardly or outwardly. The following account of how spells are learned both confirms this point and brings out how the memory is thought to be situated in a different part of the body from the mind, namely, the belly.

A man will be said to have a good *nanola*, when he can acquire many formulae, but though they enter through the larynx, naturally, as he learns them, repeating word for word, he has to stow them away in a bigger and more commodious receptacle: they sink down right to the bottom of his abdomen. (Malinowski 1961: 409; see also Munn 1986: 228, 290 n. 32)

The idea that the memory resides in the belly explains why a novice sorcerer is obliged to drink salt water to purge his belly before receiving instruction from his mentor. It also explains why the sorcerer must refrain from food while practicing his art. The belly is regarded as a receptacle for words that are interiorized by repetition, and as the place from which magic outs. For the belly to contain or yield knowledge (read: "noise-force"), it must first be empty of food.

Awareness of this antithesis between eating and "sound-thinking," as the Massim conception of cognition might be called, would appear to be on the wane. Consider the following Trobriand incident.

One day I asked some men where magic resided. Bunemiga shook his head and said, "I think our ancestors made a mistake about that because they said magic stayed in belly. If that were true, then when we defecated we would lose all the magic. Our ancestors were wrong about magic. I think it stays in our heads." (Weiner 1976: 252)

For the "ancestors," however, the digestive tract was not the only tract that led to the belly, and words were not assimilated the same way food is. The mutual exclusivity of eating and memorization is still recognized on Gawa. There, "eating" is a metaphor for forgetting (Munn 1986: 66). Bunemiga, it seems, has already forgotten how to remember.

Knowledge has to be cast in verbal formulas, such as rhymes or commonplaces, to be memorable.   Orality theorists go so far as to claim that "the metric recitation of rhythmic formulas and commonplaces provides a communicational grid to *determine* knowledge in oral culture. Only those phenomena that fit existing formulas and commonplaces can be preserved as knowledge" (Lowe 1982: 3, emphasis added). Thought therefore tends to be formulaic, rather than analytical.

There is support for this proposition in the fact that Massim magical speech is strongly formulaic, contains many puns on words, and is heavily repetitive. However, the repetition is considered to be more for purposes of intensifying presence than for storing knowledge, and the puns are typically esoteric and inventive rather than commonplaces (see Malinowski 1961: 441, 448, 452). Furthermore, it is not solely in the verbal structure of the spell that knowledge is stored and communicated. The physical medium into which the spell is spoken is of *equal* importance. Indeed, the medium is intrinsic both to the conceptualization and to the communication (or effectiveness) of the message. The spoken word is therefore more dependent on its material embodiment in Massim practice than the theory of oral mentality would allow.[7]

The theory of oral mentality may also be criticized for failing to accord adequate importance to all the other modes of thought and communication besides speech in oral societies. Knowledge may be encoded in nonverbal forms as well. For example, Patrick Glass has shown that knowledge of the male role in procreation was *emblazoned* on Trobriand war shields. The apparently abstract designs are, in fact, anatomical diagrams. Such knowledge could not be verbalized precisely "for fear of offending 'the ears of the spirits'" (1986: 60). This, then, is a case of knowledge *having* to be encoded nonverbally for cultural or religious reasons.

A further limitation of language that orality theorists often fail to appreciate is that words, particularly "hard words" (as they are called in the Trobriands—that is, words spoken in anger or that state the truth) can be all too memorable. Annette Weiner noted a marked reticence among her Trobriand informants as regards making explicit their thoughts and intentions: these are, in fact, *supposed* to remain hidden. Rather than define a situation by speaking about it, Trobrianders often prefer to express their thoughts and emotions through food prestations, kula shells, and other nonverbal (or sensual) media, such as body decoration (Weiner 1983; 1988: 39; 1976: 86–87, 212; Munn 1986: 68).

Kula shells and body decorations constitute extensions of the senses, as discussed previously. These nonverbal modes of communication may convey very detailed or "analytical" appraisals of a person's worth or a situation's significance. Where, then, does the idea that thought in oral societies is nonanalytical come from? It comes from the orality theorist assuming that speech is paramount and looking only to linguistic usage for evidence of analytic modes of thought. Not finding anything but formulas used in public oratory, magic, and mythtelling, the orality theorist concludes that thought in oral societies is "nonanalytical." But this is a foregone conclusion if those are the only places the analyst is prepared to look!

The individuation (or rational structuring) of ideas, as of people, is comparatively slight. This branch of the theory of oral mentality holds that thought in oral cultures tends to be diffuse or "participatory" (meaning emotional) as opposed to "rational." The reason for this is that "speech is assimilated directly by the ear, without the mediation of the eye. And we are moved more by sound than by sight, since the former surrounds us, whereas the latter distances" (Lowe 1982: 7). Personality structures are also deemed to be more collectivist (or sociocentric) than individualist in orientation in oral cultures because hearing is a more "social" sense (Ong 1982).

Giancarlo Scoditti's (1984/85, 1982) account of the apprenticeship of prowboard carvers on Kitava provides an instructive context for the examination of this proposition. One of the stages in the initiation rite for an apprentice carver involves the carver-initiator uttering a spell as he and the initiate bend over a pool of water. The spell is supposed to induce the apprentice to see himself as the reflection, or mirror image, of his instructor. In the course of the rite:

> The mind of the initiate, as the mind of his mirrored image, the carver-initiator, is "wrapped" or "enveloped" by an external power, sometimes thought of as the mythical hero Monikiniki . . .

The performers [who have become as one] are momentarily "blind." During the performers' blindness the hero Monikiniki, represented . . . as "Shout," spreads his creative power upon them, and they in their turn "spread" the same power, as "images," upon the commoners. (1982: 79)

The carver-initiator is the link between the initiate and the culture hero Monikiniki, just as the prowboards he has carved mediate the initiate's first "vision" of the abstract model (the ideal form of the prowboard) he will later reproduce in his own work. The purpose of the rite is to transform this relation of mediation into one of identification. Hence its strong "participatory" or "confused" character, as McLuhan and Ong—or Lévy-Bruhl (1978)—would say.

While it is certainly possible to point to various cases of "mystical participation" in Massim culture, there is an equal if not stronger accent on differentiation. People distinguish themselves from each other by means of the food taboos they keep and, significantly, by means of the sounds they make. For instance, rattling one's lime spatula in one's lime gourd is a chiefly prerogative in the Trobriands, which commoners are forbidden to emulate (Weiner 1976: 207).

People are above all differentiated by their faces. A child's face is supposed to resemble its father's visage, both in those cultures where physiological paternity is recognized and in the Trobriands where it is not (Malinowski 1929: 204; Weiner 1976: 123; Munn 1986: 142–43). The significance of this resemblance lies in the fact that it is through the father that the individual is connected with the world outside the confines of his or her own matrilineal subclan (*susu* or *dala*). As Munn puts it, facial appearance is "the domain of relationality to the other or to an extrinsic, external order" (1986: 143). The "expansion outward" of the individual is thus already visible, already implicit, in the features of that individual's face at birth. The individual's life will be spent establishing ever more interfaces with the external world through food distribution, courting, kulaing, and so on—in short, all the arenas where a person's own individual "fame" can be enhanced through exchange.

According to orality theory, and Western notions generally, the eye distances, objectifies, and judges. Sight is further held to be the most rational of the senses. Vision is constructed quite differently in the more acoustically minded cultures of the Massim. There, the eyes are divorced from ratiocination; they are, in fact, "the things of copulation." Malinowski explains: "The eyes are [considered] the primary motive of all sexual excitation . . . they are 'that which makes us desire to copulate.' In proof of this the natives say: 'A man with his eyes closed will have no erection'" (1929: 166). Sight is thus the erotic sense as opposed to the intellectual sense, by Massim standards. Vision attracts rather than distances.

The eyes are not only a seat of lust; they are themselves a focus of erotic interest. Trobriand sexual foreplay typically involves nipping at one's partner's eyelashes and, in the throes of passion, even biting them off (Malinowski 1929: 297, 342–43). This eroticization of the eyes is comparable to the eroticization of the mouth in the West, as in the practice of the kiss. Significantly, Trobrianders never kiss each other on the mouth, for the mouth is not an erotogenic zone; it is an organ of the intellect.

Besides eroticizing the eyes, the Trobrianders have eroticized the nasal apparatus: they kiss by rubbing noses, and, like other Massim peoples, they believe strongly in the erotic potential of scents.

According to Massim sensory anatomy, then, the nose, the eyes, the belly, and the genitals all form one system—the *system of desire,* as it might be called. This system is complemented by the *acoustic system,* which connects the ears, the mouth-throat (seat of the intelligence), and the belly (seat of the memory) and is concerned with the functions of the intellect. The two systems interact with each other, of course—they are not hermetically sealed—and the main point at which they interconnect, it seems, is the belly.

The sorcerer, the kula voyager, or indeed anyone preparing for an important undertaking must abstain from various foods for a prescribed period. The sensuous reasoning behind this practice is now apparent: abstention from food expands the individual's powers of thought and reduces interference with the "noise-force" contained in the belly. This "noise-force" becomes focused as it is channeled through the larynx and issues in the form of the magical words that predict and thereby control the world. Ideally, the power so unleashed goes on to resonate as thunder, as in the case of the *sulumwoya* spell.

Sound, or "noise-force," is the precondition for, and the cumulative effect of, the exercise of influence in the Massim world. The "outerance" of sound, the spreading of renown, is the ultimate goal of every undertaking. This *telos* is reflected in the way the nonaural senses are utilized as well: they too are turned outward, so that the accent is on being seen rather than seeing, on radiating a sweet scent rather than smelling, on being mobile rather than motionless, and on scourging the tastebuds with ginger (or depriving them altogether) rather than glutting one's appetite.[8]

Twisted Senses: Sensory Profile of the Massim Witch

The pattern of sensory functioning described previously is the normative one. It is most perfectly embodied in the way the big man or "man of influence" uses his senses. The sensory profile of the witch is the reverse of that of the big man and can usefully be studied as a further source of evidence regarding the indigenous anatomy of the senses and the intellect.

The witch is distinguished first of all by her sex: witches are invariably female. The witch is also distinguished by her invisibility and extraordinary powers of sight. For example, on Gawa,

> although others cannot see the witch, the latter's own vision exceeds the ordinary. The witch can see through the opaque forms of houses and other persons. In one [Gawan] folktale, a witch's visionary capacity is depicted as an actual extension of the body; an old woman sent her eyes out each day to roam in the four directions across the seas to other islands to eat. This spatial extension of seeing is the reverse of the body's capacity to *be seen* by others. (Munn 1986: 232)

Witches are otherwise distinguished by their inaudibility and extraordinary powers of hearing. The witch is "inaudible" in that, by convention, her name is never spoken in public; conversely, her special auditory powers enable her to "hear" that a person has died at such and such a place, or that a canoe is in danger (Munn 1986: 217–18; Malinowski 1961: 241). Witches may also be guided to the scene of a burial or a shipwreck by their hyperacute power of smell, while their presence at such a site is said to be betrayed by the putrid or fecal odor they give off (Malinowski 1929: 449; 1961: 242; Battaglia 1990: 59, 67). Above all, witches are distinguished by their constant desire to eat, to consume. Nothing haunts the Massim imagination more than the image of a band of witches trysting on a reef, whetting their appetite for human flesh by partaking of a special kind of coral and proceeding to dine on human corpses (Malinowski 1961: 244; 1929: 45–46).

Comparing the image of the witch with that of the big man, a range of highly significant reversals can be seen: the witch whets her appetite by eating coral, the big man is forever using magic to suppress his appetite; the witch emits an odious smell, the big man gives off a sweet scent; the witch has the power to render herself invisible (by "peeling off her skin"), the big man is constantly seeking to maximize his visibility by oiling his skin and ornamenting his body; the witch's name is unheard of, whereas the big man, through the circulation of his name in the kula, is talked about far and wide.

The contrasting sensory powers and characteristics attributed to the witch and the big man evidently have important gender connotations. The femininity of the witch links women to undesirable sensory traits, while the masculinity of the big man associates men with desirable characteristics. The Massim sensory order is inflected with gender values, whereby the most valued sensory traits are manifested in their fullest form by men. The frightening figure of the witch may, in this context, represent the fear of what might happen if women, blocked from attaining authority and influence through socially accepted avenues, were to try to acquire power through illicit means (see Classen 1998: 78–82).

The contrasting traits of the witch and the big man reflect the negative value attached to interiorization and the positive value ascribed to exteriorization in Massim culture. The witch is the epitome of the consumer, whereas the big man is the epitome of the exchanger. In the opposition between these two figures, it is possible to perceive an echo of the opposition between our own consumer-oriented society, with its understanding of perception as reception, and the exchange-oriented cultures of the Massim, with their emphasis on perception as communication. Most Westerners would be witches by Massim standards, because they consume without knowing how to give. Conversely, most Massim people seem quite profligate by Western standards, since they know not how to save.

CHAPTER 5

The Visible and the Invisible
in a Middle Sepik Society

The Washkuk Hills are situated in the Ambunti District of East Sepik Province. They are inhabited by the Kwoma. John Whiting's *Becoming a Kwoma* is probably the best known source on this Middle Sepik society. The Kwoma have also been studied by Christian Kaufmann, Margaret Holmes Williamson, and Ross Bowden, whose excellent book *Yena: Art and Ceremony in a Sepik Society* and recent *Dictionary of Kwoma* contain much information of relevance to the present inquiry into the Kwoma sensory order. The following brief ethnographic description is based partly on Bowden's books and partly on notes I took during the time I spent in Tongwinjamb Camp at Ambunti, and in the villages of Tongwinjamb and Beglam during a visit to Kwoma territory in 1990.

The Kwoma are bordered by the Nukuma to the north and northwest (who speak a dialect of the Kwoma language), the Mayo to the west, the Kaunga to the east, and the Manambu and Iatmul to the south and southeast (fig. 5). Traditionally, each of the four Kwoma tribes formed a single settlement or village located atop a mountain ridge. Each village was itself made up of a number of hamlets, occupied by the members of from one to three patriclans. Tongwinjamb and Urambanj are the only tribe-villages to retain their residential solidarity since pacification. The other tribes have splintered, whence the eight villages met with today.

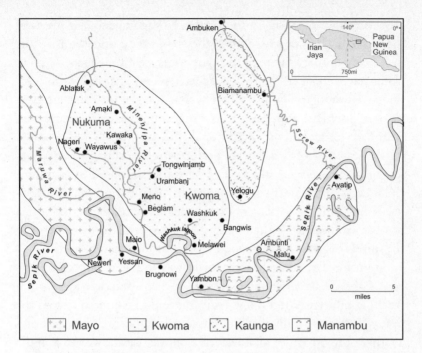

Fig. 5.   Map of Kwoma Territory, East Sepik Province. (Map by Derek Parent, based on Bowden 1983: 10.)

The highest point in each hamlet was traditionally occupied by a Haus tambaran or men's house. Each of the resident clans would affix polychrome paintings of its totemic beings to the house ceiling and carve representations of its totems on the posts and beams, so that the interior of the Haus tambaran constituted "a visual representation of the totemic composition of the community" (Bowden 1983: 30).

The Kwoma subsist on sago, which grows wild in the swamps at the base of the mountain ridges. They also cultivate yams, dry taro, and a few other vegetables in hillside garden plots. Yams are the most highly valued food, even though they are much less important to the Kwoma diet than sago. Bowden estimates that yams and other tubers constitute less than 5 percent, whereas sago constitutes close to 80 percent, by weight, of food consumed on a daily basis (1983: 30).

The disproportionate value attached to yams has a historical explanation. The Kwoma migrated into the Washkuk area from

The Visible and the Invisible in a Middle Sepik Society

the Toricelli mountains to the north. In the indigenous cultures of the latter region, yams are both the staple food and the focus of men's ceremonial (Tuzin 1972, 1980; Forge 1971; Bowden 1983: 2–3). Yams have remained the focus of men's ceremonial in Kwoma culture, even though sago has taken over as the staple. Yams are considered powerful and dangerous on account of their association with the spirits, and as a traditional rule, no yams could be eaten until a set range of rituals were performed. The rituals in question, known as *yena*, *mindja*, and *nowkwi*, were also supposed to guarantee the success of the next year's harvest, by propitiating the yam spirits. While only two villages, Tongwinjamb and Bangwis, continue to observe these rites, the memory of them remains quite vivid in the minds of most older Kwoma people from other villages.

Traditionally, every Kwoma male was initiated into either the *yena* or the *mindja* ceremonial section (or men's secret society) upon reaching puberty. After a few years, he could be invited to join the opposite section. Only if a man was an accomplished homicide and a father of many children, however, would he be allowed to join the august third section, *nowkwi*. The responsibility for planting yams was also reserved for men of the *nowkwi* cult. As the qualifications for membership in *nowkwi* suggest, Kwoma men conceive of themselves (ideally) both as creators of human beings and of yams and as killers. "These two ideas are actually related in Kwoma thought, since it is by killing enemies that men are believed to acquire the capacity to plant and grow yams. If a man who had not killed were to plant yams, people say, the tubers would simply rot in the ground" (Bowden 1990: 483).

The association between creativity (fertility) and aggression is very close in the Kwoma imaginary, and we shall be encountering many expressions of this association in what follows. This study begins, however, with an inquiry into the processes of emplacement in the Middle Sepik—that is, into how the Kwoma construct their environment, and construct themselves in the process.

Between Ridge and Swamp

The physical environment of the Kwoma consists of mountain ridges that are separated by swampy valleys and muddy streams that drain into the Sepik. It is indicative of the value the Kwoma attach to the different sectors of their environment that the name by which they designate themselves is derived from the word for "hill" (*kwo-*) and the word for "man" (*-ma*). The Kwoma thus identify both themselves as human beings and their civilization with the mountain crests, and they dissociate themselves from the watery, nether regions of the Middle Sepik environment.

It is a precarious order the Kwoma have carved out for themselves on these mountain crests. The layout of a settlement follows the dictates of topography, rather than any preconceived plan. Each hamlet belonging to a settlement, like each of the houses that make up a hamlet, is situated at a different elevation. The spaces between the houses, as well as the paths that connect them, tend to be overgrown with vegetation. When it rains, the paths turn into gushing streams, effectively severing communication.

Despite the Kwoma preference for being on high, solid ground, it is from the lowlands—the spaces *between* the ridges—that they derive the better part of their subsistence. Sago, their staple food, and fish, their principal source of animal protein, come from below. The sensory ambience of the lowlands, the valleys, contrasts with that of the mountain ridges in a number of important respects: visibility is greatly reduced in the valleys, the ground underfoot is always mushy, and each step triggers transient smells of rotting vegetation or of wildflowers. The swamp is a seedbed of corruption and fertility. It is a space in which tracks or boundaries are difficult to discern. In the swamp, everything tends either to ooze or to swarm—before one's eyes, over one's body. Insects thrive there more than humans. They also thrive *on* humans, much to the latter's discomfort.

The Kwoma conceive of the swarms of mosquitoes that make their life so miserable as issuing from the mouth of a giant crocodile. This *sikilowas*, or "bush spirit," lives somewhere in the swamp between Tongwinjamb and Beglam. Sometimes, out of frustration more than anything, the Kwoma beat out angry rhythms on their slit gongs, threatening the crocodile spirit, and commanding it to shut its mouth, usually to no avail (Whiting 1938: 27).

Other bush spirits take the form of unusual natural features, such as a hardwood tree in the middle of a stand of sago palms, or the odd boulder on a riverbank. These spirits strongly object to being touched or moved. Should they be disturbed, they retaliate by shooting invisible sago needles into the careless intruder's flesh (Whiting 1938: 26; Bowden 1983: 91). The swamp is thus not only an area of incessant corruption and rampant fertility, it is also the locus of a host of visible and invisible entities that threaten to, and frequently do, invade the boundaries of the body.

As if the various threats to bodily integrity posed by the natural and spiritual forces of their environment were not enough, the Kwoma must also be wary of sorcery attack. Sorcerers operate in two principal ways. The most deadly form of sorcery involves magically or literally poisoning a victim's food. Anxiety over the threat of food poisoning runs deep. For example, when going on a short visit to another village, people will often take their own food along and consume it just prior to arrival, so as not to have to consume any potentially poisoned food at their destination.

The other principal way a sorcerer operates is by obtaining "sorcery materials." He may either steal this material from the victim himself or have it supplied by the person who bears the grudge he has been asked to avenge.

> [He] then puts the sorcery material in a special narrow-necked clay pot and puts it on the fire. When the pot and its contents are very hot he pours some cold water in it. The result is a burst of steam. If the sorcery material completely disappears with the explosion, the victim will die; if some fragments are still left he will merely be very sick. (Whiting 1938: 68; see further Bowden 1987, 1997: 192–93)

Effective sorcery materials include a person's food leavings, the butt of a cigarette, an infant's feces, or a man's sperm or blood (including the blood of an animal he has killed or eaten). Scrupulous care is accordingly taken with respect to the disposal of these body products and wastes. Food leavings, for example, are scraped together and placed in a pile in plain view of the house and burned.

The fear of sorcery so prevalent in Kwoma life may be related to the tensions intrinsic to the Kwoma social order. Each clan consists of a residentially stable core of agnatically related men, and these men are obliged to marry women, just as their sisters must marry men, belonging to other clans. "What do you call your brother-in-law?" Bowden once asked, in an attempt to elicit Kwoma kinship terminology. "Enemy," came the answer (1990: 481). The relation between male relatives by marriage is thus a basically hostile one.

The relation between husbands and wives is an ambivalent one. Married women not only come from "enemy" groups by definition, but also remain, in certain important ways, permanently identified with those groups.

> For instance, married women regularly visit and are visited by their brothers, "enemies," who have an obligation to "look after" (*aboboy hawa*) them throughout their adult lives, and all men believe that if they alienate or persistently antagonize their wives the latter will not hesitate either to divorce them or secretly to send some of their leavings to their brothers with instructions to perform sorcery against them. (Bowden 1990: 481)

It is the structurally anomalous position of women in the Kwoma social order that both stimulates and exacerbates sorcery fears. Women are intrinsic outsiders, permanently displaced persons. Were the Kwoma to adopt a nonlineal descent principle, or an alternative residence rule, there would not be the same constant distrust in the relations between spouses or friction between affines, and sorcery fears would abate substantially. But such an eventuality appears unlikely.

The anomalous position of women in the Kwoma social order resonates with their ambiguous position in the Kwoma cosmological and sensory orders. Men are stable, like mountain ridges, whereas women are mobile or fluid, like water. Women accordingly tend to be associated with the space *between* the mountain ridges, which is to say, the low-lying swamps. As Williamson notes, "In [Kwoma] narrative women are usually carrying out some activity in a swamp, while men are working in gardens or resting in villages, both located on ridges or upper slopes. The women's activities in these stories are always the same—fishing or working sago" (1990: 386).

The association between the female sex and swamps is otherwise reflected in the idea of women as intrinsically "cold," like water, in contrast to men, who are distinguished by their "heat" (on which more later). It is further reflected in the idea of women as polluting, particularly during their menses. For instance, it is taboo for a woman to handle or cook food for her husband while she is menstruating. It is thought that the "bad blood" in her body would somehow contaminate the food and make her husband sick if he consumed it (Whiting 1938: 96; Bowden 1983: 102). The notion of menstrual blood as at once fertile and contaminating ties in with the association between women and swamps.

Scarification: Hardening the Skin

The plethora of natural, spiritual, and human threats to bodily integrity that the Kwoma recognize in and project onto their surroundings has led them to place a premium on "strength" and "hardness" in women as in men. One of the ways in which the "hardness" considered necessary to withstand the rigors of the Middle Sepik environment is built up is through ritual scarification. Upon reaching puberty, girls are cicatrized with elaborate oval designs around the navel, while boys are carved with half-moon shapes above each nipple (Whiting 1970: 71–72; Williamson 1979a). The scars are regarded as a kind of prophylaxis against pain. I was told (boastfully) by one man that once having undergone the ordeal of scarification, "if you are stabbed in a fight, you won't feel a thing."

In addition to promoting physical strength by literally fortifying the skin (in that the horned ridges of the designs have a different, harder feel from the rest of the epidermis), cicatrices are regarded as evidence of physical strength. A particularly ornate scar carries moral and aesthetic connotations as well. Williamson explains:

That a woman's scar demonstrates physical endurance is easy to appreciate. This endurance has moral connotations also because scars are supposed to be beautiful, and the girl's cooperation is necessary to the beauty of her scars. Beauty in all forms pleases the bush spirits, who reward the beautiful with prosperity and health. A woman who has suffered to be beautiful is thus morally good as well as strong. (1990: 389)

The designs carved on women's bellies are supposed to represent various animals and plants in nature, but it requires familiarity with the cicatrizer to know exactly what a given scar represents. In any event, Williamson found that her informants were not much concerned with the identification or referential meaning of a mark; what they emphasized was its uniqueness (1979a: 40–41).

The meaning of Kwoma female (and male) rituals of body scarification is primarily in their doing. It is not what the designs carved on the skin can be said to "say" that is significant ("this is an oval, that is a moon," etc.), but what they signify about the qualities of the person who bears them. The scars are signs of moral endurance. Significantly, in Kwoma narratives, reference is often made to the condition of a character's skin. Good characters have dark and well-decorated skins, while bad characters have skins that are "blotchy with streaming sores and an unpleasant smell" (Williamson 1983: 17). This contrast illustrates the importance Kwoma attach to strong bodily boundaries, or in other words, "hard" skin. To have a "weak," permeable skin is a not only a sign of despicable physical decrepitude, but of moral corruption as well.

The Circulation of Blood

To remain "strong," Kwoma individuals have not only to fortify themselves against corruption from without by developing "hard" skins, they must also protect themselves from the corruption that they perceive as internal to their bodies. "Rotten blood" is cited as the cause of illnesses ranging from headaches to sprains (Whiting 1938: 67). All such illnesses are treated by making incisions in the skin around the ailing part and draining off the stagnant blood.

In addition to modulating sickness, bloodletting once played a central role in modulating growth and gender, as appears from a consideration of the traditional Kwoma male initiation ritual. This rite, known as *handapia-sugwia*, used to be held every five years. It provided uninitiated boys with the opportunity to enter the first grade of the traditional age-grade system, which consisted of four grades in all. It also gave previously initiated youths the chance to advance their status in the system.

On the appointed day, the youths of two or three adjacent hamlets would march together with the senior men down to a stream at
the base of the ridge. There, each boy would be assigned a sponsor
or "ceremonial father." These men proceeded to slash the initiates'
tongues and penises, letting the blood flow away in the stream; they
would then rub salt or ashes in the wounds. A two-day ceremony
involving all of the inhabitants of the hamlets followed, marked by
sexual license. During this ceremony, the youths showed off the
ornaments they were newly entitled to wear in accordance with
their change in status.

On the morning of the third day, the sponsors took the youngest
grade of initiates to the men's house. There the boys would remain
for the next two months, taking care to avoid being seen by women
and always wearing their penis sheaths when they ventured out.
During this period, the novices were fed "hot" food, cooked in the
men's house by the initiators, and given ginger to chew while they
were taught the myths and songs belonging to their respective
clans. While secluded from women, the initiates also engaged in
hunting competitions and were cicatrized. At the end of the period,
a small ceremony was held in which, according to Whiting, "each
boy puts his phallocrypt over a growing bamboo shoot, which in
time splits the ornament and is supposed to symbolize and induce
magically the growth of the lad's penis" (1941: 65–67; see further
Kaufmann 1972: 179).

The *handapia-sugwia* ritual is of considerable interest, for it brings
out a range of Kwoma conceptions relating to blood, food, growth,
masculinity, heat, and space. It should be noted first that the ceremonial slashing of penis and tongue in the context of this ritual was
typically preceded by many years of "private" penile phlebotomy
by the boys themselves:

[For a boy was] taught that growth depends upon the renewal of
the blood, and that food produces blood, which promotes
growth as long as it is fresh. When blood has been in the system
for a time, however, it begins to grow stale and finally rotten,
and the growth ceases until the bad blood is removed from the
body . . . [The] best method of removing this bad blood is
through the penis . . . Boys frequently go into the bushes and

scrape their penises with nettle leaves so that the blood may flow out. (Whiting 1941: 64)

The Kwoma conceive of the inside of the male body as no less "swampy," or prone to stagnation and decay, than the inside of the female body. They also consider women to have a certain advantage over men in that the latter possess a "natural mechanism" for purging their bodies of stagnant blood—namely, menstruation. Men and boys, by contrast, must resort to artificial means—bleeding their penises—for this purpose. The Kwoma explicitly liken this male practice to female menstruation (Williamson 1990: 391; Bowden 1983: 105; Whiting 1938: 62).

When the sponsors bled the penises (and tongues) of the initiates in *handapia-sugwia* they were not simply imitating women, however. Rather, they were making men of the boys by purifying the latter of "a female aspect of themselves" (Williamson 1990: 391). Children are thought to inherit their blood in equal parts from both parents, the blood from the mother being "cold," that from the father "hot." It was to rid the boys of this "cold," feminine aspect of themselves that *handapia-sugwia* was performed. The boys were then literally fed their masculinity in the form of the "hot" food cooked by the initators, which became male, "hot" blood to replace the blood that had been drained from their bodies.

It is significant that the boys were bled in the low, marshy area of the stream, then removed to the high, solid area of the men's house to be fed. This spatial displacement both emphasized the opposition between the female and male domains of Kwoma existence and formed an integral part of the transformational process by which the boys came to acquire the ideal masculine qualities of "heat" and "hardness." Their seclusion from the gaze of the women and their participation in exclusively masculine pursuits, such as the hunting competitions, helped to further solidify and give definition to their emergent masculine identities.

The exclusively masculine, perfectly bounded existence, which the youths enjoyed during their initiation into manhood, could not endure indefinitely. Within a few months, they were forced to descend again into the relatively "feminine" everyday world and consume the food prepared for them by women. Williamson notes that "ordinary cooked food is tepid or cold when eaten" (1990: 391). The consumption of lukewarm food, coupled with more intimate contact with women, was believed to drain the youths, and men in general, of their "heat" by cooling the blood and causing it to stultify. If allowed to go unchecked, this degeneration is thought to sap men of their physical, intellectual, and spiritual potency. Hence the necessity of periodically purging themselves of the blood in their systems that had become "cold" through daily contact with women, thereby "reheating" their bodies.

We have seen that the Kwoma place a premium on corporeal boundedness and seek to promote this through "hardening" the skin. At the same time, they conceive of the bounded body as prone to stagnation and so must periodically bleed themselves to ensure health and growth. "It is believed, furthermore, that any blood, once it has left the body of an individual, is very harmful to him should it return" (Whiting 1938: 94). It is for this reason that the initiates in *handapia-sugwia* were bled into a stream that flowed out of the tribal territory. They were also prohibited from eating fish for a certain period, so that there would be no danger of their blood reentering their bodies through the fish that might have ingested it. To eat one's own blood was thought to constitute the most serious possible threat to a person's health, for it represented a total confusion of boundaries.

Blood and Generation

The taboo on eating one's own blood also informs the alimentary prohibitions that must be observed by hunters and those men who plant yams. Both hunting and planting yams are classified by the Kwoma as male generative acts, for a man's blood is believed to enter (and actually nurture) the yams he plants, as well as to enter the animals he spears. For a man to eat of his own harvest or of his own kill would therefore be equivalent to eating his own blood, with the result that he could sicken and die (Whiting 1941: 110, 113; compare Gell 1979: 137). To avoid this danger, a hunter never eats the game he kills himself, but rather distributes it in a feast, and yam-planters arrange among themselves to plant sections of each other's gardens, from the harvest of which they may eat without fear of falling ill.

These taboos have the effect of promoting social exchange, but the rationale for them, significantly, is not framed in terms of reciprocity. Rather, they are understood to protect the body from invasion by exteriorized aspects of the person's *own* generative potential. This understanding contrasts sharply with the situation in the Massim world (chap. 3): there, as the reader will recall, people engage in exchange in order to enhance their fame—that is, to *extend* the boundaries of their persons. We shall come back to this point later.

Among the Kwoma, a man's blood is also thought to circulate outside his own body in the form of the children he generates. It is the "one blood" relation of the father with his children, and of the latter among themselves, that forms the basis of the Kwoma incest taboo. The rationale for this taboo again takes an interesting turn when expressed in Kwoma terms, since the idea is not "marry out or be killed off" (which would place the emphasis on alliance, on exchange), but rather "to partake of one's own blood is deadly"— an alimentary rationale for exogamy, as it were. Of course, this peculiarity of the Kwoma is one of emphasis only, since the Kwoma do contract matrimonial alliances. Significantly, however, they have also elaborated a complex system of "friendship" alliances.[1]

It might seem contradictory that spearing animals is included in the category of male generative acts, since we do not normally think of killing as an act of generation. However, as Williamson points out, "there is a relationship between spearing, on one hand, and planting and impregnating on the other, in that all involve insertion of one thing in another" (1979b: 215). The association between procreating, planting, and killing is further borne out by the notion that "if a man is engaged in generation of one kind [e.g., planting yams in his garden], he should refrain from other kinds [e.g., sexual intercourse] lest he divert his generating energy and spoil both enterprises" (Williamson 1979a: 36).[2]

The taboos that a man must observe when his wife is pregnant (or has just given birth) are identical to those that a yam-planter must follow until the tubers germinate and to the taboos that must be respected by a man who has just speared an enemy. These taboos include not washing, not drinking water, using a stick to scratch oneself, and smoking cigarettes with tweezers rather than one's fingers (Whiting and Reed 1938/39: 211; Newton 1971: 36). All of these taboos emphasize the "heat" of the man's condition. In effect, he is so "hot" that it is dangerous for him to touch himself; at the same time, he does not want to dissipate this "heat" by washing or drinking water since the success of the enterprise depends on him remaining in a "heated" condition.

We have seen that the Kwoma conceive of masculine productive activities, from generating children to spearing pigs, as involving an outering of the blood. It is because male blood is "hot" that it has this generative potential. What of the productive activities of women, such as bearing children, processing sago, cooking, weaving net bags? Here we encounter the curious fact that women are not supposed to have any generative potential because of the "coldness" of their blood (Williamson 1979b: 215; Bowden 1983: 101). This ascribed "coldness" renders everything about them, and everything that they produce, destructive of "heat."

This disqualification of women from playing any sort of creative role in Kwoma society is connected to the way in which women are imagined to "produce" in Kwoma culture. Women produce through absorbing things (food, semen) into themselves or their environment, in contrast to men, who produce through the insertion of one thing into another. Women's receptivity seems to be a source of some disturbance to Kwoma men. This is perhaps partly because of the men's concern with establishing boundaries (which the women have little interest in defending, given their intrinsic outsider position in their matrimonial village) and partly because men perceive the absorbing ways of women in light of the image of the swamp, which sucks and drains. This image is the very antithesis of men's existence as *kwo-ma*, "mountain-men"—that is, as firm instead of swampy, and as visibly outstanding instead of enveloping.

Visual Domination

In Kwoma society, relations between the sexes are intimately bound up with the regulation of looking behavior. This was especially true when the Kwoma still went naked. As Whiting and Reed (1938/39: 209) aptly put it, "conventions function[ed] in place of clothing." These conventions, the visual code of Kwoma society, were remarkably elaborate and entailed, among other things, a complete disjunction between speaking to and looking at another person of the opposite sex.

> When men and women meet on the path the woman steps aside and stands with her back to the path until the man passes. Only after they have passed and are facing away from one another do they speak. When a man visits the house of a friend he must keep his gaze fixed on the ground until he has taken a seat facing away from the women present . . . On the woman's part, she must always sit with legs together, either straight in front of her or bent up to one side. For a man to have an erection in public is a very shameful thing and was never observed by us. (Whiting and Reed 1938/39: 209–10)

In theory, then, the sexes were invisible to each other, or rather, they occupied the peripheral field of each other's vision. Only husbands and wives were permitted to look at one another directly. For anyone else to do so was considered a sexual advance. In the case of a man, such advances were punished by the woman's protectors sorcerizing the man, or seeking to seduce his sister in return. In the case of a woman, the punishment consisted of a beating, for her protectors conceived of themselves as having an "economic interest" in her chastity—that is, in the bridewealth she would bring—and did not want her to acquire a loose reputation (Whiting 1941: 76, 87; 1938: 59, 96–99). In practice, these taboos on looking were constantly, if surreptitiously, breached—for both men and women prided themselves on their sexual conquests.

The regulation of looking behavior began in infancy. Training was more strict in the case of a boy than of a girl. The girl had primarily to learn how to control her posture (keeping her legs pressed together when sitting, for example), "sitting properly" being one of the defining characteristics of womanhood. The boy had to learn to keep his eyes strictly to himself. His female relatives would scold him if they caught him staring at their genitals; if a boy were to have an erection in his sister's presence, she would take this as an "insult" and hit his penis with a stick. At puberty, the taboo on staring at a woman's genitals extended to all parts of a woman's body (Whiting 1938: 96–100; 1970: 41).

The relations of visual control and domination established in childhood are reversed in adulthood: men come to dominate what women can see. For instance, it is strictly forbidden for a woman to see the musical instruments and sculptures associated with the yam cults. When new initiates are first shown these instruments and carvings, they are warned very seriously that the mere knowledge of the secret of the cult—the secret being that the spirits are made of wood, and their voices are the men playing instruments—may "kill" members of the female sex, as well as noninitiated members of the male sex (Whiting 1941: 89).

The basic pattern, then, is that men are prohibited to look at women's reproductive organs, while women are forbidden to see the male organs for the regeneration of nature and the cosmos— the latter "organs" being the flutes and gongs, carvings and flat paintings, that the men use to propitiate the yam harvest spirits. By propitiating the spirits, the men ensure the fertility of the yam plots (compare Tuzin 1980, 1995).

That men dominate sight is the fundamental social fact of Kwoma society. Various myths legitimate this male-visual dominance, such as the myth of the origin of the Haus tambaran. This myth relates how two brothers, seeing some people come out of a hole in the ground, went down into it themselves and "looking round" saw a men's ceremonial house for the first time. After memorizing the design of the building and the flat paintings on its ceiling, they returned from what was, in fact, the village of the spirits of the dead and made a copy of the building in their own hamlet. Bowden comments, "By attributing a supernatural origin to . . . men's houses, this myth thereby invests them with a sanctity and authority in social and ritual life that is beyond question. Men's houses, that is, form part of the divine order of things" (1990: 485).

The divine order of things is a visual order of things. This is apparent from a consideration of the power the Kwoma ascribe to the representations of spirits that decorate the cross-beams of the men's ceremonial house. These carvings are believed to *be* the spirits they represent.

Located as they are above the center of the men's house, the spirits are thought to look down on and preside over the activities
that take place in the building. For instance, if a man were to
strike another in anger during a meeting in the building (something that is strictly prohibited), these spirits, it is believed,
would immediately afflict him with disease. (Bowden 1990: 487)

Thus, the men *visualize* the spirits (or in other words, make representations of them) and are in turn *watched over* by them. It is in a
related way that men are required to "look after" their married sisters, watching out for their welfare (Bowden 1997: 134).

The Origin of the Flutes

Another myth that deals with male-visual dominance, and also provides the charter of Kwoma gender relations, is the myth of the origin of the bamboo flutes (Bowden 1983: 125–26). According to
myth, these instruments were inadvertently discovered by some
women while they were fishing. Realizing that the flutes were powerful spirits, the women kept their discovery a secret from the men.
The following day, they told their husbands that they were going
fishing, but in fact went and built a ceremonial house high in the
branches of a hardwood tree.

Each day the women would go to this house and play on the
flutes, leaving the men to do the work of gardening, fishing, and
caring for the children. As the men did not know any ceremonies at
this time, all they could do was stand at the base of the tree and listen, without being able to see. The women soon began ordering
their husbands to cook and bring food for their ceremonies. One
day, after a man was brutally beaten for failing to fulfill his wife's
orders, the men decided to retaliate. They allied themselves with a
borer beetle, which ate through the trunk of the tree, causing it to
topple. As the women fell to the ground, the men speared them and
proceeded to appropriate the flutes for themselves.

This origin myth depicts a situation that is the reverse of the
conventional Kwoma social and sensory order: women above men,
men not being able to see, and men having to play the role of cooks

and porters of food for the women and spirits. Especially significant is the way the myth represents social dominance as dependent on control of the means of communication with the spirits—as opposed to, say, control of the means of production, or any innatist doctrine of men as "naturally" superior to women. Indeed, the men are portrayed as *usurping* their power and position from the women by an act of treachery (teaming up with the borer beetle). As the myth also suggests, it is by artifice that the men perpetuate their position of dominance.

There is clearly a great deal of ambivalence concerning gender roles and status in Kwoma society. As this myth attests, men are conscious of the fact that they rule by artifice, not natural right (which if anything is on the side of the women). This ties in with men's consciousness of the artificiality of the means they employ to maintain their health (bleeding their penises), in contrast to women, whose health is naturally superior to men's on account of their menstrual cycle. Another sign of the depth of Kwoma ambivalence as regards gender roles and status is manifest in the sex of the spirits of the Kwoma pantheon. Most of them are *female*. Moreover, while all Kwoma spirits are aggressive and destructive (like men, in contrast to women, who are ideally submissive), the highest and most destructive spirit of them all, Nankwi, is female (Williamson 1983: 19–20; Bowden 1983: 77–82, 93).

The myth of the origin of the flutes poses an interesting epistemological question, which goes to the heart of Kwoma culture. Who bears the greater burden: the women who see nothing and therefore remain ignorant of the men's secret, while cooking and transporting the food that the men have ordered for the spirits? Or, the *nowkwi* (third-level) initiate, who has seen everything there is to see, knows that "the secret is that there is no secret" (Tuzin 1980: 259), yet must protect this hidden knowledge while keeping up appearances because the regeneration of the gardens is represented as directly dependent on him playing his role with conviction? Of course, there can be no determinate answer to this question, because Kwoma culture is itself profoundly ambivalent on this score—an ambivalence that is in turn motivated by what Carol Laderman (1987) has called "the ambiguity of symbols."[3]

Yam Harvest Ceremonies: The Struggle for Adequate Form

We next explore how the Kwoma sensory order is articulated and sustained through the yam harvest rituals. The following analysis will confirm the broad strokes of the picture that has already begun to emerge of a strongly ocularcentric society. It will also fill in some details concerning the role of hearing in the Kwoma way of sensing the world.[4]

There is a taboo on loud noises in the village for the three days leading up to a yam harvest ceremony, whether it is *yena, mindja,* or *nowkwi* that is being celebrated. Dogs are muzzled, no one is allowed to play the slit gongs, and it is strictly prohibited for voices to be raised in argument. The reason for this is that the yam spirits are believed to be "irritated" by such noises and will have nothing to do with the ceremony if they are so offended.

The work of carving the figures to be displayed at a ceremony is carried out during the months leading up to it at a work site away in the forest (out of the sight and hearing of women and noninitiates). During the three days prior to the ceremony itself, the carvings are transported to the Haus tambaran to be painted and decorated. A special screen fence is constructed around the men's house so that no uninitiated eyes can see what goes on inside.

All of the cult figures used in the ceremonies are owned by specific clans and either are copies of existing figures or give expression to the revelation of a yam spirit that a clan member has had in a dream. In fact, the term for "ceremony," *sukwiya,* is the same as that for "dream" (Bowden 1997: 204), as if the rituals involved acting out the men's dreams of power and control over natural, spiritual, and social forces.

The men must be in fit condition to carve and paint the figures. This means that they must avoid close contact, particularly sexual contact, with women. Such contact is believed to drain them of their creative power or "heat," with the result that the designs painted on the figures would "not come out straight" or the carvings themselves would fracture. There is a further taboo on any man whose wife is pregnant taking part in the preparations. He is thought to be contaminated by her "coldness," which could in turn contaminate the sculptures, with the same results described previously. These taboos are rationalized in terms of the yam spirits, who are "hot" like men, being "irritated" by female influences—specifically, women's "coldness."

As Kaufmann observes, Kwoma painted sculptures are collaborative rather than individual efforts and "the result of a conscious artistic struggle for adequate form" (1979: 322). The *epi* or "father" (leading artist, commissioner) of a work makes a sketch of the figure directly on the wood. This sketch is sometimes critiqued by his peers, and he corrects it accordingly. He then proceeds to execute it, assisted by other artisans of varying talents and training.

All the while the figure is being carved and later painted, the men's work is scrutinized by others. The latter comment on the formal aspects of the sculpture but, significantly, are not permitted to inquire after the meaning of the individual design elements or the figure as a whole (Kaufmann 1979: 329). In other words, there is never any question of "What is that?" but only "Shouldn't that be more like this . . . ?" A carving may simply be abandoned if the nose comes out too short, or painted over with black slip and painted again if the design is not "correct" according to the estimation of peers.

There is a period at the beginning of each ceremony, once all of the sculptures have been placed in position in the altar in the Haus tambaran, that is specially set aside for the benefit of the artisans. All of the ritual participants "examine the carved wooden figures on the altar and comment on their excellence, those who have made them standing by to receive the praise" (Whiting 1941: 131). As the setting aside of this period attests, the Kwoma are committed art critics.

It is the way a cult figure *looks*, as opposed to what it represents, that matters most according to Kwoma cultural-aesthetic standards. There is a marked emphasis on color and form over content or "meaning," much as Anthony Forge (1979) found among the Abelam. Consider the way the Kwoma conceptualize "power" (*ow*): "The 'power' that is attributed to *yena* (and other yam harvest) spirits is not thought of as automatically inhering in the sculptures that represent them; rather they develop it slowly in the course of being carved and decorated" (Bowden 1983: 93). In other words, the figures derive their power from their execution, not from any external source, not from that which they represent, for example.

Three occasions are said to be especially important to the development of this power. The first is when a figure is blackened immediately after having been carved. The second is when it is blackened again just prior to being painted and decorated in the men's house. The third is when the sprays of chicken and bird of paradise plumes, called *chey ap*, are added to it at the start of the ceremony proper.

> When the *chey ap* feathers are placed in position, . . . men prance around the stage in a battle stomp spitting magical juices over their shoulders. This spitting, as in other ritual contexts, is thought to impart efficacy (*ow*) to the act . . . it accompanies. (Bowden 1983: 94)

The act in question is the act of decorating. The figures get their power by association with and from the very cult adepts whose body decorations they copy: significantly, only homicides—the most respected and powerful individuals in traditional Kwoma society—were permitted to paint their upper bodies and faces black (the color of hostility and aggression) or wear the *chey ap* headdresses.

The Kwoma emphasis on "aesthetic" considerations—that is, considerations of form and color over any semantic or moral considerations, for example—is further reflected in the conventional explanation for why men used to go out on killing raids. Spearing a person was thought to result in the victim's *mai* or "soul" entering the body of the homicide, where it remained until the latter's death.

> The virtue of acquiring others' *mai* is that it enhances one's ceremonial decorations. The Kwoma with whom [Williamson] discussed this denied that another person's *mai* would endow the killer with the victim's intelligence, knowledge, or skills. It simply makes him . . . dazzling to look at when got up for a ceremony [on account of the decorations he is therefore entitled to wear]. (Williamson 1983: 16; see further Harrison 1993: 82)

The ulterior reason for killing—namely, pleasing the spirits—pandered to a similar penchant for the decorative.

> Ceremonies of any kind have as a primary purpose to please the
> *sikilowas,* who are therefore supposed to provide the Kwoma with
> such benefits as good harvests, . . . easily captured game, and pro-
> tection from enemy attack. The splendid decorations of the men
> at a ceremony contribute as much to the happiness and benevo-
> lence of the *sikilowas* as do the songs, dances and feasting.
> (Williamson 1983: 16)

Thus, men killed so as to be able to put on a good spectacle for the
spirits. The show was the thing.

Seeing Things: The Epiphany of Masculinity

The *yena, mindja,* and *nowkwi* ceremonies proper always begin at
dawn. The men belonging to the ceremonial section sponsoring the
rite are summoned to a prearranged spot in the forest by a slit gong
signal. From there they proceed into the hamlet, singing harvest
songs. In the case of the *nowkwi* ceremony, this procession is to the
accompaniment of flutes and bullroarers. The din is heard by the
women and noninitiates, who have been forewarned to keep their
distance. They think, or at least have been told to think, that the
noises are made by Nankwi (the female deity who presides over
nowkwi) as she makes her way to the men's house. Upon entering
the hamlet, the men rip thatch from the houses and smash pots—
evidence of Nankwi's power and aggressiveness, to be remarked
upon by the women and noninitiates when they reenter the hamlet
later on.

After a brief lull, a deafening cacophony of drumming bursts
forth from the men's house, and the ceremony officially begins. It
is at this point that the *chey ap* feather sprays are put on the main
cult figures, as the men do a stomping dance around the stage or
altar in the middle of the Haus tambaran. This stomping dance is
resumed periodically throughout the rest of the day and night.
Otherwise, harvest songs and chants recounting clan histories are
sung, the sacred flutes are played, and rhythms are beaten out on

the slit gongs and other percussive instruments. At midafternoon, a meal is brought by the women, who afterward remain dancing and singing in front of the (screened off) Haus tambaran until well into the night. The men continue until dawn the next day, when there is another deafening cacophony of drums, and the ritual stops. The ceremonial stage is then dismantled, and all of the ritual paraphernalia carefully stored away out of sight.

Each ceremony involves an induction of new initiates into whichever ceremonial section is sponsoring the rite. The induction procedure in *yena* is as follows. Some months prior to the ceremony, the boy is taken to a clearing in the forest where youths initiated in previous years practice gong beating and flute playing. He is told that the sounds from inside the Haus tambaran, which so terrified him as a child, are man-made, not the voices of spirits, and he is instructed in how to produce these sounds himself on the gong and flute (in preparation for his upcoming debut). He is also told that he must keep this knowledge a secret (Whiting 1941: 89).

On the day of the ceremony, the boy paints his face after the fashion of the *yena ma*. He is taken to the Haus tambaran by his sponsor, or "ceremonial father," who "warns him that when he enters the building he will see the [*yena* spirits], who will be on an altar in the center of the dance floor. The sponsor especially warns him not to look up at the altar too quickly lest the shock kill him" (Whiting 1941: 90; see further Bowden 1983: 112). The two then enter the Haus tambaran through a hole in the screen, and the sponsor dances the boy around the altar, holding him by the arm. The cacophony of the bullroarers, flutes, and gongs is deafening. For two rounds the boy keeps his eyes on the ground, then the sponsor tells him to "look up"—and after the initial shock he sees that the yam spirits themselves, like the sounds they make, are all created by men. At the same time, he is warned that this secret must be carefully guarded from the women and children.

To sum up, among the Kwoma, knowledge, power, and status are determined principally by how far an individual can see inside the Haus tambaran. Those who belong to the *nowkwi* ceremonial section can see the farthest (in that their vision is never blocked), whereas women and children cannot see in at all. They can only hear. Moreover, the women and children are fooled by the sounds that emanate from the Haus tambaran into thinking that there are spirits present, whereas those who have seen the instruments know that the so-called voices of the spirits are in fact produced by men. Sight is thus regarded as a superior way of knowing to hearing. The principal way in which men's knowledge differs from women's is that women can hear but may not see, whereas men can see and thus know the truth, but must keep what they see a secret.

Men dominate sight. They are the ones who produce the sculptures and other visual representations of the spirits (e.g., the flat paintings). As noted earlier, they are also the ones who determine who may and who may not see inside the Haus tambaran at different times. In short, men are the guardians of the visual order of Kwoma society. This order is both recognized as artificial—that is, as a human (male) creation—and as having an integrity that must be protected at all costs. The formal integrity of the images men make of the cosmos is understood to be contingent on the physical (tactile) separation of the sexes. If any man involved in the production of a cult figure were to infringe the taboo on sexual contact with women, for example, it is believed that the sculpture would fracture, or the designs painted on it would come out crooked. Women's touch is thus antithetical to men's visual powers. In the next section, we shall see how women's smell is also perceived as inimical to the visual structure of the Kwoma cosmos.

The Odor of Things

The role of smell in Kwoma culture is in many ways the opposite of that of sight. For example, smell is thought to reveal identities that visual appearances sometimes mask. In one myth I recorded, the human identity of a female flying fox is discovered as a result of the protagonist smelling a breadfruit tree leaf on which the flying fox had urinated. In another myth, a man who used to trick his wives by changing his skin (appearing to them as an old man at home and as a radiant warrior when he would cavort with them in the bush) has his true identity exposed when the women bring their dogs along with them to the place where they work sago. The dogs immediately recognize the radiant young man as the women's husband by his smell, despite his transformed appearance (Bowden 1983: 107, 130–34). These myths imply that the Kwoma conceive of persons as having an olfactory identity that endures despite changing appearances.

Smell is also opposed to sight by virtue of its association with women as opposed to men. There is a special term, *mukushe gwonya*, for the scent of the armpits and genitals of a pubescent girl, which Kwoma men consider especially enticing sexually (Bowden 1997: 138). Women otherwise produce smells when they cook food and when they menstruate or have just given birth. The odor of menstruation and parturition, *maba gwonya*, is considered unpleasant and harmful if interiorized by the men, which is why women in either of these conditions are not permitted to cook (Bowden 1990: 109). Women are further identified with odor due to the fact that the principal locus of their work activities is the rotten-smelling swamp. Men, by contrast, produce visual representations and are associated with the high, solid, and relatively inodorous ground of the mountain ridges.

A third opposition between the two senses relates to the way sight is regarded as generative of order because of the way it establishes boundaries, while smell is conceived of as destructive of order because of the way odors cross boundaries.[5] The myth of the origin of Yambon Gate testifies to this point. According to myth, there was once a span of solid ground across the Sepik at the spot fifteen miles upriver from Ambunti where the village of Yambon now stands. However, people started to cross the Sepik too freely, and one day a woman broke the taboo on women using the bridge when menstruating. The resident spirit, irritated by the smell of the woman's blood, caused the bridge to collapse. The stretch of the Sepik where this catastrophe occurred remains one of the more turbulent sections of the river to this day.

The preceding myth gives expression to *the* most pervasive concern of Kwoma culture: namely, the control of geographic, social, and bodily boundaries. The destruction of the bridge established a barrier where people had previously been able to cross the natural boundary presented by the Sepik with ease. The myth implies that there had already been too much crossing of boundaries (i.e., that too many people had been using the bridge). The last straw, however, was the escape of smell from the menstruating woman's body. The spirit reacted to this olfactory transgression of boundaries by creating a geographic barrier to any further social movement.

Olfactory pollution is evidently a matter of grave concern to the Kwoma, given that it can result in natural and social catastrophes of such great magnitude.

Of related significance is the Kwoma belief that a yam-planter must refrain from sexual intercourse for the duration of the time it takes the tubers to germinate. Yams are said to find the smell of human sexual fluids irritating, with the result that their growth will be stunted, or they will simply rot in the ground. This taboo gives expression to the rule regarding the separation of creative activities—that is, the prohibition on a man investing his energy or "heat" into two opposing generative categories simultaneously. Bowden records another taboo that is grounded in the same set of ideas.

> Men believed that if they went into battle after having had sexual intercourse, the aroma of the woman's sexual fluids would still be adhering to their skins. During the fight, they said, the enemy's spears would "smell" the aroma and be overcome by an irresistible desire to "penetrate" the bodies that were emitting it. In their desperate bid to reach their targets, furthermore, the spears would fly over and around any objects in their way. (1983: 103)

It is indicative of how centrally the olfactory sense looms in Kwoma consciousness that the Kwoma should attribute powers of smell to inanimate objects and plants, spears and yams. The main interest of the preceding examples, however, lies in the way they bring out how the Kwoma conceive of category confusion in terms of olfactory pollution. Even though there is nothing visually distinctive about the appearance of a man who has infringed the taboo on directing his energy into two opposing creative activities at once (impregnating women/planting yams/spearing game or enemies), *his odor betrays him.*

Note also how contravening the taboo on sexual intercourse prior to a battle is represented as in some way "feminizing" the body of the warrior. The spear (as phallic symbol, perhaps) is possessed by a desire to "penetrate" the warrior's body on account of his bearing the smell of a woman. This implies that the Kwoma conceive of gender identity as modulated not only by the temperature of the blood, as discussed earlier, but also by the smells that the body either gives off or acquires through interaction with others.

The boundary-crossing power of smells leads the Kwoma to conceive of odors as dangerous to the boundaries they wish to maintain and as constituting an ideal channel for destroying the boundaries they wish to overcome. It seems that ginger is the favorite vehicle for crossing boundaries and thus working magic, on account of its penetrating smell when crushed and its "hotness" when chewed. The Kwoma distinguish fifteen different varieties of wild ginger. One variety, called *asakwase* in Tok Pisin, is mixed in with sago grubs and fed to hunting dogs to make them "strong" and able to outfight wild pigs. It is also said to "pull" the pigs to the dogs and hunters. *Polkwase*, "pig ginger," is tied to the blade of a spear and thought to exert a similar effect.

Other sorts of ginger are tied to the digging stick used for ferreting out sago grubs, rubbed on the hands when searching for fowl eggs, spit on the garden when a man goes to plant yams, and tied to fishing nets when women go fishing. All of these different sorts of ginger are said to guarantee an abundant harvest or catch. Traditionally, when a village prepared for war, one of the senior men would retire to his secret herb garden, dig up a "fighting ginger" (*owkwase*), utter a spell over the root, and fling it three times in the direction of the enemy. This action was believed to stun the enemy and thus ensure a successful raid.

As appears from these examples, ginger is understood to establish an irresistable channel of olfactory communication between sender and addressee: it prepares the way for the penetration of the addressee's body, be the latter the soil of a garden, a fowl's nest, a pig, an enemy, or a woman. There are spells to go along with some of these uses, but not all, which suggests that ginger is believed to have virtue in its own right rather than always being dependent on the magical power of words. As for those uses that do have accompanying spells, it is apparent that, according to Kwoma magical practice, the power of a spell is in its smell, its aroma, not simply its verbal structure (see Gell 1977; Howes 1986: 29–31).

The power of a spell is also in its spittle. Bowden was alerted to the importance of spitting as a means of imparting efficacy to a spell by an incident at the Manambu village of Avatip. After watching a sorcerer utter a spell and then spit to disperse a storm, Bowden jokingly informed his companions that the English also have spells for quelling storms. In proof of this he proceeded to chant "Rain, rain, go away," and other rhythmical phrases: "When I finished, a Kwoma man who had come to Avatip with me promptly scoffed at my performance and said 'Your spell won't work; *you didn't spit*'" (1983: 162 n. 7).

The fiery sensation in the mouth when one chews ginger is part of the reason the spittle worked up incanting some spell is considered "hot." Spittle is also considered powerful because of the symbolic association between it and semen, an association that is inspired by the symbolic equation between the tongue and the phallus. The latter equation is apparent in the way the tongue and the penis were treated identically in the context of the *handapia-sugwia* ritual—that is, both organs were bled. Kwoma men say that the reason they bled their tongues on this occasion (as well as before going into battle) was to "make ourselves strong." The most salient expression of this strength was thought to lie in a man's power to "talk up" fellow warriors and yell down the enemy, a power that the Kwoma believe to be localized in the tongue. The tongue is thus a symbol of masculine potency, identical in many ways to the phallus. It follows that the tongue should also be conceived of as a generative organ (see further Bowden 1983: 114 on the marvelous tongue of Sasap the culture hero).

A Fitting Meal

The Kwoma diet basically consists of sago or yam and fish. Depending on the occasion, it may also include pork or turtle or cassowary meat as well as grubs (which taste rather like peanut butter). Tinned or packaged goods from the local trade stores, most notably tinned meat and rice, have begun to make inroads into the diet. As in other parts of Papua New Guinea, betel chewing is ubiquitous, and something of an addiction.

The ingredients of a betel-chew include the nut of the areca palm, which has a strong, pungent taste; a betel pepper called "*mustad*" in Tok Pisin; and some lime. The lime is made of the ashes of burnt coral or seashells, and it easily burns the mouth of the inexperienced chewer. Chewing betel is an art. It takes skill to get the proportions of a chew just right. It also takes practice to be able to talk with a wad of betel-chew in one's mouth, and to be able to spit out the dark red juice in the form of a jet or spray, as opposed to a gob. There are very few "Colgate smiles" in the Sepik region (or Papua New Guinea generally, for that matter) because of the way the juice stains the teeth red and even black. Betel nuts, as the areca fruit are erroneously called, vary in strength. Most times, the sensation is only mildly stimulating, but when one bites into a particularly potent nut, the feeling in one's skull is like that of a mild sunstroke. On account of its hot, biting flavor and its effects, betel nut is often referred to as "PNG beer."

Beyond everyone's obvious liking for betel nut, when I inquired about people's other gustatory passions, the typical response was "sago and fish." When I pointed out that sago and fish are staple foods and raised the further question of whether people might not prefer to eat yam and pork, the typical response was that "when yam and pork are available we eat them; when sago and fish are available we eat sago and fish." It quickly became apparent that the idea of a person *choosing* to eat one food rather than another out of preference was not very developed.

Sago is consumed in two distinct forms: in its jellied form, it has a slightly sour taste, while in its baked form it has one of the blandest tastes imaginable. Personally, I did not find sago at all delectable and so rather pestered people about how they could like it themselves. The response was always that "it fits our stomachs." The reason given for this "fit" is that people were accustomed to eating sago almost from the moment they were born. This notion of "fit" went beyond taste and had more to do with the feeling of fullness.

Kwoma attitudes toward food are helpfully thrown into relief when compared with those we encountered in the Massim world, where food is not considered to have any nutritive value and to feel full is regarded as distinctly disempowering, not a valued state at all. The Kwoma, by contrast, like to feel full, which is why a starch like sago is so popular, so "fitting." Among the Kwoma, furthermore, food is considered to have an essential role to play in producing blood and thus promoting growth as well as strength. Eating is therefore regarded as an act of empowerment, rather than disempowerment. This idea is further expressed in the practice of men consuming a ritually prepared hot soup prior to engaging in specifically masculine activities, such as warfare or planting yams (Whiting 1941: 109; Bowden 1983: 105). What makes this soup "good to eat," however, is the temperature at which it is consumed, rather than its flavor. In the Massim as in the Middle Sepik there is, thus, the same privileging of edible "heat," while the value attached to feeling full is diametrically opposed in the two culture areas.

Kwoma Anatomy of the Senses

The Kwoma way of sensing the world can be adduced from the manner in which the Kwoma themselves represent the senses in the carving of a *yena* head. It should be noted that *yena* sculptures, like the one to be considered here (fig. 6), represent "a highly condensed and *idealised* symbolic expression of what it is to be a man in Kwoma society—a man, that is, as distinct from a woman" (Bowden 1983: 87). As we shall see, it is indeed a masculine experience of the Kwoma sensory order that finds expression in the exaggerated proportions of some sense organs on the head in figure 6 and diminutive proportions of others.

Yena heads can range anywhere from three to nine feet in length and typically take the form of elongated ovals with horizontal undercut brows and concave face-planes. One or more long spikes usually protrude from the backs of the heads. According to Douglas Newton, the spikes "represent the [*yena's*] daggers of human thigh bone such as were carried by important men" (1971: 84). The spikes may thus be analyzed as an extension of the hand, of the touch.

The features of the face itself typically include two large conical projections for eyes; a long spindle shape hanging from the brow and detached from the plane of the face for the nose; small U shapes for the ears, or in some cases nothing; a small U shape for the mouth; and an arc or series of arcs extending downward from the mouth for the tongue (for further examples see Bowden 1984; Newton 1971: 97, 102; Hodgkinson 1982; Thomas 1995: 40).

At first glance, the sensory profile presented by the *yena* head is one in which the senses of touch, sight, and smell appear to be

Fig. 6.   Yena head. (Drawing by George Classen, based on Bowden 1983: plate 6.)

fields of extensive cultural elaboration (given the exaggerated manner in which the corresponding sense organs are brought out), whereas that of hearing is comparatively restricted or even absent. But then there is the puzzle presented by the conflicting proportions of the tongue and the mouth: what can it mean that the tongue is elongated while the mouth is truncated? To resolve this puzzle, and to deepen our understanding of each of the other sensory features of the *yena* heads, let us proceed by cross-referencing the manner in which the senses are portrayed in sculpture with the information on the senses that can be culled from the ethnographic record.

To begin with touch, the haptic sense (including temperature) is definitely one of the more elaborated senses in the Kwoma sensorium. It is from this sense that the metaphors of "hardness" versus "weakness" (or mushiness) and "hotness" versus "coldness" are derived. These metaphors play an extensive role in ordering and regulating experience. According to Kwoma tradition, only by developing a "hard" skin can people be able to withstand the rigors of the Middle Sepik environment, with its innumerable insults to bodily integrity; and only by virtue of the "heat" in men's bodies is cultural creation possible. The fact that touch is signaled by a spikelike protuberance that symbolizes a bone dagger in turn evokes a physically aggressive stance toward the world (on which more later).

Turning now to sight, the bulging conical eyes of the *yena* figure are peculiarly apt as symbols of the ocularcentrism of Kwoma society. This ocularcentrism finds expression in, among other things, the way Kwoma ritual art emphasizes form and color over content or "meaning," the spectacular (in both senses) nature of Kwoma rituals, and the various visual taboos that serve to underline the transgressive power of sight. Indeed, the order of Kwoma culture is essentially a visual order. Knowledge and status are explicitly linked to how and what one can see. Men rule not by natural right, but through their exclusive visual access to the sacred, and Kwoma men believe that if any of the cult figures and instruments were to be seen for what they are by the women, the foundations of male authority would immediately crumble (see further Gourlay 1975; Tuzin 1980, 1997; MacKenzie 1991). Male dominance in society is thus intimately related to visual dominance.

It is not only women who are excluded from viewing the mysteries of Kwoma culture, however. Other men are excluded as well. The hierarchical sequence of cult initiation, whereby *yena* men are permitted to see inside the Haus tambaran on one ritual occasion, those initiated into both *yena* and *mindja* on two occasions, and those initiated into *nowkwi* on *all* occasions, gives rise to a society that is composed of multiple vantage points, each more penetrating than its predecessor. The viewpoint of the *nowkwi* initiate is the most penetrating of them all. What the *nowkwi* initiate sees, however, is the constructed character of all vantage points, including his own. *The* secret of Kwoma culture is that the very possibility of culture depends on the erection of visual barriers—beginning with the barriers designed to exclude women's gaze.[6]

As for the sense of smell, the extended nose of the *yena* head also fits with our understanding of Kwoma culture, insofar as the exaggerated proportions of the nasal apparatus may be taken to signify acute olfactory sensitivity. The Kwoma are indeed very sensitive to odors, and they imagine various entities in their environment, such as yams and spirits, to be equipped with equally discriminating powers of olfaction. The reason the Kwoma are so sensitive to smells is that in Kwoma culture the odor of things is regarded as a threat to the order of things. For example, in myth, smells often play the role of revealing identities that persons would prefer to conceal, thereby undermining the order constructed through vision.

Smells continually escape from bodies and enter into other bodies, thereby confusing the boundaries between distinct entities. It is consistent with the emphasis on the maintenance of bodily boundaries in Kwoma culture that odors—particularly body odors—are credited with great destructive potential. Odor management is, in fact, regarded as a virtue, and when persons fail to control the escape of smell from their bodies, there is inevitably disaster: yams rot in the ground, land formations collapse (as at Yambon), a warrior is speared in battle. The order of things thus quite literally depends on keeping the odors of persons in their place. This is accomplished by periodically avoiding activities, such as sexual intercourse, and persons, such as menstruating women, that are generative of contaminating odors.

In the book *Yena*, Bowden compares the way the nose is represented on *yena* heads with the way the penis is represented in other Kwoma sculptures and concludes on the basis of the visual similarity betweeen the two that the nose is a phallic symbol (1983: 111). The visual resemblance between the nose and the penis in Kwoma art is undeniable, but this does not obviate the form of the nose being a carrier of other meanings as well.

Consider the way Kowma men look upon their spears. A spear is an obvious phallic symbol, and "spearing" is, in fact, a common euphemism for sexual intercourse in Kwoma speech. However, the spear is not simply a phallic symbol. It is also a nasal symbol. Enemy spears are supposed to be able to "smell" the scent of a woman on a man who has failed to observe the taboo on sexual intercourse prior to battle and be overcome by an irresistible desire to "penetrate" the body of the man who emits this sexual odor. Thus, the spear functions *both* as a symbol of masculine potency *and* as a symbol of olfactory acuity in Kwoma thought. The same goes for the nose on the *yena* head, I suggest. It too is symbolic of masculine potency and olfactory sensitivity at once.

Bowden's iconographic approach to the interpretation of Kwoma art needs to be supplemented by what could be called a sensographic one—that is, an approach that is sensitive to all of the sensory channels that are symbolized or engaged in Kwoma material culture. Bowden may be correct to see Kwoma art as expressing various symbolic associations of a sexual nature "in direct visual terms" (after Forge 1979), as he claims. However, the visualism of this approach puts him at risk of screening out other meanings that "resonate" in other sensory registers, such as the way a spear or phallus can double as a nose (see further Howes and Classen 1991: 264–68).

The protruding tongue of the *yena* head could signify various things,[7] but we have it on record that the Kwoma see the jutting tongues on *yena* heads as indicating "that *yena* spirits are 'hard,' . . . that they are quick to anger and will strike a person down for the most trivial of reasons" (Bowden 1983: 112). The sensuous basis for this association is given in the stance that a man assumes in a debate, when he wishes to express extreme anger and aggression: "This [stance] involves holding the arms slightly apart from the body and bent inwards, hopping slowly from one foot to the other, glaring at the opponent, and *extending the tongue as far as it will go*" (Bowden 1983: 112, emphasis added). The extended tongue is, therefore, a sign of self-assertion, a mark of "hardness"—the highest moral quality in the Kwoma ethos, as in the mores of other Middle Sepik societies (Roscoe 1990; Harrison 1985).

The elongated tongue is also associated with masculine potency, as may be inferred from the way it serves as a substitute for the phallus in Kwoma myth and from the fact that it was bled along with the penis in the context of the *handapia-sugwia* ritual. Kwoma men practiced lingual and penile phlebotomy in order to drain off the blood grown "cold" through daily contact with women, and thereby they "reheat" as well as fortify their bodies. In ritual and symbolic terms, therefore, Kwoma lingual symbolism has more to do with tactile and thermal sensations than, say, strictly gustatory sensations.

It would appear that the lolling tongue of the *yena* head may signify oral potency as well as thermotactile potency. "Part of being a 'hard' man," Bowden records, "is having a powerful voice—one with which a man can literally shout down opponents in debate in the men's house" (1983: 113). In addition to indexing the "hardness" of an individual's character, the volume of a man's voice is thought to reflect the condition of his blood—specifically, its temperature (compare Roscoe 1990). Lingual phlebotomy, by heating up the blood, therefore also serves to augment the voice. The protruding tongue of the *yena* head can thus be said to represent vocal power along with the ideal qualities of "heat" and "hardness"—or thermotactile potency.

This brings us, finally, to a consideration of what the proportions of the ears on the *yena* head might signify. As suggested earlier, the smallness (or in some cases absence) of the ears may be taken to imply that hearing is a relatively restricted or secondary sense in Kwoma culture. In keeping with this, it will be appreciated that Kwoma men are more given to shouting than to listening. As we have also seen, it is a point of honor in Kwoma culture that while women believe their ears, men do not. Men only believe what they can see. Thus, the minuscule proportions of the ears on the *yena* head may constitute a reflection of the way Kwoma men are ill-disposed to believe what they are told.[8]

The last interpretation may not be very satisfying. Surely an oral society like that of the Kwoma will be aurally minded! But as noted in chapter 2, it is important to guard against projecting Western stereotypes of the role of the senses in nonliterate societies onto the interpretation of the sense lives of other cultures. Nor is it warranted to assume that the senses are essentially the same everywhere, for different qualities of and uses for the senses may be emphasized by different cultures.

Something of the significance that attaches to the auditory register in Kwoma culture may be inferred from the way two of the most prominent paths to distinction involve either skill at singing the song cycles or skill at playing the flutes and other instruments (Whiting 1941: 131–33; Whiting and Reed 1938/39: 189–91). Knowledge of the song cycles is especially important, since up and down the Sepik the recitation of the cycles is just as integral to the performance of a ceremony as the display of the cult figures (Harrison 1990). The salience of the auditory register is also underlined by the extraordinary number of verbal and quasi-verbal channels of communication the Kwoma have developed; for example, in addition to regular and ceremonial language, there is a whistling language, a shouting language, and a drum language (Whiting and Reed 1938/39: 176–78; Gardi 1960: 91; Zemp and Kaufmann 1969).

If oral-aural communication is a field of such extensive elaboration in Kwoma culture, then why is it not ascribed the same symbolic weight as vision or touch in terms of the proportions of the sense organs on the *yena* head? A brief excursion to examine concepts of the person among the neighboring Manambu-speaking people of Avatip may help answer this.

At Avatip, every person is viewed as having two aspects, *mawul* and *kaiyik*, or what Simon Harrison glosses as Understanding and Spirit (life force). The *mawul* is associated with hearing. It is that "aspect of the self predisposed to 'hear' others: 'hearing' covering a range of ideas—comprehension, obedience, pity, desire—which have in common the implication of the capacity to identify with others" (Harrison 1985: 119). While the Understanding "hears," the Spirit "speaks." The *kaiyik* is associated with the mouth and with speech (or rather, quarreling)—that is, with self-assertion as opposed to comprehension. Significantly, a vital and self-assertive style of behavior is called "sharpness" (as in the sharpness of a knife-blade), which is analogous to the Kwoma idea of "hardness" (*ow*).

The primary meaning of *kaiyik*, however, lies in the visual domain. *Kaiyik* means "an 'image' of something: a shadow or reflection, a carving or painted design, or nowadays also a photograph" (Harrison 1985: 119). It is in ritual contexts, including warfare (or in recent times, intervillage sports contests), that the life force in men comes to the fore.

> Avatip men regard their life-force as gaining, in ritual contexts, an intensity such that they and their acts are no longer assessable by moral criteria but only by aesthetic ones. . . . It is regarded as in the nature of men to rise—precariously and for limited periods—above the status of moral subjects and become objects of intensely significant display. (118)

Thus, mundane existence is associated with being in the world aurally, which is also to say morally, whereas ritual existence involves being in the world visually, aesthetically.

Harrison's analysis of concepts of the person at Avatip resonates strongly with all that we have learned of Kwoma constructions of the person and the senses in this chapter. We may conclude that the *yena* head appears the way it does because it symbolizes self-assertion and autonomy, which are ways of being in the world visually. Hearing, or being in the world aurally, by contrast, means letting down the boundaries that separate the self from others. Listening to others compromises the hardness and impermeability that Kwoma men try so diligently to cultivate in themselves. The "hard man" must, therefore, have small ears—or better, none at all.

CHAPTER 6

Comparison of Massim
and Middle Sepik Ways of
Sensing the World

The purpose of this chapter is to present a synthetic account of the ways in which the senses are customarily distinguished, characterized, and articulated to each other in the sensory orders of the Massim and Middle Sepik regions of Papua New Guinea. Comparison of the two sensory orders will in turn bring out how the manner in which the senses are socialized (or "enculturated") mediates the ways in which society and the cosmos are sensed. In effect, the systematic relationships between sensations within and among different modalities provide the model in terms of which selves are constituted and the relationships between persons are grasped. Similarly, the structure of intersensory relations supplies the framework in terms of which the universe is constructed and cosmic processes are held to unfold. Walter Ong has a point when he writes, "Given sufficient knowledge of the sensorium exploited within a specific culture, one could probably define the culture as a whole in virtually all its aspects" (1991: 28).

Let us begin with an examination of the contrasting sensuous geographies of the two regions. Both the Middle Sepik and Massim environments divide naturally into opposing geographic domains: swamp and mountain ridge in the case of the Middle Sepik, and land and sea in the case of the Massim. In both cases, the contrasting domains are assigned contrasting cultural values.

The Kwoma perceive the swamp as a negative area because of its instability: the ground is soft, rivers and streams constantly overflow their banks, and corruption and decay are rampant. The mountain ridges, on the other hand, are positively valued because of their hardness and stability. It is on the ridges that the Kwoma locate their settlements—small outcroppings of order in a pre-dominantly swampy universe.

In the Massim, land is devalued relative to the ocean, which is perceived as an endless, alluring expanse. The peoples of the Mas-sim, therefore, prefer to locate their villages not high and dry on the mountains of the interior but along the coast, where they have access to the sea. In the Middle Sepik, the basic opposition is one of above/below, in the Massim it is one of exterior/interior. In the former area, culture is associated with being above on the moun-tain, in the latter it is associated with going out on the sea.

In general, the environment is experienced as invasive in the Middle Sepik, while in the Massim it is perceived as expansive. These contrasting constructions of space are related to the social history of each culture area, as well as to physical setting. In the Middle Sepik, territorial boundaries were constantly overrun and needing to be redrawn in the period prior to pacification. The Kwoma took the Washkuk Hills by force and have had to continue to use force to defend their mountain settlements from being over-run by enemy outsiders, as well as by enemy Kwoma tribes. While overt violence was outlawed within each tribe, it was and continues to be assumed that clans practice homicidal sorcery against each other. Thus, every social boundary that the Kwoma have set up remains subject to attack and can only be maintained by force.

In the Massim, by contrast, territorial boundaries were reason-ably secure in the prepacification period. It was rather the lines of communication *between* territories, the kula routes, that were liable to rupture by enemy attack and required constant effort to keep open. The fact that the kula established alliances between distantly situated communities, and travelers could rely on their kula part-ners for protection and hospitality, has contributed substantially to the perceived openness, or outward focus, of the Massim physical and social universe, in contrast to the inward focus of the Kwoma physical and social milieu.

In both the Massim and the Middle Sepik, there are qualitatively distinct kinaesthetic and tactile sensations associated with the domains of sea and land, and ridge and swamp, respectively. In the Massim, the ideal bodily state is one of buoyant lightweightness. This state is primarily associated with the experience of lifting over the waves in a dugout canoe. It is reproduced on land in the form of the graceful bobbing and swaying motions Massim people perform as they dance, and in the form of the elongated curlicues that adorn the carved wooden prowboards. Being on land is otherwise associated with a feeling of heaviness and lethargy in the head and limbs. This generalized feeling becomes acute when a person eats too much or falls sick. Individuals in either of these conditions of pronounced heaviness confine themselves to the house. The interior space of the house is associated with states of minimal bodily mobility and vitality.

In addition to being a buoyant space, the sea is a smoothing place. It is constantly grinding and polishing the shells that it deposits in the shallows. In the early evening, when the winds have died down, its smooth, undulating surface provides a glorious reflection of the heavens. Likewise, the cultures of the Massim are cultures of smooth sensations. People stroke their faces with mother-of-pearl shell to make them smooth and reflective of light like the shell, and they rub their bodies with coconut oil to keep their skin moist and gleaming. There is, significantly, no tradition of body scarification, although tattooing is practiced. The fine blue lines of the tattoos accentuate the natural features of the face, but do not disrupt the smoothness of the skin. To have an oiled, gleaming skin is considered a mark of beauty. Smoothness is, furthermore, one of the most important criteria by which kula valuables are classified and ranked: the older a shell is, the smoother it will be on account of having been ground and polished by each of the men through whose hands it has passed.

Kwoma culture is a culture of hard and rough sensations. The stiffness and aggressivity of the Kwoma dance style, which consists basically of stomping the ground and charging around in a circle, contrasts starkly with the fluidity and buoyancy of the Massim dancer. In the Middle Sepik, the ideal bodily state is one of hardness, analogous to the obduracy of the hardwood trees that grow on the mountainsides. Sickness is thought to be brought on by having a "weak" skin—that is, a skin that is permeable, like the unstable ground of the swamp. In order to harden the skin and strengthen their bodily boundaries, the Kwoma practice scarification. Scarification brings out ridges on the skin that are rough to the touch and in a way resemble mountain ridges. These scars are valued as signs of moral as well as physical endurance and are considered attractive.

This process of hardening the body can be compared to Kwoma pottery techniques. Making pots involves taking wet, formless clay from the valley, modeling it, and then baking it in a fire until it becomes dry, hard, and permanent.[1] The Kwoma incise the pots in the same way they incise their bodies; the texture of the pots is a mirror of the dry, rigid qualities they strive for in their skin. The Kwoma accent on rough sensations is also reflected in their shell money, which consists of tiny *kina* shells sewn onto pendants woven from bark fiber (fig. 7). The overall texture of these pendants is distinctly rough and uneven to the touch, in contrast to the smooth surface of an age-worn kula valuable.

In the Middle Sepik, there is grave concern over the protection of the body from invasive sensory stimuli. In the Massim the concern is rather to extend the surface of the body (or person) through different sensory media. Therefore, while the Kwoma strive for a protective, hard, rough exterior, in the Massim, people want their skins to be smooth and reflective.

The contrasting sensory values and orientations of the two cultures can be seen as arising from the contrasting environments. However, there is no intrinsic reason why either society should privilege one geographic domain (sea or land, ridge or swamp) and its associated kinaesthetic and tactile qualities over the other. Hence, the contrasting orientations are to some extent arbitrary and should be seen to reflect the influence of culture on environment even as they reflect the influence of environment on culture. The contrasting sensory orientations should also be seen as related to the contrasting sociological orientations: the focus of Massim society is outward, and the emphasis is on exchange, whereas the focus of Kwoma society is inward, and the emphasis is on defense.

In addition to stressing different aspects of tactility—smoothness in the Massim versus hardness in the Middle Sepik—touch is evaluated quite differently in the two culture areas. Physical contact

Fig. 7.   Kwoma woven pendant. (Drawing by George Classen.)

between the sexes is regarded as a source of pleasure in the Massim, whereas it is construed as a source of danger among the Kwoma. Whiting records that a young Kwoma married couple "never sleep in the same bed but lie alone on separate bark slabs, joining only for copulation, which is performed with a minimum of embracing and foreplay. All informants insisted that a husband and wife should not sleep together" (1941: 102).

The reason for this separation is that prolonged physical contact between men and women is believed to weaken men physically and intellectually. Menstruating women are thought to be especially polluting and must accordingly observe numerous restrictions, such as not touching any of their husbands' effects and not cooking or serving food, for the duration of their menses. To the best of my knowledge, such strict restrictions are not found in the Massim, for there bodies are not held to be so vulnerable to invasion through touch.

The power of touch is a subject of considerable symbolic elaboration in the Middle Sepik. For example, the Kwoma distinguish between women's touch and men's touch. These contrasting touches are seen as reflected in the characteristic modes of production of each sex: women absorb things through touch, while men create things through touch. Thermal symbolism is another aspect of tactility that is quite developed in the Middle Sepik. Generative potential is conceptualized in terms of the temperature of the blood. It is the "heat" of men's blood that is supposed to account for their capacity to generate children, gardens, and representations of the spirits. Women are not considered to have any generative potential, because of their "coldness."

Women's coldness is, furthermore, conceived of as actively destructive of men's heat. It is believed that men must periodically reheat their bodies to maintain their intellectual and physical vigor. One way of reheating the body involves making cuts in the tongue and penis to drain off the blood that has grown stagnant and cold through daily contact with women. Another is to consume a ritually prepared hot soup, which is usually done immediately prior to engaging in an activity that requires that men be in a particularly hot condition, such as yam-planting, warfare, or sorcery.

Unlike the Kwoma, Massim people do not conceive of themselves as living in a corrupt universe, constantly verging on stagnation. Massim practices of purification are predominantly of an aesthetic, rather than a prophylactic or therapeutic, character. For example, they involve washing the skin to remove the "hiding darkness" of the dirt that normally coats the body—the better to *extend* the body in light. The skin is also rubbed with smooth or sometimes prickly substances, such as nettles, but never to the point of lacerating its surface. The primary concern of the Massim subject is with regulating the reflective condition of the skin, as opposed to modulating the thermal condition of the blood.

Just as bloodletting has no place in Massim ritual, neither does the consumption of special foods in preparation for an undertaking. On the contrary, the Dobuan sorcerer, for example, deliberately *abstains* from eating: he does not want the ingestion of food to interfere with the expulsion of the "noise-force" that he has stored in his belly. Indeed, virtually every important ritual or social occasion in the Massim, from going out on a kula expedition to holding a memorial celebration (*sagali*), is preceded by a period of fasting.

There are various reasons for this fasting. One is that, unlike in the Middle Sepik, food is not thought to have any role to play in sustaining the body or replenishing the blood. Another is that eating is felt to weigh a person down and induce lethargy: on ceremonial occasions a person wants to feel and appear buoyant and quick, not heavy and slow. A third is that eating is supposed to spoil or dull the luster of a person's body decorations. The principal reason for the strictness with which food in-take is regulated in the Massim, however, is that eating is perceived as an act of interiorization, and as such it is considered antithetical to the *exteriorization* of the person, which is the underlying goal of virtually every field of human endeavor in Massim culture.

In the Middle Sepik, the consumption of food is believed to generate blood and thus contribute to a person's growth, or fullness. Eating is a positively valued act, because it fosters solidity. In the Massim, by contrast, eating is a negatively valued act because it decreases visibility, reduces bodily mobility, and also (in the case of the sorcerer chanting spells) interferes with audibility. Ultimately, Massim people take such a dim view of food consumption because eating reduces the amount of food available for distribution to others. It is through giving away food that persons acquire "fame"— conceived of as the circulation of the name apart from the body. Hence, distribution must always take priority over consumption. To this end, Massim people have elaborated numerous different forms of appetite-suppressing magic.

Taste is thus the sense most singled out for repression in the Massim, whereas in the Middle Sepik the most repressed of the senses is touch. The rationale for the repression of gustation in the Massim is that eating counteracts the extension of the body in space. The rationale for the circumscription of touch in the Middle Sepik is that touch, specifically woman's touch, threatens the integrity of (male) bodily boundaries. Hence, Massim peoples have devoted as much attention to the invention of techniques to restrict the appetite as the Kwoma have invested in the development of techniques, such as scarification and bloodletting, for regulating the effects of physical contact between the sexes and between people and the environment. Significantly, a Massim carver must not eat boiled bananas or other slippery foods, or his ideas will slip away instead of becoming fixed in the wood; a Kwoma carver must avoid sexual contact with women or the sculpture he works on will fracture. Thus, in both regions, cultural production is represented as contingent on individuals displaying the requisite sensory mastery.

Just as the cultures of the Massim and Middle Sepik differ with respect to the sense they single out for repression, so do they differ with regard to the sense they single out for honors. In the Middle Sepik, sight is the most valued sense, and Kwoma culture is itself constructed on a visual scaffolding. The visual field is created and controlled by men. Men create the visual field by virtue of the fact that they alone produce the carvings and paintings of the spirits. The latter are said to oversee the fertility of the gardens and watch over the safety of the village. The visual field is controlled by men through the construction of screens that prevent women and children from ever seeing, and other men from sometimes seeing, the cult figures and musical instruments that are used in the yam harvest ceremonies.

Among the Kwoma, knowledge gained through the eye is held to be superior to that gained through the ear. Women and noninitiates can hear the sounds that emanate from the Haus tambaran, and they are led to believe that these sounds are made by the spirits, whereas male initiates, because they have *seen* that these sounds are made by men, know not to trust their ears or believe what they are told. It is significant that new initiates are shown the instruments of the cult before they are allowed to see the cult figures: the acoustic mystery is exposed before the deeper, visual mystery (that the spirits are made of wood) is revealed. The ascendancy of sight is otherwise attested in the marked emphasis on color and form over content (or "meaning," narrative explanation) in Kwoma art. Significantly, the cult figures are thought to derive their power from the act of men blackening and painting them. The most powerful medium in the Kwoma universe is thus the *visual* medium of paint.

Massim people do not make carvings of any of the powers of their universe. For example, there is not a single representation of Kasabwaibwaileta, the guardian of the kula: he is approached through speech alone. The visual arts are thus comparatively "underdeveloped" in the Massim, though by no means absent. For example, there are the ornately carved wooden prowboards. In the Massim, however, visual representations always have an auditory basis: the idea for a prowboard is supposed to originate in the "shout" of the mythical culture hero Monikiniki, which the carver proceeds to translate into a visual image. The carver does not use any visual aids in this process: he does not, for example, sketch the design on the wood before executing it. He carves directly from his mind, transforming sound into sight. This is in contrast to the situation among the Kwoma, where the idea for a carving occurs to the artisan in a dream (i.e., as a visual image); he makes a sketch of it on the wood before carving it; the sculpture is not named until it is completed; and it is only given sound, a "voice," when it is displayed.

Sound is the most powerful medium in the Massim universe: the sorcerer animates and controls the world through his voice. The spells he uses are supposed to have come into being *together with* the things and forces to which they refer. It is on account of this intrinsic connection that he is able to summon them to do his bidding through the repetitious chanting of their names. Generating heat is no less fundamental to the sorcerer's art in the Massim than it is in the Middle Sepik, but the most essential thing in Massim magical practice is that the sorcerer give vent to the noise-force contained in his belly (where the magical words are stored). In the Middle Sepik, the emphasis is rather on the sorcerer venting his heat, which is built up by scraping the tongue with nettles and expelled by spitting.

In the Massim, names matter more than visual appearances. The "man of influence" or "big man" is one whose name is known on other islands, even though people there have never seen his face. The kula career of a big man will have involved a progression from being seen and remarked upon for the splendor of his body decorations, through listening to and gradually learning how to master "kula talk," to having his name circulate completely apart from his physical presence in connection with the shells of note that have passed through his possession.

In the Middle Sepik, men are ranked not according to the extension of their names, but according to how much of their upper bodies they are permitted to paint black. This blackening is the primary insignia of the homicides they have committed (other insignia include feather headdresses and tassels). This brings up the subject of warfare and the reasons men killed. In the Middle Sepik, men killed to enhance the body decorations they were allowed to wear on ceremonial occasions. In the Massim, men killed to obtain bodies that they could then exchange for kula valuables. This contrast brings out nicely the emphasis on spectacle in the former culture versus the emphasis on exchange in the latter.

Another means of ranking men in the Middle Sepik is by reference to the loudness of their voices. The Kwoma "big man"—or "hard" man, as they say—is one who is able to shout down opponents in debate. The ultimate expression of "hardness," however, is the nonverbal gesture of sticking the tongue out—the same pose that is captured in the expression on the faces of the *yena* heads.

The Massim big man sends out his name, the Kwoma big man sticks out his tongue. This contrast nicely illustrates the difference between the emphasis on the extension of boundaries (bodily surpassment) in the former culture and the stress on the affirmation of boundaries (bodily entrenchment) in the latter.

There is a significant gender dimension to the sensory orders we have been considering. In the Middle Sepik, where gender dualism is quite pronounced, men are associated with the power of sight while women are associated with the power of touch and to a lesser extent smell. Women's touch is perceived as inimical to the integrity of the visual creations of the men. Women's smell, particularly during menstruation, is also regarded as polluting.

Gender dualism is less pronounced in the Massim. There too, however, we find that the sexes are associated with different senses. Munn records that on Gawa: "It is said that, in contrast to men, women are 'consumers,' a description for which there is a special label, *vila-kamkwamu* (female-eat)" (1986: 220). While women are thus stereotyped as "consumers" (i.e., identified with the field of gustation), men represent themselves as "speakers." It is the ambition of every Massim man to establish himself as a "name," which in Massim terms means one to whom others should "listen" or to whose requests they may be influenced to "agree." Massim men thus identify themselves with the field of speaking and hearing.

There is a further partitioning of the sexes by geographic domain and by association with different kinaesthetic and tactile sensations. In the Middle Sepik, men are associated with the mountain ridges, women with the swamps. Men's bodies are conceived of as ideally hot and hard, while women's bodies are thought of as cold and permeable. In the Massim, men are associated with the exterior domain of the sea, women with the interior domain of the land, and in particular the house. Men's bodies are conceived of as buoyant and mobile, like boats on the sea, whereas women, who are supposed to dislike sea travel, and whose bodies grow heavy with child, are identified with the heaviness and immobility of the land.

It will be observed that in both regions, men are associated with the most culturally important sense—sight in the Middle Sepik, speaking/hearing in the Massim—whereas women are associated with the stigmatized senses of touch and taste respectively. These sensory associations are both reflective and constitutive of the social position of the sexes. The question arises, What do the women themselves think of their social and sensory status in these male-dominated societies? Do they simply accept the male devaluation of their sensory qualities and abilities? Have they elaborated an alternative social and sensory order? Unfortunately, the data is too scanty at present to allow the question of "women's sense" to be resolved in a definitive way. It is to be hoped that future research in these societies will bring out more clearly what the women themselves make of their senses, and their real or alleged sensory characteristics.[2]

As appears from the preceding analysis, the five senses are invested with contrasting significance in relation to the scale of self-constitution and the production and reproduction of the social and symbolic order. This significance is always relative, but can nevertheless be characterized as "cultural" or "anticultural" in orientation.

What defines a field of sense as "cultural" in the Massim is the capacity of the sense in question to extend the boundaries of the person. The most salient sense in this regard is hearing, the medium of which is sound. Sound is both the most capacious and the most powerful medium in Massim experience. At the opposite pole is tasting something. Eating is understood to detract from the extension of the person in space, because it induces lethargy (reducing mobility), dulls body decorations (reducing visibility), and so on. Hence, Massim culture is predicated on the repression of gustation and the extension of the individual in space through each of the other senses, especially hearing. The emphasis throughout is on the opening up of sensory channels, an emphasis that is consistent both with the overriding value attached to exchange in Massim culture and with the relative absence of concern as regards the protection of bodily and social boundaries. (The protection of trade routes is a different matter.)

What defines a field of sense as "cultural" in the Middle Sepik is its capacity to be restricted. Seeing is the most salient sense in this regard. Sight can be restricted by erecting screens, or through internal controls, such as the elaborate code of looking behavior that traditionally functioned in place of clothing. Hearing (including speech) is another channel that is readily restricted: people have only to keep their mouths closed. Secrecy is, in fact, the keynote of Kwoma culture. At the same time, there is always the danger of an initiate divulging cult secrets, or of a conversation being overheard, hence hearing is considered less "cultural" than sight.

It is by way of opposition to the quintessentially "anticultural" senses of touch and smell that the cultural character of sight and hearing in the Kwoma sensory order emerges most clearly. The body is always "in touch" with the environment: the tactile sense can never be entirely closed off, despite the considerable lengths to which the Kwoma go—fortifying the skin through scarification, for example—in an effort to seal themselves off from the world. So too with smell: smells are constantly escaping from bodies and entering into other bodies in Kwoma experience.

The sense of taste is regarded with ambivalence by the Kwoma. Eating is both cultural, insofar as it strengthens the body and blood, and anticultural, insofar as it can introduce elements of disintegration—for example, coldness or poison—into the body.

The most anticultural of the senses in the Massim scheme of things are tasting and touching. Eating is denigrated because it is associated with interiorization. Touching (or kinaesthesia) is viewed a bit more positively because being mobile enhances presence. Smelling is yet more cultural because of the way this sense operates at a distance and thus surpasses the physical boundaries of the person.

Whereas Massim people are passionately interested in *extending* themselves in space, the Kwoma are above all concerned with *protecting* themselves from invasion. This concern on the part of the Kwoma may be related to the emphasis on defense. It is also related to the comparatively minor role played by exchange in relation to the external world on account of the way "friendship" relations under the totemic system subsume alterity and transform trade into sharing (see chap. 5, n. 1). Thus, the Kwoma present neither an exchange-oriented society, like that of the Massim, nor a consumer-oriented society, like our own. Rather, they present a *boundary*-oriented society.

The boundary-mindedness of Kwoma society is well illustrated in the case of the Kwoma hunter. The Kwoma believe that a hunter's blood enters the animals he kills, and that if he were to consume these animals he would sicken and die. The hunter makes a distribution of the meat, therefore. This taboo has the effect of promoting exchange, but it is rationalized in terms of protecting bodily boundaries. The same reasoning is used to justify the incest taboo and the taboo on eating self-planted yams. In Kwoma culture, one must constantly protect oneself from being polluted by one's own blood circulating outside one's body.

The idea of blood circulating outside the body is the mirror opposite of the Massim conception of the name as circulating apart from the person. It could be said that people feel themselves to be constantly overspilling their boundaries in the Middle Sepik, whereas in the Massim, people feel that they can never extend their boundaries far enough. The Kwoma conceive of the blood that circulates outside their bodies as dangerous to their health, whereas such detachment (and autonomous circulation of elements of one's person) is precisely what Massim people strive for, since to them it spells fame.[3]

In contrast to the contagious environment of the Kwoma, that of the Massim is disjunctive, and constant effort is required on the part of Massim people to enter into and stay in communication with each other. The people of the Massim therefore strive to link islands, while the Kwoma continually seek to preserve the structures they have created from being swamped.

PART 3

Libidinal and Political Economies
of the Senses

CHAPTER 7

Oedipus In/Out of
the Trobriands

A Sensuous Critique of Freudian Theory

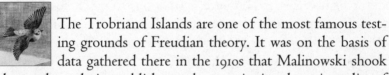 The Trobriand Islands are one of the most famous test-ing grounds of Freudian theory. It was on the basis of data gathered there in the 1910s that Malinowski shook the psychoanalytic establishment by questioning the universality of the Oedipus complex. In the Trobriands, Malinowski (1924) claimed, it is not the case that the male child wishes to kill his father and marry his mother, but rather that he wishes to marry his sister and kill his mother's brother. Malinowski represented this alternative complex as consistent with the matrilineal social organi-zation of the Trobrianders and suggested that the Oedipus com-plex proper be seen as tied to the "patriarchal" organization of the family in the West.

Malinowski's challenge provoked a strong attack from one of Freud's disciples, Ernest Jones (1925). Jones's critique led Mali-nowski to qualify his position. For example, he came to allow that father hatred could underlie the hostile feelings toward the mater-nal uncle and that these sentiments were simply "displaced" onto the latter (see Malinowski 1960: 135–41). Malinowski's original position received another blow when Géza Róheim (1932) pub-lished his account of what appeared to be a full-blown Oedipus complex among the matrilineal Duau people of nearby Normanby Island.[1] However, the hardest blow came in 1982 when Melford Spiro published *Oedipus in the Trobriands*. Spiro used Malinowski's own material against him to "prove" that the Oedipus complex was just as firmly implanted in the Trobriand psyche as in the Western psyche, if not more so.

In recent years, Spiro's refutation of Malinowski has been questioned by Stanley Kurtz (1991). Kurtz challenges Spiro for failing to make use of Malinowski's detailed data on early childhood sexual activity and development, and presents a highly acute analysis of this material in support of his own interpretation of the "Trobriand Complex." That body of material also provides the principal basis for the present intervention in the Trobriands Oedipus debate, which stands Freudian developmental theory on its head.

At issue is the applicability of Freud's "erotogenic zone" theory of psychosexual development to Malinowski's Trobriand material. Freud first articulated the erotogenic zone theory in the course of revising his *Three Essays on the Theory of Sexuality* in 1915 and considered it one of his most important contributions to psychology. While Freud's theory purports to be universal, it is in fact grounded in a particular (Western) construction of the sensorium. The biases inherent in this construction cause the theory grief when the attempt is made to apply it to the interpretation of facts informed by a different arrangement of the senses, such as Trobriand culture presents. The sensory organization of the Trobriand psyche during the period ranging from infancy to the end of adolescence diverges in certain key respects from that of the Western psyche (as described by Freud), and these divergences are conducive to the emergence of the alternative *social* organization of the psyche described by Malinowski in his original 1924 paper on the Trobriand complex. Instead of simply dismissing Freud, however, this chapter shows how Freudian theory can be adapted to the Trobriand context. It is true that what emerges from this process of adaptation may no longer be recognizable as Freudian theory in the eyes of those who remain committed to extending that theory transculturally with all of its sensory and other biases intact (e.g., Róheim 1950; Spiro 1982; Lidz and Lidz 1989; Gillison 1993). The counterposition, which I tend to favor, is that we should seize the opportunity to critique, emend, and otherwise nuance Freudian theory in light of the resistance it encounters in cultural contexts like that of the Trobriands.

A few caveats should be registered before proceeding. First, to bridge the gap between Freudian-Western and Trobriand or Massim psychology and to permit some sort of dialogue between the two traditions, I have taken the liberty of coining a range of new psychoanalytic terms, such as "nasality" (the Trobriand equivalent of "anality" in Freudian theory) and "exuberancy period" (the Trobriand equivalent of Freud's "latency period"). These terms are certain to sound strange at first, but should become familiar with use. Second, the discussion that follows only concerns the male Oedipus complex; this restriction is primarily for want of adequate data on the so-called female Oedipus (or Electra) complex. Third, it will be noted that, as in the chapters of Part 2, this chapter incorporates data from other Massim societies besides the Trobriands, such as Duau and Dobu. These extraneous references are included partly to bridge gaps in the Trobriand material and partly because my aim is to show that the developmental pattern described here is not unique to the Trobriands, but rather appears to have some currency throughout the Massim world.

Being in Bad Odor

One of the distinguishing features of Trobriand (and Massim) gender relations is that "Trobriand women are not considered polluting agents and their sexuality is not thought to deprive men of their strength" (Weiner 1976: 15, 118). This is very different from the situation found elsewhere in Papua New Guinea, where all sorts of debilitating effects are attributed to the presence of the female sex, in particular the smell of menstrual blood (Meigs 1984; Biersack 1987; Lidz and Lidz 1989).

The most repulsive smell in the Trobriand olfactory register is that of excrement: "Unpleasant smells and unclean matters disgust them, especially if they are of an excretory nature" (Malinowski 1929: 444). Thus, for example, the greatest hardship of mourning is said to lie in the prohibition on leaving the house to defecate. The widow's or widower's relatives by marriage must dispose of the bereaved one's excreta for the duration of the mourning period, which lasts anywhere from six months to a year (1929: 157–58). Similarly:

The duty of receiving the excreta of small children in receptacles, with the liability of becoming soiled and the necessity of carrying the dirty matter into the bush, is often mentioned as one of the hardships which give to parents, and especially the father, a permanent claim on the gratitude of the child. It is also quoted as a reason why the child should look after the parents later on, and incidentally repay these particular services in kind should they fall ill. (1929: 444)

As this quotation attests, the profound repulsion Trobrianders feel toward the stench of excrement makes risking olfactory pollution by caring for a child a source of "permanent" obligation—one grounded in feelings of gratitude that, according to Trobriand psychology, the child can never forget.

The father's olfactory self-sacrifice in caring for the child is comparable to the gustatory self-sacrifice involved in eating sparingly. The latter act makes more food available for sharing with others, principally children and overseas visitors. Parents—especially fathers—are, in fact, remembered for their generosity as providers of food (Malinowski 1929: 156; Weiner 1976: 125; Munn 1986: 50; Thune 1980: 177–78). Nonetheless, their highest claim on their children's gratitude would appear to be the one based on cleaning dirty bottoms. It is in recognition of this sacrifice that, as part of the traditional mortuary ritual, the sons suck the decaying flesh from the bones of the exhumed corpse of the father, prior to laying the bones to rest permanently (Malinowski 1929: 156–57, 444; 1965 I: 206). Similar practices have prevailed elsewhere in the Massim region, such as on Duau where the "belly" of the deceased is eaten by the kin (Róheim 1950: 204–5).

This last rite of anthropophagy may seem a rather exaggerated way to express filial gratitude, and it *is* regarded as excessive and disgusting by the Trobrianders (Malinowski 1929: 156). There is reason to it, however, when one considers how deeply conflicted and shame-ridden the act of eating is in the Massim world. The only thing a person is thought to derive from eating is pleasure, not nutrition or energy, and the only thing eating leads to, besides heaviness and sleep, is having to defecate; there is no positively valued result, such as beauty or fame, to eating one's fill (chap. 3). In fact, the way to fame is precisely through not eating and thus being able to distribute food to others, which explains why there are so many forms of appetite-suppressing magic to be found in the Massim world (Malinowski 1961: 169; Young 1983). The Trobriand adult is, therefore, acutely conscious of the act of food consumption as being intrinsically "wasteful." Its negativity is summed up in its most salient effect or "yield," the stench of excrement.

Could it be that the motivation behind the ritual act of sucking the father's bones clean is the overwhelming feeling of shame that the adult son experiences at the thought of his father having had to clean his bottom when he was a babe in arms? While admittedly speculative, this construction nevertheless makes strong sense. One of Malinowski's informants rationalized the ritual as follows: "It is right that a child should suck the father's ulna. For the father has held out his hand to its excrement and allowed it to make water on to his knee" (1929: 156–57; see also 1965 I: 206). The emotions that the mourner works through while performing this most odious of rites are thus rooted in the memory of a scene from childhood—that of excreting on the father—which appears to leave an indelible mark on the Trobriand psyche. It is as if the picture of children excreting were the "primal scene" of Trobriand psychology.

Primal Scenes

According to conventional Freudian theory, the "primal scene" consists of the image of the parents copulating. This vision is said to arouse such conflicted sentiments in the child (wanting to sleep with the cross-sex parent and murder the same-sex one) that the only way to cope with them is to banish the scene from consciousness. Hence the onset of the "latency period" at age four to six, which is shot through with repression and amnesia.

As suggested earlier, the Trobriand version of the "primal scene" would appear not to fit this picture and to center around the image of children excreting instead. The evidence for this consists not only of the memory at the core of the traditional mortuary ritual, but also of two other practices. The first has to do with what the Trobrianders call "copulation amusement," which will be treated next, and the second with the socialization of the excretory functions and the child's birth into language, which will be discussed a bit later on.

In the Trobriands, sexual acts are not shrouded in secrecy or necessarily hidden from young eyes. One indication of this is the term "copulation amusement." It is used to refer to the sexual antics of children aged three to six when they play at imitating the sexual behavior of their seniors (Malinowski 1960: 55–56). For the Trobriand child, therefore, the sexual activity of the parents is not a source of conflict-ridden angst, as Freud would have it. Rather, it is a source of amusement, in that children find that they can make people laugh by imitating the sexual behavior of their elders. This implies that the "latency period" of Freudian-Western psychology corresponds to what can only be described as an "exuberancy period" in the Trobriands. The "exuberancy period" is marked by heightened bodily and social awareness, rather than repression.

According to Freudian theory, the "latency period" represents the culmination of a process that begins at birth, when the infant's "sexual instinct" or libido is already present, but exists in an undifferentiated or "polymorphously perverse" state. The first orifice to which the libido attaches itself in a definitive way is the mouth, followed by the anus, and then (by around age three) the genitals, as each of these "erotogenic zones" is discovered by the child to yield more pleasure than the preceding one, and thus assumes primacy (Freud 1959 VII: 156–57).

Notably missing from this list of bodily orifices is the nose. The exclusion of the nasal apparatus would be considered a major lacuna, from a Trobriand perspective. Indeed, the nose, and not the oral cavity or mouth, is the primary "erotogenic zone" of the Trobriand body. This ranking can be seen reflected in the way Trobrianders express affection by rubbing noses, as opposed to kissing each other on the lips. In fact, like numerous other Melanesian peoples, they find the idea of kissing rather silly and insipid (Malinowski 1929: 330–31). Another reflection of the privileged role of the nose in Trobriand erotica is the belief that genital odors are a major motive of sexual excitement. For example, one informant pointed out to Malinowski that "the olfactory sense can sometimes replace the eyes, for 'when a woman discards her grass petticoat in the dark, desire may be aroused'" in her male partner, even though the latter cannot see her genitals (1929: 166).[2] This suggests that the Trobrianders would have little difficulty accepting the theory that human sexual behavior is governed by the exchange of chemical signals called pheromones. By contrast, it has been a struggle for this theory to win much support among Western scientists to date (Wright 1994; Jacob 2002).[3]

The anus is not counted among the erotogenic zones of the Trobriand body. Indeed, the Freudian interested in finding evidence of "anality" in Trobriand culture is bound to be frustrated. Malinowski baldly states, "Feces have no place in magic, custom, or ritual; nor do they even play any part in sorcery" (1929: 448). The roots of this dismissal can be traced to early childhood, for as Malinowski notes elsewhere, "I have failed to find any traces of what could be called infantile indecencies, or of a subterranean world in which children indulge in clandestine pastimes centring around excretory functions or exhibitionism" (1960: 38). Trobriand culture is thus characterized by a certain "denial of anality." There is no pleasure, not even sublimated pleasure, in elimination or its products.

Probing further we find that parents typically shame their children into observing proper excretory etiquette by means of the standardized expression (translated literally): "Odour of excrement! Not thou wipest thy remnant of excrement, odour we (excl.) smell!" (Malinowski 1929: 446). The intensity of the Trobriand sensitivity to smells may be attributable to the formidable impact this expression would have on the child's sense of group membership. The child henceforth associates the use of the addressee-exclusive form of the pronoun "we" with *itself* as the source of an excremental odor. This "expulsion from language" coming at a time when the child has only just discovered its own ability to communicate through language must prove a traumatic experience. The child wants to *identify* with other language-users, not be individuated from them! It is easy to imagine how a wish *never* to smell of excrement (perhaps never even to defecate) again could take shape in the young one's mind as a result of this incident.[4]

The "olfactory anxiety" instilled in the child as of the moment it learns the meaning of the addressee-exclusive form of the pronoun "we" has clearly had an impact on the development of the Trobriand psyche—to the point of eliminating any trace of an anal phase from the maturation process. Such is the importance attached to "being in good odor" in Trobriand culture that anal erotism is ruled out and a kind of "nasal erotism" comes to take its place—or to put this another way, "nasality" eclipses anality.

Interestingly, when Géza Róheim mentioned to Freud that Malinowski said there was no evidence of anal erotism in Trobriand culture, the latter was shocked. "*Was, haben denn die Leute keinen Anus?*" (What, have the people no anus then?) the father of psychoanalysis exclaimed (Róheim 1950: 159, 236–37). It was simply unthinkable to him that any people (or individual) could somehow bypass the anal phase. From the standpoint of Trobriand psychology, of course, the question would be whether Freud had any nose. How else to explain Freud's failure to recognize the rightful place of the nose among the erotogenic zones of the body? How else to account for his perverse "denial of nasality"? The question of Freud's denial of nasality is a legitimate one, with far-reaching implications, but let me reserve further comment on it until the conclusion to this chapter.

Olfactory Anxiety

Given the existence of a sort of exuberancy period in the Trobriands, as documented earlier, the question arises, Does castration anxiety have any role to play in the formation of the Trobriand psyche? According to Freudian theory, castration anxiety works visually. The sight of female genitalia provokes the fear of being castrated in the boy, because the latter interprets this sight as the consequence of castration. This fear induces the boy to give up the wish to kill his father and start to identify with him instead. The desire to have the mother as a sexual partner is also relinquished as of this moment, supplanted by the desire for somebody to function as her substitute.

The situation in the Trobriands is quite different. Visual images do not have the same horrific grip on the unconscious there. For example, the vision of the father copulating with the mother, so emphasized by Freud, carries very little weight. Indeed, the son's primary recollection of this scene is probably tinged with the laughter he remembers having provoked in his elders when he used to play at imitating it with his friends. As for the sight of female genitalia summoning up fears of castration, it is difficult to say if the link is made (however much Spiro [1982: 109–13] may protest). What we do know with certainty, however, is that the one memory that makes every son cringe with guilt is the thought of having excreted on his father as a child. Indeed, the son is reminded of his own selfish pleasure (and his father's kindness and self-sacrifice) every time he himself defecates, by the odor of his excrement. Rather than castration anxiety, therefore, the Trobriand subject is burdened with acute olfactory anxiety linked to defecation.

While the hypothetical character of the preceding remarks must be underlined, the conclusion nevertheless follows that the sensory conditions of childhood in the Trobriands are not conducive to the formation of an Oedipus complex, for there is not the same stress on forbidden sights or the same omnipresent threat of castration that is allegedly found in the West. It remains to be seen how the alternative organization of the senses in the Trobriands combines with the alternative organization of society to produce a differently configured psyche.

The Olfactory Origin of Desire

Malinowski (1924) hypothesized that the matrilineal organization of Trobriand society had a profound effect on the organization of the Trobriand psyche, and he found evidence for this in the local mythology. There is no trace of the male in the role of husband or father in any of the origin myths: it is rather the "spontaneous" procreative powers of the "ancestral mothers" that are celebrated. Nor is there any trace of conflict between father and son in the myths. Instead, the focus is all on the antagonism between maternal uncle and uterine nephew (Malinowski 1960: 110–14). These preoccupations are as one would expect of a *matrilineal* society, particularly one in which the physiological role of the father in procreation is "ignored" or "denied" (Malinowski 1929: 179–95; Austen 1934). Under a matrilineal regime, jural authority is vested in the maternal uncle, rather than the father, hence the greater presence of friction in the uncle-nephew pair.

Another departure from the Western Oedipal pattern, according to Malinowski, may be seen in the way it is the sister, rather than the mother, who provokes incestuous desires in the boy. The reason for this is that the sexual attachment, if any, to the mother is given up spontaneously by a boy, since normal erotic impulses find an "easy outlet" throughout the period during which, according to Freudian-Western psychology, the mother is supposed to emerge as the "primary love object." The result is that the selection of a primary love object is postponed until puberty. By this time the boy is conscious of how he has been forced to avoid his sister all his life, which makes the mystery and desirability of having her as a sex partner all the more intense, according to Malinowski (1960: 523).

It is consistent with these social facts that the theme of mother-son incest is absent from the Trobriand myth that accounts for the origin of sexual desire, and that the theme of brother-sister incest takes its place. The myth in question is called the *Sulumwoya* myth (Malinowski 1929: 537–72; 1960: 125–29). In *Oedipus in the Trobriands*, Melford Spiro provides the following summary.

> According to the relevant aspects of this myth, a boy prepared a concoction of love magic in his hut. Later, his sister entered the hut and accidentally brushed against the vessel containing the concoction, causing some of it to fall on her. As a result she was consumed with lust for her brother and, despite his repeated attempts to elude her, she relentlessly pursued him until, finally, he capitulated to her desire and they committed incest. (1982: 27)

Spiro's summary is admirably succinct, but unfortunately leaves out the two most relevant aspects of the myth, from a Trobriand perspective—namely, what happened to the couple after they committed incest and what the specific ingredients of the concoction were in the first place. As we shall see, failing to take these two aspects into account seriously undermined the integrity of Spiro's interpretation of the myth.

To begin with what happened to the couple after they committed incest, it is recorded that,

> ashamed and remorseful, but with the fire of their love not quenched, they went to the grotto at Bokaraywata where they

remained without food, without drink, and without sleep. There also they died, clasped in one another's arms, and through their linked bodies there grew the sweet-smelling plant of the native mint (*sulumwoya*). (Malinowski 1960: 127–28)

Following a vision, a man from the island of Iwa went and discovered the mint plant growing out of the lovers' chests and passed it, together with the spell that activates its power, on to his kinfolk, who continue to receive royalties for its use.

Spiro was not impressed with the *Sulumwoya* myth. He felt that it did not support the interpretation Malinowski placed on it: "rather than reflecting the special power of the libidinal attraction of the boy for his sister [as Malinowski claimed], the myth shows the special power of this type of love magic to overcome *inhibitions* arising even from the incest taboo" (Spiro 1982: 27, emphasis added). Spiro is, of course, correct to protest that the myth does not disclose any special *instinctual* attraction between siblings. Had he only followed his nose he would perhaps have understood why (the attraction is magical, as we shall see later). In any event, Spiro goes on to rest his own claim that the boy never stops burning with passion for the mother on Malinowski's "failure" (by Spiro's standards) to provide convincing evidence of incestuous desire for the sister.

The first problem with Spiro's interpretation is that he assumes—in total disregard of Trobriand or Massim conceptions—that love is something physical rather than magical. We get a sense of just how magical love *is* from a remark of Fortune's concerning the Dobuan theory of sex: "Without a love charm to arouse and create desire, desire does not exist according to native theory" (1963: 235). By way of illustration, Fortune records that the men of Dobu were not in the least concerned about their womenfolk being sexually attracted to him, for they knew this to be impossible (as long as he had no charms).

A further problem with Spiro's interpretation is that he assumes that lust can exist prior to the culturally coded signals that evoke— that is, create—and channel it. This is where the significance of the actual ingredients of the love potion comes in. The potion was made from the leaves of the sweet-scented *sulumwoya* and *kwayawaga* plants boiled in coconut oil. As Malinowski observes:

Whenever a substance is to be medicated for the purpose of charming, seducing or persuading, as a rule *sulumwoya* is used. This plant figures also in several myths, where it plays a similar part, the mythical hero always conquering the foe or winning a woman by the use of *sulumwoya*. (1961: 135; see also 1929: 312; Fortune 1963: 237)

Thus, in the Trobriands as in Dobu, desire does not exist unless and until it has been evoked and directed by the smell of *sulumwoya*.

The most serious problem with Spiro's interpretation has to do with the centrality he ascribes to the act of sex. This fixation on the sex act causes him to ignore the sensory experiences that, according to Trobriand aesthetics, should lead up to having sex and those that should follow after. Reviewing the *Sulumwoya* myth with particular attention to how the senses are engaged in the course of a sexual encounter, we find the myth lays down a definite order. That order is that smelling leads to copulating, while eating and drinking (i.e., sharing a meal) should come afterward, or a couple will never enjoy any peace. As will be recalled, in the myth, the brother-sister couple *do* go without rest. This is because their liaison was an illicit one, and they were therefore barred from ever sharing the meal in public that would consummate their relationship and seal their marriage (see Malinowski 1929: 75 and Róheim 1950: 175–76 on Massim marriage customs). Thus, it was not because they were too interested in making love to think of anything else that they died, but because they knew that they could *never*, according to Massim custom, sit down and share a meal. Their last thoughts would thus have been of food, not more sex: the "impossible object" of their love was a marriage feast.

The suggestion that having sex is *not* the *telos* of human psychosexual development in the Trobriands, while sharing a meal *is*, flies in the face of Freudian orthodoxy. The Freudian is committed to regarding the search for "oral gratification" as "pregenital." In the Massim world, however, it is the reverse: youths are free to engage in a wide range of sexual activities but must on no account indulge in cross-sex commensality, *until* they are grown-up enough to marry (Malinowski 1929: 86). This means that genital gratification is typically "preoral" in the Massim world.

Figure 8 shows how Trobriand and Freudian-Western psychology diverge with respect to the discrimination of the erotogenic zones of the body and the ordering of the phases of "psychosexual development." The rationale for positing a nasal phase at the outset of the developmental process is given in the *Sulumwoya* myth. The myth is clear in stating that genital desire (i.e., true lust) is unknown until it has been evoked and directed by the magic of *sulumwoya*—that is, by the scent of mint. Given that it is not until adolescence that youths are initiated into the use of love magic, it follows that sexual (in the sense of genital) attachments between individuals do not take shape until *after* puberty, just as Malinowski suggested.

The *Sulumwoya* myth also explicitly states that the initial progression from smelling to copulating should have been followed by a further progression, from copulating to eating together. However, this outcome was arrested on account of the sister accidentally brushing the oil of mint prepared by her brother (and therefore being consumed with sexual desire for the boy) instead of it being used on the foreign woman, as the brother had intended. Barred from ever indulging their gustatory impulses in concert, the couple starved to death. While the brother-sister pair may have broken the incest taboo, therefore, they nevertheless comported themselves in strict conformity with the (apparently even stricter) taboo on pre-marital food-sharing relations.

The preceding account suggests that "orality" is a greater focus of repression and anxiety than sexuality in Trobriand psychology. This can be seen in the way the *Sulumwoya* myth is as much about "forbidden orality" as it is about forbidden sex. It also makes sense that orality constitutes a more central preoccupation than sexuality in Trobriand culture given the paramountcy of orality in terms of the phases of the developmental process. It is interesting in this regard to note that Spiro was able to discover only two Trobriand myths suggestive of "castration anxiety" (neither of them very compelling), whereas myths that are not simply suggestive of, but explicitly about, "cannibal anxiety" abound in the Trobriand corpus (see Spiro 1982: 109–13; Malinowski 1960: 114–15). This is as one

	TROBRIAND	FREUDIAN
Phase 3	Oral	Genital
Phase 2	Genital	Anal
Phase 1	Nasal	Oral

Fig. 8. *Contrasting constructions of the erotogenic zones of the body*

would expect of an "oral culture" (in the Freudian sense of the term).

For the Trobrianders, the regulation of oral gratification is the essence of civilization, just as in the Freudian view of things civilization depends on the regulation of the sexual instinct. It is by overcoming one's immediate desire for food that one is able to engage in social exchange and display in the Trobriands, just as in the West everything is said to depend on the sublimation of sexual desire.

The Polysexualization Thesis

Stanley Kurtz (1991) has advanced a "new approach" to the Trobriands Oedipus debate, which is of interest both for its critique of Spiro's universalist position and for its affinities with the approach advocated in this chapter. Kurtz does not question the universality of the Oedipus complex, but he does urge us to consider how different cultures may have developed different ways of resolving it. Central to Kurtz's approach is the concept of "polysexualization," defined as the process whereby "attachments to infantile pleasures and objects are broken by means of multiple sexual relationships at higher stages of sexual development" (1991: 70). The concept of polysexualization—sometimes also referred to as "group seduction" by Kurtz—is meant to alert us to the possibility of there being other actors involved in the Oedipal drama (and the stages leading up to it) than those we are familiar with in the West. It is also meant to suggest that the stages of infantile sexuality (with their distinct kinds of pleasures and emotional interests) are more varied in content than the traditional psychoanalytic account would allow.

Kurtz accepts Spiro's argument that the question of how and why the Trobriand boy relinquishes his phallic attachment to the mother is not very satisfactorily explained by Malinowski's "natural maturation" theory, and he proposes an alternative theory to account for this transition. Briefly, Kurtz's hypothesis is that the Trobriand boy is drawn out of his incestuous attachment to the mother by virtue of his entry into the Trobriand play group at some point in his third or fourth year. The play group is a troop of boys and girls age three to six whose relations with each other are characterized by a "precocious genital sexuality, by Western standards" (1991: 70). Right from the moment of first admission to the group, when one of the older girls steps forward and takes the new boy in hand, various forms of genital stimulation are practiced, including intercourse—or as close an approximation to intercourse as the little boy is capable of. Hence, Kurtz concludes, "the group seduces a child out of immaturity by offering and imposing on that child multiple experiences of sexual pleasure at a level more mature than that to which it is attached" (1991: 70). It should be noted that Kurtz's approach assumes that genital pleasure is more "mature" than the "other" pleasures of an oral and anal nature to which the child would up till then have been attached.

In support of his thesis Kurtz points to the Trobriand depiction of life on Tuma, the isle of the dead. On Tuma, everything revolves around sex. Kurtz suggests that the "erotic paradise of Tuma is a conscious depiction of the adult Trobriander's unconscious childhood memories" of initiation into the play group (1991: 80). When one considers how orgiastically the recently deceased spirit is greeted on Tuma, this suggestion makes good sense. The Trobrianders say that the new spirit still yearns for his earthly spouse, but the other spirits, knowing this, conspire to break this attachment by aggressively seducing him. They send the most beautiful one of their company, a "hostess-spirit," forward, and her first act is to wave a magical scented potion (*bubwayata*) under his nose.

The scent enters his nostrils, carrying with it the magic of *bubwayata*. As with the first sip of the water of Lethe, so this scent

makes him forget all that he has left on earth, and from that
moment he thinks no more of his wife . . . Erotically inspired by
the *bubwayata* spell, he yields [to the entreaties, caresses, and vio-
lent yanks of the hostess-spirit] and a scene is enacted. (Malinowski quoted in Kurtz 1991: 79)

The "scene" in question involves the newcomer copulating with
the hostess-spirit right on the beach, in open view of the other spirits. This sight is said to stimulate the latter to do the same, and the
reception quickly transforms into a sexual orgy.

There could well be something to the parallels Kurtz identifies
between the initiation of the new spirit on Tuma and the initiation
of the child into the play group. However, it is troubling that Kurtz
fails to make any sense of the scented potion the hostess-spirit uses
to arouse the newcomer's desire; that is, while Kurtz takes the trouble to quote the preceding passage from Malinowski at length, he
does not work this sensory fact into his interpretation, choosing
(like Spiro before him) to pass over it in silence.

Kurtz's attempt to enlarge the discourse and focus of psychoanalysis did not meet with the approval of Melford Spiro. The latter shot back with the essay "Oedipus Redux," which basically
contradicted and denied all of the points Kurtz had tried to make.
This did not help the Trobriands Oedipus debate, but one good
thing to come of it was that it provoked Kurtz to publish a rejoinder in which, among other things, he elaborated upon the role of
the father in the "Trobriand Complex," as he dubbed it.

According to Kurtz, "early Trobriand [child] rearing is radically
unlike Western rearing in that much of what we think of as 'moth-
ering' is actually performed by the Trobriand father" (1993: 99).
The Trobriand father (in contrast to the father of Freudian theory)
is *intimately* involved in the physical care of the child, feeding it
mashed food while it is still breast-feeding, replacing the mother in
the child's bed during the period of weaning (which occurs at
around age two), and often continuing as the child's bedmate afterward. In Kurtz's view, the father thus "seduces" the child away
from its infantile attachment to the mother's breast and draws it
into the next stage of psychosexual development. In Freudian

terms, this next stage would be the anal phase, but in the Trobriand case, Kurtz suggests, we should call it "the *kopoi* phase," after the Trobriand term for paternal care. The ultimate symbol of this care is the image that has surfaced again and again in the course of this analysis—the symbol of the father receiving the child's excreta into some receptacle (or failing that, his own hands) and otherwise attending to the child's cleanliness.

Kurtz goes on to speculate concerning what meanings the child derives from the father's care.

> I argue that the Trobriand child subjectively equates the food he receives from the father's hands with the urine and feces that he returns to the father's hands . . . the Trobriand child's subjective experience of the father's early nurturance, or *kopoi*, centers around the idea that father and child are exchanging pleasing and/or dangerous edible gifts. (1993: 99)

These speculations are, in turn, worked by Kurtz into a novel interpretation of the unconscious roots of one of the principal institutions of Massim society—the Kula Ring.

In his rejoinder to Spiro, Kurtz goes on to break with the olfactory silence of his first article on the Trobriand Complex and proceeds to weave certain speculations about the *kopoi* phase into a general explanation for why smell magic figures so prominently both in the context of kulaing and in Trobriand representations of the orgiastic reception that awaits them in the next life. "In my view," he states,

> beneath the image of the most beautiful female spirit on Tuma, carrying a sweet-smelling potion that can draw a man away from his previous lover, there lurks the seductive Trobriand father, whose early physical care helps to draw the child away from his mother and toward the larger group, and whose feeding and cleansing of the child is experienced as a pleasant-smelling exchange of anal gifts. (1993: 101)

As we shall see presently, this is a view no Trobriander would be able to share.

Stanley Kurtz makes a strong case for the importance of recognizing "numerous, culturally particular paths of [psychosexual] development where before we have tended to see various cultures making either tenuous or confident advances along a single, universal path to maturation," and hence for "the need to culturally reshape psychoanalytic theory" (1992: 248). However, to allow that there are different paths while at the same time assuming that there is only one destination, "psychosexual maturity," may not go far enough. My principal critique of Kurtz's approach is that he fails to subject the standard Freudian assumption that maturation is a process of growing into one's sex to the same critical scrutiny as the other tenets of Western psychoanalytic theory he treats. But before delving into this critique, let me comment briefly on what I consider to be the principal theoretical advances made by Kurtz's "new approach."

Kurtz's most basic insight is that "child 'training' practices, traditionally classified as harsh or mild by Western standards, are best conceived as motivated by culturally specific principles—principles not necessarily animated by Western-style relations of love and discipline between individuals" (1991: 70). The search for the pertinent "culturally specific principle" in the Trobriand case led Kurtz to the concept of polysexualization or "group seduction," which is noteworthy for the way it revises conventional psychoanalytic assumptions about the identity and number of actors involved in the Oedipal drama, as well as the roles they perform.

In addition to being sensitive to the cultural variations in the social relations that underpin the Trobriand complex, Kurtz's approach is sensitive to some of the cultural variations in the sensual content of the phases of psychosexual development; for example, he picked up on the challenge to Freudian theory posed by the Trobriand equivalent of the latency period being one of exuberance (or "precocity") and of the anal phase being one of cleanliness (*kopoi*). He even picked up on how pervasive and persuasive a role smell plays in Trobriand erotica, although here, I would argue, he showed a failure of imagination. For Kurtz treats the Trobriand smell data within the framework of an unreconstructed Freudian theory instead of listening to what the Trobrianders have to say about the power of smell in human affairs, and revising his model accordingly.

The crux of the problem here is that Freudian psychology, including Kurtz's restatement of it, does not make sufficient allowance for how the different senses may be weighted or constructed differently in different societies, and it therefore fails to comprehend how alternative sensory orders may impact on the experience of the body, obviating some erotogenic zones (for example, the anal) and creating others (for example, the nasal), while at the same time rearranging their sequence. As we have seen, the endpoint or *telos* of the developmental process in the Trobriands is not sexual maturity but "oral maturity"—the mastery of gustatory impulses.[5] We were able to see this because we did not simply assume that maturation is a process of growing into one's sex, but instead sought to interpret and give effect to Trobriand definitions of the developmental process as one of growing into one's senses. Had Kurtz been more resolute in his search for "culturally specific principles," I suspect he would have come to the same conclusions.

One "principle" he certainly would have discovered is that the origin of desire, as of repulsion, in the Trobriand scheme of things is to be looked for in the olfactory domain. Recognizing this would have saved him from committing a number of fundamental errors (from a Trobriand perspective). For example, he would have seen how culturally implausible it is to posit any sort of connection between excreta and the sweet-smelling *bubwayata* potion (given what we now know of the Trobriand denial of anality). He might also have come to recognize how culturally impossible it would be for any two individuals to form a genuine sexual attachment without recourse to the aphrodisiacal power of the smell of mint (as is very clearly laid down in the *Sulumwoya* myth). Following his nose in this way, Kurtz might even have come to suspect that Freud's theory of the erotogenic zones of the body was missing some organs (in particular, the smell organ), which brings us back to the question of Freud's "denial of nasality."

Freud's Nose, or The Denigration of Olfaction and the Birth of Psychoanalysis

Did Freud have a nasal complex? Did some event or series of events in his personal life cause him to deny or repress his nasality? Supposing Freud did have such a complex would explain why, for example, he devotes a section to "Touching and Looking" but says nothing of smelling in his *Three Essays on the Theory of Sexuality.* It would account for the dearth of references to smell in Freud's published work generally.[6] Above all, it would help explain the virulence (or overdetermined character) of Freud's denigration of olfaction in a pair of footnotes to chapter IV of *Civilization and Its Discontents,* which he added near the end of his career—as if to rationalize the olfactory silence of all his previous writings.

"The organic periodicity of the sexual process has persisted, it is true, but its effect on psychical sexual excitation has rather been reversed," writes Freud in the first footnote.

> This change seems most likely to be connected with the diminution of the olfactory stimuli by means of which the menstrual process produced an effect on the male psyche ... The diminution of the olfactory seems itself to be a consequence of man's raising himself from the ground, of his assumption of an upright gait; this made his genitals, which were previously concealed, visible. (1961: 46)

The gist of Freud's argument (incorporating the second footnote as well) may be summarized as follows: (1) the assumption of an erect posture and exposure of the genitals made sight paramount among the senses as well as the primary vehicle of sexual excitation, and relegated smell to a diminished and devalued position in the human sensorium; (2) the fact that visual excitation is continuous, whereas olfactory excitation is intermittent or cyclical, meant that henceforth males would find their female mates sexually attractive all the time—a development that paved the way for the emergence of the family as the basic unit of social organization; (3) the original "organic" antipathy toward menstrual effluvia extended to include excremental smells; eventually all odors that emanate from below—that is, from the genital region—came to bear the same stigma in the interests of advancing civilization.

Freud's account of the displacement of smell (like some other elements of his theory of human sexuality) has become part of Western popular wisdom, an idée fixe, as it were. Never has any critical attention been paid to the soundness of Freud's arguments, or the biographical reasons for his nasal-loathing, or, for that matter, the historical reasons for the initial acceptance and subsequent popularity of his denigration of olfaction. In what follows an attempt will be made to correct these various oversights, and in the process a hidden history of psychoanalysis will be revealed.

Let us begin our examination of the soundness of Freud's arguments by briefly reviewing the empirical basis (or lack thereof) for Freud's three claims, starting with the third. Freud saw the taboo on menstruation as an "organic" expression of disgust, but recent anthropological research into menstrual taboos contradicts this suggestion. It appears that rather than exemplifying repression, and being rooted in disgust, the taboos on women cooking for or having contact with men during their menses may well constitute "sex strikes," and occasions for women to develop culture independently of men (Knight 1991: 385–87). For example, in certain West African societies the "cuisine of menstruation" is said to possess a particularly delectable aroma and taste, but one that can only be enjoyed by women (men not being allowed to partake) (Buckley and Gottlieb 1988). Thus, Freud was simply wrong to assume that menstrual taboos possess the same valence everywhere. The Trobriands are a case in point. There, as will be recalled, menstrual effluvia are not supposed to have any ill effect on men, and it is in fact excremental smells toward which Trobrianders feel the deepest antipathy.

Freud's second claim may also be disputed on the basis of the Trobriand material. Trobrianders say that the eyes are "that which makes us desire to copulate" and "a man with his eyes closed will have no erection" (apparently confirming Freud's suggestion), but they also hold that the nose can sometimes replace the eyes, such as "when a woman discards her grass petticoat in the dark" and desire is aroused in her male partner just the same (Malinowski 1929: 166). According to Trobriand theory, then, olfaction is continuous, whereas vision is an intermittent motive of sexual excitation, susceptible to being interrupted by darkness.

Finally, Freud's first claim, which holds that sight took over from smell as the sense of sexual excitation in some long-ago period of human evolution, can also be contested from a Trobriand standpoint. According to Trobriand theory, olfactory excitations can overcome visual inhibitions. Malinowski records the case of Gomaya, who liked to boast of his amorous successes: "I am ugly, my face is not good-looking. But I have magic, and therefore all women like me" (1929: 375). The magic in question would have involved the native mint plant, *sulumwoya*, the most seductive scent in the Trobriand olfactory register. Being a master of this magic, Gomaya's unsightly appearance was no barrier to his being a great seducer.

Freud situated the decline in the valence of olfactory stimuli—or visual eclipse of smell—in the prehistory of the human species. However, his speculations on this subject belong to a specific historical moment and are, in fact, laced with a number of biases that were peculiar to the European culture of his time. For example, the idea that olfaction is an animal sense whereas humans rely more on vision, or the way in which—on Freud's account—men look while women smell, are not so much biological facts as ideological constructs, manifestations of the visualism and sexism that were so deeply embedded in nineteenth-century Western culture (Classen 1998). Rather than pertaining to the "natural history" of the species, therefore, Freud's speculations should be analyzed as *projections* that were motivated by the *cultural history* of the senses and the sexes in fin de siècle Vienna.

Cutting Off the Nose

But before exploring further the cultural and historical context of Freud's projections, there are some considerations of a personal or biographical nature that merit attention by way of explaining his curious denigration of olfaction. Let me preface this glimpse into the development of Freud's thought by noting that according to E. M. Thornton in *The Freudian Fallacy*, Freud would never have arrived at his theory of the sexual origins of the neuroses had it not been for the pioneering example of Wilhelm Fliess's theory of the nasal origins of the neuroses.

Wilhelm Fliess was Freud's closest friend and confidante during the watershed years of 1892 to 1900, when most of the germinal ideas of psychoanalytic theory occurred to Freud. Fliess was a medical man, like Freud, only his specialty was in ear, nose, and throat medicine, with a side interest in sex. The two men tended to be highly effusive in their praise for each other's ideas and accomplishments. They held "congresses" (because they lived in separate cities) and produced a copious correspondence (which was published posthumously). However, Freud and Fliess had an extremely bitter falling-out in the spring of 1900, largely over the issue of Freud's appropriation and careless dissemination of Fliess's novel theory of bisexuality, which resulted in another of Freud's associates beating Fliess into print with it (Brome 1984: 1–13).

While Freud apparently did appropriate Fliess's notion of bisexuality and saw fit to develop it, after their split he came to dismiss the two other major ideas associated with Fliess's name that had been formulated during the period of their intimacy—the idea of a naso-genital relationship and the idea of periodicity. As we shall see, this dismissal (or denunciation, really) of his former friend's pet theories actually forms the subtext of the footnotes in *Civilization and Its Discontents* where Freud discounts smell.

Fliess formulated his theory of a naso-genital relationship, or more specifically "nasal reflex neurosis," in 1892. Physicians had long recognized that nasal congestion frequently accompanies menstruation (and the later stages of pregnancy), and that nosebleeds occur in both sexes at puberty and sometimes during sexual activity (Stoddart 1990: 80–81). However, Fliess went further. He claimed to have found evidence that a wide range of symptoms were caused by swelling of the nasal mucosa and pathology of the turbinate bones in the nose, and that they could be cured (or at least diminished) by either cauterizing or anesthetizing these "genital spots" with cocaine. The symptoms ranged from heart trouble and respiratory difficulties to various gynecological complaints including dysmenorrhea (painful menstruation) and hysteria in women, and neurasthenic complaints such as migraine (which at the time was associated with masturbation) in men.

The "Fliess Syndrome," as it became known, created a flurry of interest in "naso-sexual medicine." Over 220 articles and books, mainly in German, were published on the subject over the next few decades (Stoddart 1990: 80). One of the consequences of the heightened attention to the naso-genital connection, however, was its dissolution. Scientific medical research disclosed that the cause of Fliess's syndrome was, in fact, the method of its cure.

The effects Fliess attributed to reflex action were . . . in reality, those of the action of cocaine on the brain. The dramatic amelioration of the pains of such conditions as dysmenorrhea or migraine by nasal applications of cocaine resulted from the action of the drug on specific brain centers and had no connection with the nose itself. No reflex mechanism was therefore involved. (Thornton 1984: 120; see also Stoddart 1990: 79–93)

Fliess's theory of periodicity grew out of his research on the relationship between the nose and the sexual apparatus, and was published in a book entitled *The Relationship between the Nose and Female Sexual Organs* in 1897. In keeping with the prevailing fashion for incorporating mathematics into biology, Fliess postulated a twenty-eight- and a twenty-three-day cycle—the former being linked to the menstrual cycle in women and the latter to a corresponding cycle in men—both of which were present in all human beings, and indeed every living cell. The action of these cycles was believed by Fliess to be manifest in all life's fluctuations. The rhythms determined everything from dates of illness and other life crises or "critical periods" to the date of death, not to mention a person's sex (Fliess 1979). More numerological than mathematical, and mystical than biological, the grandiose generalizations that made up Fliess's theory of periodicity in human life were not well received by the scientific community, and his calculations were found to be all too easy to pick apart (Schur 1972: 143–44).

The validity of Fliess's theories was never an issue for Freud during the early to mid-1890s, when their friendship was at its peak. Indeed, Freud believed in Fliess's "laws of periodicity" so completely that he worried himself sick about the forecasted date of his own death and other "critical periods" predicted by Fliess's magic numbers (Anzieu 1986: 437–41). Freud also suffered from many nasal complaints, as well as migraines and heart trouble, during this period and entrusted himself to Fliess's care. His correspondence with Fliess is dripping with references to suppurations, congestion, and pains in his nose (Masson 1985). While some of Freud's nasal complaints would have been alleviated by Fliess's surgical operations on his turbinate bones and by Freud's frequent applications of cocaine to his nasal mucosa (also prescribed by Fliess), it is probable that these treatments did more to exacerbate Freud's nasal and other conditions than cure them. Nevertheless, Freud found solace at being able to attribute the migraines and heart troubles to his diseased nose, since this etiology at least held out the possibility of treatment (i.e., more cocaine, more operations), whereas there was no cure for the migraines or heart disease per se.

A decisive moment in the Freud-Fliess friendship and major turning point in the history of psychoanalysis came when Freud called in Fliess to treat one of his female patients, Emma Eckstein, who presented various neurotic symptoms that Freud diagnosed as having a sexual etiology. Fliess duly operated on Eckstein's nose, and in a horrific case of medical malpractice, left a long string of gauze in the wound when he sewed up. Another surgeon had to be summoned to diagnose the cause of the alarming hemorrhages from which the patient suffered following the operation. Freud was present and fainted at the sight of the gauze being extricated from Eckstein's nose. It turned out that she had been conscious throughout the operation and, when Freud came round, greeted him with the "patronizing" (to his ear) remark, "So this is the strong sex."

This episode in turn gave rise to the famous "dream of Irma's injection," which Freud had in the early hours of July 24, 1895. That dream, with its strange scene of a laryngeal-cum-gynecological examination of Irma's throat by Freud, and of an injection with an unclean syringe by a certain Otto, was the inspiration for Freud's elaboration of the "wish fulfillment" theory of dreams—a cornerstone of psychoanalytic theory. Freud interpreted the dream as expressing the wish to exculpate himself of responsibility for Irma's malady. But as Freud's personal physician and disciple Max Schur has pointed out, this interpretation concealed a deeper wish—the wish to exculpate Fliess—which Freud either remained unconscious of or willfully suppressed in the account that appears in *The Interpretation of Dreams* (Schur 1972: 80–81; see also Anzieu 1986: 135–55).

Of all Freud's sense organs, there was probably no organ that gave him more pleasure (when he treated it with cocaine, for example) or more pain and discomfort (when it seeped pus and catarrh) than his nose. It was a mutual "medical" (but also curiously sexual) interest in noses that drew Freud and Fliess together as friends, and it was a botched operation on a nose that caused the rupture of their relationship. The dream of Irma's injection was inspired by the latter incident, and so Freud owed one of the most fundamental insights of psychoanalysis to this event. But this event was also perhaps the most traumatic incident in his life: given his embarrassment at having fainted at the sight of the bloody gauze being extricated from Eckstein's nose; given Eckstein's taunt to his masculinity; given how his confidence in his friend Fliess (whom he had worshipped up to that point) was shattered; and given how torn he felt between needing Fliess and blaming him.

In light of all this baggage, is it any wonder that Freud chose to cut the nose out of psychoanalytic theory, and to seal off that whole painful period of his life? A sort of nasal taboo took the place of the fascination with nasality that had so occupied him and Fliess throughout the 1890s. As a result, Freud never did come to terms with his own nasality, and, it appears, he even projected his own arrested development in this domain onto the human species![7]

The Decline of Smell in the West

But it was not simply for biographical reasons (influential as these may have been) that Freud privileged visuality over nasality, and continuity over periodicity, in the footnotes of *Civilization and Its Discontents* where he put forward his theory of the assumption of an erect posture leading to the "diminution of olfactory stimuli." There are also reasons of a historical nature for his denigration of nasality and cyclicity.

As regards cyclicity, Donald Lowe has shown how "development-in-time" emerged as the dominant "epistemic order" of bourgeois society in the nineteenth century. "The temporalization of reality underlay such new conceptualizations as the evolution of species, the ages of human life, and the development of society" (1982: 49). Henceforth, changes in reality had to be accounted for immanently—that is, by reference to causes from within the temporal process itself. This had the effect of obviating explanations in terms of, for example, teleology, eschatology, or cyclicity. The Freudian theory of phases of psychosexual development fit nicely with this new epistemic order, whereas Fliess's notion of cosmic periodicity was doomed to appear archaic and outmoded. Similarly, the conflict between Fliess's view that periodic processes of a biological nature are the precipitating factor in neuroses and Freud's view that psychic conflict is the decisive etiological factor was bound to be resolved in the latter's favor, because Freud had history (read: "development-in-time") on his side (see Schur 1972: 95; Anzieu 1986: 528).

As regards nasality, Freud's views on smell were also very much in keeping with historical trends. There had occurred a precipitous decline in the cultural significance of smell during the nineteenth century. Many of the meanings formerly invested in smell were stripped from it during this period. For example, whereas bad smells spelled disease and good smells served as cures in premodernity, Louis Pasteur's discovery of the germ theory of disease severed the connection between olfaction and infection, and smells lost their life-and-death significance (Classen, Howes, and Synnott 1994: 89). As another example, the meaning of the odor of sanctity, which in premodernity was a sign of spiritual grace, was inverted and came to be interpreted as a sign of mental and physical illness—a hallucination, or the emanation of a condition such as diabetes (Classen 1998: 57). Or again, the deodorization of the environment brought on by advances in personal hygiene and sanitation and the new fashion for vegetable scents (in place of animal ones) laid the foundation for "the bourgeois control of the sense of smell and the construction of a schema of perception based on the preeminence of sweetness" (Corbin 1986: 141).

The net result of these developments was the destruction of the elaborate olfactory semiotics of premodernity and its replacement by an olfactory hedonics—a simple calculus of relatively pleasing and displeasing aromas and stenches. A significant by-product of this shift was the way in which the nose came to be conceived of completely independently of its function as the smell organ and exclusively in terms of its visual shape in the "scientific" classifications of races promulgated by Freud's contemporaries. "Look at the nose and you will see the basic sign of humanity in all its variety!" (quoted in Gilman 1993: 96; see further Bijlmer 1923). Thus, the nose assumed prominence as a visual sign of racialized difference just as the significance of olfactory differences in and to the European imagination receded.

This decline in the meanings carried by smell made conditions ripe for the reception of Freud's argument concerning the "diminution of olfactory stimuli." Of course, Freud's argument also contributed to the decline by forging an association between an overactive interest in smells, particularly strong smells, and man's animal past, as well as perversion. This animalization of the sense of smell pushed it beyond the pale of culture. Freud's personal inability to come to terms with his own nasality has thus been transformed into a cultural legacy.[8]

Saving Fliess

Anthropology can sometimes show how what is animalized, considered mad, or supposedly lodged in the unconscious in one culture may be treated as civilized and the subject of extensive (and quite conscious) cultural elaboration in the next (Lévi-Strauss 1992). Wilhelm Fliess's theories are a case in point. They were ridiculed by his contemporaries; and even modern sympathizers, like Sander Gilman, feel compelled to say that they "appear to us as more than slightly mad" (Gilman 1993: 95).

Fliess could have found a more receptive audience for his ideas had he gone among the Melanesians. For example, his fascination with nasal swellings would not have been considered so bizarre among the Ommura of the Eastern Highlands of Papua New Guinea. The Ommura are constantly watching each other's noses for signs of swelling. They differ from Fliess, however, in the way they ascribe a social as opposed to purely sexual etiology to such manifestations. According to Ommura conceptions, a swollen nose is a sign of blockage in a man's exchange relations with his relatives by marriage (Mayer 1982).

Fliess's theory of the periodic nosebleeds of men and women as expressions of "general body rhythms" akin to menstruation would also have enjoyed far more currency in Melanesia than it ever did in Berlin. For example, Kwoma men periodically phlebotomize (i.e., bleed) their penises and tongues in explicit imitation of women, whom they consider to have a certain advantage over them in terms of health (chap. 5). Women are understood to possess a "natural mechanism" for purging their bodies of stagnant blood, namely, menstruation, whereas men and boys must resort to the artificial (but also therefore more cultural and valued) technique of phlebotomy.

The Kwoma also introduce an interesting twist to the naso-genital relationship discovered by Fliess. As will be recalled, they posit a connection between the nose and the penis that is the reverse of the conventional interpretation of the nose as a sign of the penis. To the Kwoma, the penis is a nose, as evidenced by the manner in which the two members are represented identically in Kwoma sculpture, and the notion that "phallic objects," such as a spear, have the capacity to sniff out their targets.

As a final example, the link between nasality and periodicity is a subject of extensive cultural elaboration among the Ongee of the Andaman Islands in the Bay of Bengal. The Ongee conceive of time in terms of a cycle of smells (their calendar is a calendar of scents) and attribute a wide array of life processes to the ebb and flow of odors. For the Ongee, *the* identifying characteristic and life force of all living beings resides in their smell (Classen 1993b: 126–31). Unfortunately, none of these connections can have much resonance for most contemporary Westerners due to the primitivization of olfaction and deodorization of sexual attraction by Freud and his contemporaries, although there are some signs that this trend may now be turning around (Drobnick 2000).

The Material Body of
the Commodity

Sensing Marx

The production of guides to reading the work of Karl Marx has become an industry unto itself over the years, with some of the finer titles including *For Marx* (Althusser 1969) and *Reading Marx Writing* (Kempel 1995). This chapter proposes not another reading but a sensing of Marx's life and works, keyed to the play of the senses in Marx's writings and personal circumstances. It traces the origin of some of his most critical insights into the life of the senses under capitalism to the works of the materialist philosopher Ludwig Feuerbach and the utopianist Charles Fourier. It then goes on to document the "transcendence of sensuousness" in Marx's mature works on the capitalist mode of production and exchange, where the senses, like the material bodies of the commodities Marx ponders, appear to transform into ghosts of themselves.

The chapter proceeds by tacking "diathetically" between Marx's analysis of "the social circulation of matter" (money and commodities) in mid-nineteenth-century industrial capitalism and the modern-day reception of transnational commodities and consumer capitalism in Papua New Guinea. This procedure, by virtue of its historical and cross-cultural focus, throws into sharp relief the lacunae and hidden assumptions in Marx's analysis.[1]

Three conclusions emerge. First, Marx never challenged the sensory status quo, whereas without sensory transformation there can be no social transformation, as Fourier and Feuerbach illustrated so well. Second, Marx sacrificed the senses on the altar of science and to that extent committed no less an abstraction of sensory value (or infraction of human sensibility) than the system he critiqued. Third, by analyzing commodities exclusively in terms of their use- and exchange-value, Marx elided what could be called their sign-value—namely, the sensuous contrasts that set one commodity off from another and give expression to cultural categories as well as express differences in social location. Recognizing sign-value, conversely, opens the way for a full-bodied, multisensory theory of the commodity and of consumption.

Sensory Deprivation and Industrial Capitalism

There are few more dramatic ruptures in the history of Western thought than Marx's apparent break with the idealist tradition of German philosophy (Synnott 1991). "Man is affirmed in the objective world not only in the act of thinking, but with *all* his senses" proclaimed the young Marx in the *Economic and Philosophic Manuscripts of 1844* (1987: 108). Whereas Hegel had interpreted world history in terms of the progressive unfolding of Spirit, Marx held that "the *forming of the five senses* is a labor of the entire history of the world down to the present" (1987: 109). He was inspired to accord such primacy to the senses by the writings of the materialist philosopher Ludwig Feuerbach. In his doctrine of sense perception, Feuerbach argued that it is not only nature or external objects that are experienced by the senses but *"Man, too, is given to himself only through the senses;* he is an object for himself only as an object of the senses" (1966: 58).[2]

Marx's portrayal of the state of the senses in nineteenth-century bourgeois society was in turn influenced by the writings of the utopianist Charles Fourier. Fourier (1851) believed that societies could be judged according to how well they gratified and developed the senses of their members. He argued that the senses were debased by the civilization of his day, in which most people were unable to afford any sensory refinements and in which all people, no matter their rank, were continually confronted with disagreeable sensory impressions, such as the stench and din of the streets. Furthermore, even if sensory pleasures were to be made more available, most people would be unable to appreciate them as their senses remained brutish and undeveloped. These sensory ills, according to Fourier, were the result of a society obsessed with the accumulation of personal wealth to the detriment of the general well-being.

There are numerous echoes of Fourier in Marx's discussion of the condition of the proletariat in the *Economic and Philosophic Manuscripts*. For example, Marx describes how the senses of the worker, living amid "the *sewage* of civilization," are deformed until he loses all notion of sensory refinement and "no longer knows any need ... but the need to *eat*" (1987: 117). Marx returned to this theme of the stripping of the senses in *Capital*, where he described the conditions of factory work.

> Every organ of sense is injured in an equal degree by artificial elevation of temperature, by the dust-laden atmosphere, by the deafening noise, not to mention danger to life and limb among the thickly crowded machinery, which, with the regularity of the seasons, issues its list of the killed and the wounded in the industrial battle ... Is Fourier wrong when he calls factories 'tempered bagnios'? (1954 I: 401–2)

The sensory deprivation of the proletariat was to be expected, given the grueling conditions of factory work, but Marx insisted that not even among the bourgeoisie are the senses fulfilled. All of the capitalist's senses are ultimately fixed on one object—capital; and while the enjoyment of wealth is one of the supreme goods of capitalism, even better is sacrificng pleasure in order to accumulate more capital. "The less you eat, drink and read books; the less you go to the theater, the dance hall, the public-house; the less you ... sing, paint, fence, etc., the more you *save*—the *greater* becomes your treasure which neither moths nor dust will devour—your *capital*" (1987: 118–19).

Developing Fourier's diagnosis, Marx laid the blame for the alienation of the senses in capitalist society on the dehumanizing demands of private property, and envisioned a world in which "the transcendence of private property [would entail] the complete *emancipation* of all human senses and qualities" (1987: 139). Only through the negation of the demeaning and oppressive tyranny of capital could humankind's "species being" come into its own.

> Only through the objectively unfolded richness of man's essential being is the richness of subjective *human* sensibility (a musical ear, an eye for beauty of form—in short *senses* capable of human gratifications, senses confirming themselves as essential powers of *man*) either cultivated or brought into being. (1987: 108)

In the *Communist Manifesto*, Marx and Engels heralded the collapse of the capitalist economic order. The portents of this dissolution included, among other things, the concentration of the proletariat in ever-greater masses, the increasingly agitated character of all social relations due to the constant revolutionizing of the instruments of production, and the reduction of personal worth to commodity status. In short, all of the contradictions of bourgeois society had become manifest on its surface, and the illusion of society could no longer hold.

Reading the *Communist Manifesto* now, from the standpoint of the present world economic order (when the capitalist system seems more firmly entrenched than ever), what most stands out about this text is how accurately (if unwittingly) Marx and Engels foretold *the future of capitalism*, rather than its demise. For example, Marx and Engels wrote:

> The bourgeoisie has through its exploitation of the world market given a cosmopolitan character to production and consumption in every country. . . . In place of the old wants, satisfied by the productions of the country, we find new wants, requiring for their satisfaction the products of distant lands and climes. In place of the old local and national seclusion and self-sufficiency we have intercourse in every direction, universal interdependence of nations. And as in material, so also in intellectual production. The intellectual creations of individual nations become common property. . . . The bourgeoisie, by the rapid improvement of all instruments of production, by the immensely facilitated means of communication, draws all, even the most barbarian, nations into civilization. (1967: 84)

This passage encapsulates a remarkably prescient description of the phenomenon that has in recent years come to be known as globalization (Featherstone 1990). The fine food halls of Europe and America filled with produce "from distant lands and climes" (see, e.g., Bell and Valentine 1997; James 1996), the global flow of capital (and people) that has resulted in the "universal interdependence of nations" (see, e.g., Robbins 1998), the Hollywood movies and other elements of American popular culture that have become the "common property" (or transcultural patrimony) of everybody from Chile to Kathmandu (see, e.g., Dorfman 1983; Iyer 1989; Appadurai 1996) all speak to the truth of this passage. Summing up their vision of globalization as cultural homogenization, Marx and Engels wrote: "In one word, [the bourgeoisie] creates a world after its own image" (1967: 84).

Nevertheless, the apparent flash of insight that this passage contains must not be allowed to distract attention from the limitations of Marx's analysis of capitalism's laws of motion. Marx's gaze always remained centered on the factory and the stock market, and while he may have succeeded at exposing the secrets of the capitalist mode of production through his penetrating analysis of the labor process (on which more later), he neglected an equally salient development—namely, the *presentation* of commodities in the department stores and world exhibitions that sprang up in the mid–nineteenth century (Bowlby 1985; Cummings and Lewandoska 2000). The birth of these "palaces of consumption" heralded a transformation in the nature of capitalism with far-reaching implications—the transformation from industrial capitalism (as Marx knew it) to the consumer capitalism of today. For capitalism does not work by the extraction of the labor power and value of the worker alone, it also works by generating consumer desires of all sorts in all people, including the worker (Galbraith 1958, 1967).

Sensory Stimulation and Consumer Capitalism

It has fallen to others working within a materialist framework to theorize the ongoing history of sensory and social relations under capitalism—that is, to theorize capitalism as a mode of presentation as well as production, and as a mode of consumption as well as exchange. Walter Benjamin, Rémy Saisselin, and Stuart Ewen have each contributed to this theoretical project, and their respective views on the organization of the sensorium in consumer culture will be considered in this section.

The growing social importance of consumption in the nineteenth century was evident in the new venue for shopping, the department store. With its theatrical lighting, enticing window displays, and floor after floor of entrancing merchandise—"each separate counter . . . a show place of dazzling interest and attraction" (Dreiser cited in Saisselin 1984: 35)—the department store presented a fabulous spectacle of consumer plenty and accessibility. Previously, goods had been kept behind counters, and it was presumed that a customer would enter a shop with the purpose to buy. In the department store, by contrast, goods were largely out in the open, and anyone could enter simply with the purpose of having a look. The expectation was that the display of goods in such abundance would prove so seductive that even those who were "just looking" would be lured into buying, particularly given the atmosphere of pleasurable self-indulgence that prevailed. In his novel *Sister Carrie* Theodore Dreiser described the bewitching effect of the department store displays on a potential customer.

> Fine clothes . . . spoke tenderly and Jesuitically for themselves. When she came within earshot of their pleading, desire in her bent a willing ear. . . . "My dear," said the lace collar . . . "I fit you beautifully; don't give me up." (cited in Saisselin 1984: 36)

The department store thus appeared on the scene as an enormous candy store with a cornucopia of goodies to satisfy the taste of the bourgeoisie for fashionable but affordable style. It was able to do so thanks to advances in mass production—specifically, the mechanical reproduction of styled or imitation goods. Mass production brought previously exclusive luxury items within the reach of the bourgeoisie, and even the working class. As Walter Benjamin (1969) noted with regard to art, what such imitation goods lose in authenticity they gain in mobility: "fine" art, "fine" furniture, "fine" clothes can now go anywhere and everywhere as mass production finds its perfect match in mass consumption.

The counterpart to the (often female) shopper in the new consumer palaces was the *flâneur*, the voyeuristic idler who treated the whole city as though it were a department store, a variegated spectacle of goods to be viewed and occasionally sampled (Benjamin 1973; Tester 1994).[3] "The prime requisite of an expert *flâneur*," according to the American novelist Henry James, was "the simple, sensuous, confident relish of pleasure" (cited in Saisselin 1984: 19). Yet, as a suitable admirer of the new society of spectacle, the *flâneur* found his primary sensory pleasure simply in watching, the watching that in a visualist age would increasingly seem to offer a total sensory experience in itself. In his study of the aesthetics of nineteenth-century consumption, Rémy Saisselin writes: "The *flâneur* [was] a conscious observer for whom the word *boredom* had become meaningless: he animated all he saw; admired all he perceived. He strolled, observed, watched, espied" (1984: 25).

As Saisselin goes on to point out in *The Bourgeois and the Bibelot*, the phenomenon of the *flâneur* went hand in hand with that of the photographer, both aesthetic observers, insiders and outsiders at once, both constantly skimming the surfaces of urban life for their rich bounty of visual impressions. The photographer, however, was equipped with the technological means to fix visual impressions on paper, turning the images themselves into objects of display and desire. The mass production of images that occurred in the 1800s thus complemented the mass production of styled goods or imitations. With this proliferation of images and imitations, appearance increasingly came to overshadow—and even obliterate—substance (Ewen 1988; Boorstin 1962).

In an essay on photography published in 1859, Oliver Wendell Holmes wrote:

> Every conceivable object of Nature and Art will soon scale off its surface for us. Men will hunt all curious, beautiful, grand objects, as they hunt cattle in South America, for their skins and leave the carcasses as of little worth. (cited in Ewen 1988: 25)

The analogy to hunting here is significant as it indicates that the photographic reproduction of the world is not a passive multiplication of images but an active appropriation of all "curious, beautiful, grand objects." The notion of the "carcasses" of objects being left behind "as of little worth" once their photograph was taken points to a state of affairs in which photographic (and shortly, cinematic) imagery would become more powerful and influential than objects themselves. In *All Consuming Images* Stuart Ewen states that Holmes correctly "laid out the contours by which the phenomenon of *style* operates in the world today" (1988: 25). Style deals exclusively in surface impressions, hence the "right look" becomes all-important.

If the primary sensory mode of consumer culture was (and remains) that of visual display, however, the nonvisual senses were not left to one side. As Ewen notes, the sense of touch was also appropriated by marketers as a crucial medium of sensory persuasion. Thus, in a 1930s book entitled *Consumer Engineering*, the business professors Sheldon and Arens wrote:

> Manufacturing an object that delights this [tactile] sense is something that you do but don't talk about. Almost everything which is bought is handled. After the eye, the hand is the first censor to pass on acceptance, and if the hand's judgement is unfavorable, the most attractive object will not gain the popularity it deserves. On the other hand, merchandise designed to be pleasing to the hand wins an approval that may never register in the mind, but which will determine additional purchases. . . . *Make it snuggle in the palm.* (cited in Ewen 1988: 49–50)

Consumer capitalism, in fact, would make it its business to engage as many senses as possible in its seduction of the consumer. The "right look" must, depending on the kind of product being sold, be reinforced by the right feel, the right scent, the right sound, and the right taste. This multisensory marketing, or "technocracy of sensuality" as Wolfgang Haug (1986) dubbed it, would reach its height in the late twentieth century with artificial scents added to a range of products from cars to crayons, and with Muzak and fragrances wafting though the plushly carpeted aisles of department stores and boutiques, creating a state of hyperaesthesia in the consumer (Classen, Howes, and Synnott 1994: 180–205).

The hypersensuality of the contemporary marketplace has been theorized by a new generation of business professors. In a *Harvard Business Review* article entitled "Welcome to the Experience Economy," Joseph Pine II and James Gilmore assert that forward-thinking companies no longer produce goods or supply services, but instead use services as the stage and goods as props for creating "experiences" that are as stimulating for the consumer as they are memorable. The authors identify a series of "experience-design principles" that include: *Theme the experience* (e.g., "eatertainment" restaurants such as Planet Hollywood or the Rainforest Cafe); *Mix in memorabilia* (e.g., an official T-shirt for a rock concert); and, above all, *Engage all five senses.*

> The more senses an experience engages, the more effective and memorable it can be. Smart shoeshine operators augment the smell of polish with crisp snaps of the cloth, scents and sounds that don't make the shoes any shinier but do make the experience more engaging. . . . Similarly, grocery stores pipe bakery smells into the aisles, and some use light and sound to simulate thunderstorms when misting their produce.
>
> The mist at the Rainforest Cafe appeals serially to all five senses. It is first apparent as a sound: Sss-sss-zzz. Then you see the mist arising from the rocks and feel it soft and cool against your skin. Finally, you smell its tropical essence, and you taste (or imagine that you do) its freshness. What you can't be is unaffected by the mist. (Pine and Gilmore 1998: 104)

Capitalism has evidently come a long way since the days when production was the key value and the reproduction of capital seemingly depended on stripping the senses of the laborer and curbing those of the bourgeoisie. Now the focus appears to be on seducing the senses of the consumer in the interests of valorizing capital. This sea change is aptly symbolized by the increasingly widespread phenomenon in European and North American urban centers of abandoned factories in the city core being renovated to house amusement palaces and luxury condominiums.

Entering the Capitalist World of Goods

The introduction of consumer products and life-styles has provoked significant transformations in the indigenous social and sensory orders of Papua New Guinea. For one thing, gift exchange forms the basis of most "traditional" economic orders in Melanesia. The new consumer products, however, can only be acquired through commodity exchange (at least in the first instance). Describing the difference between gift exchange and commodity exchange, Chris Gregory writes:[4]

> Commodity exchange is an exchange of alienable objects between people who are in a state of reciprocal independence that establishes a quantitative relationship between the objects transacted, whereas gift exchange is an exchange of inalienable objects between people who are in a state of reciprocal dependence that establishes a qualitative relationship between the subjects transacting. (1983: 104)

A good example of a product that is strategically employed to create "a state of reciprocal dependence" is the *bilum* or string bag, which is used extensively throughout Papua New Guinea. Maureen MacKenzie (1991) has studied the role of the bilum among the Telefol, a Mountain Ok people of central New Guinea, where girls symbolically grow into womanhood by learning to make bilums. MacKenzie reports that the bilum represents the nurturing life-giving capacities of the woman who made it. When a Telefol woman gives a string bag she has made as a gift, it is with the purpose of establishing or confirming a reciprocal relationship with some other person by giving something of herself. Thus, an adolescent girl will give a small bilum to a male youth as a sign of her interest in him. If the youth accepts the gift he agrees to enter into a relationship with the girl and must respond by giving her a gift in return, such as an armband. Presented as gifts to friends and relatives, the bilum is at once extremely useful in a practical sense—"It is like our car and our workshop," MacKenzie (1991: 157) was told—and the means of uniting the members of a community in a web of relationships. By making and giving away string bags, women symbolically weave the community together in a social bilum, which is at once nourishing and protective.

Many Papua New Guineans' first experience with Western commodities and commodity exchange came in the late nineteenth and first half of the twentieth centuries. It was during this period that contact with Westerners (administrators, missionaries, prospectors for oil and gold, coffee and copra exporters) intensified, albeit unevenly due to the rugged geography of the country. Westerners were perceived as having unlimited access to "cargo" or manufactured goods. According to reports, their interest in such commodities led some Papua New Guineans and other Melanesians to develop elaborate "cargo cults" (Worsley 1970). These cults centered on ritual practices—such as building mock jetties or airstrips, constructing mock storehouses or temples (modeled after mission churches), erecting flagpoles, and writing "letters"—intended to attract a cargo of Western goods to the cult participants.

The avid desire for Western products that these cults expressed might seem to indicate that Papua New Guineans were primed for entry into a capitalist economy, but the reality was more complex.[5] The private property regime of the whites puzzled many Papua New Guineans. As Kenelm Burridge relates, in Tangu the presence of whites was explained by reference to a myth of two brothers. The clever brother, who was the ancestor of the whites, was "well endowed with brains, ability and inventiveness, whilst the other was dull and could only copy" as a result of some "sin" he committed in the mythic past (1969: 64; 1960: 147–76, 203–7). Nevertheless, one interpretation of the myth held that "since the two men were in fact brothers, and brothers normally shared their assets, white men would come round to sharing their goods, privileges and capacities with black men"; and, if they did not, they should be made to withdraw from Papua New Guinea (1969: 64).

In Tangu, a series of prophets arose who prescribed various ritual procedures (such as donning European clothes, undergoing baptism, and destroying crops) that, the cult members were assured, would bring about either the desired pooling of assets in accordance with the moral norms of brotherhood or else the expulsion of the whites. In a further twist, it was held that the ultimate source of these attractive new goods was not the whites at all, but the Papua New Guineans' own ancestors, who wanted to bestow them on their descendants (Gosden and Knowles 2001: 6–10).

Fast-forward to the twilight of the twentieth century and it appears that Papua New Guinea has gone the way of most societies in the world today and is developing into a Western-style consumer society. Port Moresby, the national capital, is a sprawling metropolis with numerous distractions from beer halls to beaches. Clothes and other merchandise from around the world are on display in the windows of the stores in the Waigani shopping district of Port Moresby. A good number of these products are imitation Western goods from China, so their prices are relatively low. There are department stores in most of the provincial capitals as well, such as Wewak in East Sepik Province or Alotau in Milne Bay, and these emporiums serve as more local entrées to the capitalist world of goods.

Men and women from the "grass roots" or "bush," as the hinterlands are called, flock to Port Moresby, or the provincial capitals and other towns, as well as to the mines and plantations, where they work for wages. Due to a pattern of circular migration, these same men and women normally return to their native hamlets after a spell, bringing new consumer values and goods with them. Some return migrants will use their savings to try to break into the import business by opening a tradestore. Such stores typically consist of a one-room shack with sparsely stocked shelves of packaged goods, and a Trukai rice, Benson and Hedges, or other brand-name sign outside. Tradestores now have a ubiquitous presence in Papua New Guinea. Michael O'Hanlon describes them as "raw intrusions of commercial morality into a pastoral landscape" (1993: 39). Many such ventures fail, however, due to the overwhelming demands of kin (*wantoks*) for material assistance. Mission-run tradestores tend to do better because they are purposely staffed by outsiders.

In addition to the tradestores, traveling vendors visit remote villages with a range of exotic wares: peanut butter, mosquito repellent, laundry detergent, rice (already a staple for many). These vendors will put on shows to convince prospective consumers of the value of their goods.[6] In one skit, an actor mimes disgust at the smell of his own shirt, followed by delight at its scent after it has been washed with detergent to remove any trace of body odor. In another such skit, a schoolboy wails in protest at being subjected to a meal of taro for the fifth straight day. His howls are silenced when his mother produces a bag of Trukai rice; the advantages of the product are extolled (it is the boy's real favorite—not taro—has lots of vitamins and will make him grow big); and the youth goes on to boast that he can carry his mother and his father on his biceps, thanks to Trukai turning him into a muscleman. The general aim of these shows seems to be to induce or accentuate a dissatisfaction with the status quo that can only be relieved by the consumption of the goods for sale. The appeal in most cases is made directly to the audience's senses—peanut butter tastes good, rice makes you strong, laundry detergent gives your clothes a pleasing smell.

The techniques of the traveling vendors can also be found in the burgeoning domain of mass media advertising. Thus, a newspaper ad for Pepsi-Cola shows a row of young female Papua New Guinean dancers in traditional attire blissfully downing cans and bottles of Pepsi, as though this synchronized act were one more, and perhaps the best, part of their performance (Foster 1998: 79). Companies marketing products in Papua New Guinea, in fact, are urged to consider "the natives" as potential consumers. One ad directed at generating more advertising revenue for the newspaper *Wantok* displays a man in stereotypical native dress—grass skirt, feather headdress, bone through the nose—carrying a briefcase bulging with money. The text asserts that "he SHOPS at major department stores, buys different FOODS, likes SOFT DRINKS, enjoys SMOKING CIGARETTES, has a family to feed and CLOTHE," and so on (Foster 1995: 163–64). The idea is clearly that members of traditional Papua New Guinean societies should not be presumed to be outside the market economy, as they have money to spend and lots of consumer desires to be satisfied.

These mass-marketing techniques seem to be aimed at reducing local differences and creating a generic consumer with common tastes. Thus Pepsi is advertised as "The Choice of All Papua New Guineans." While encouraged to participate in a new national identity through sharing common consumer products, Papua New Guineans are also invited to define themselves not as members of communities bound by webs of social relations and cultural traditions, but as autonomous individuals making personal "life-style" choices. Therefore, even though Pepsi may be the drink of "All Papua New Guineans," this situation is presented as the result of personal "Choice" (Foster 1996/97: 4–5; Gewertz and Errington 1999).

In a similar way, the indigenous musical traditions of Papua New Guinea, such as that of the Kaluli (Feld 1982, 1984), with their polyrhythmic complexity and decided preference for interlock, overlap, and alternation of vocal parts (to the exclusion of unison), are gradually being drowned out by commercial audiocassette tapes and compact discs produced in recording studios in towns along the coast. A group such as Kales out of Madang sings in monotonous unison to a mechanical beat and the twang of acoustic guitars—but their imitation Australian string-band music sells.

Melanesian Mode of Domestication

At first glance, it appears that traditional Melanesian practices and products are disappearing under a blanket of consumer goods and values, and that the sensory models described in earlier chapters will soon be replaced by a taste for Pepsi and an ear for string-band music. Yet on examining the ways in which mainstream consumer goods are actually employed by Papua New Guineans a somewhat different picture emerges, one in which consumers are at times able to incorporate new products into traditional life-styles. A telling example here is that of Johnson's Baby Powder as analyzed by John Liep (1994) in his fascinating study of the recontextualization of this particular consumer item in different parts of Papua New Guinea. While aware of the conventional uses of baby powder, Papua New Guineans have accorded it particular local uses, ranging from purifying corpses and mourners, to asperging the heads of dancers and singers, to serving as body decor. In one instance from the Trobriand Islands, female mourners, dressed in black and forbidden to bathe, mark the end of their mourning period by being ritually dressed in colorful clothes, rubbed with coconut oil, and sprinkled with Johnson's Baby Powder.

In some of these cases baby powder is being used in place of a traditional substance. In the Western Highlands, for example, baby powder provides an alternative to traditional clays for body decoration. Among the Mekeo of Central Province, Johnson's Baby Powder is sprinkled over dancers in place of crushed seashell powder and is itself now being replaced by Mum 21 deodorant, presumably also in powder form (Liep 1994: 66–67). Thus, new commodities do not necessarily have to support new consumer values, they may also be incorporated into traditional life-styles.

In his analysis of the unconventional uses of baby powder in the Massim region, Liep finds an association with the Massim version of a widespread trickster myth. In this myth, Kasabwaibwaileta (the trickster) fools people by wearing the malodorous, wrinkled, diseased skin of an old man. He later casts off this ugly covering to reveal himself as a youth with smooth, bright, light skin. The smooth, white, bright, fragrant baby powder seems to possess a similar transformative significance. Applied to corpses it purifies and counters the harshness of death and decay. Applied to mourners it transforms darkness and uncleanliness into brightness and fragrance. The sensory symbolism of baby powder in the Massim is hence in keeping with the traditional sensory model of the region with its emphasis on the "expansion outward" of the individual (see chap. 3). Furthermore, the fact that baby powder is a product created primarily for babies creates an association between baby powder and youthfulness. The ritual use of baby powder implies a symbolic rebirth, as when in the myth Kasabwaibwaileta magically transforms from an old man into a young one, or as when mourners leave the sphere of the dead and return to the world of the living.

These examples of local Melanesian appropriations and transformations—or "domestications"—of the meanings and uses of transnational commodities could be multiplied (Thomas 1995). For example, Rena Lederman records of her experience among the Mendi of the Southern Highlands:

> The Mendi we know do not see [consumer] objects in the same way as we see them: their purposes supplied *for* us . . . In our objects, they perceive multiple possibilities for satisfying needs the manufacturers never imagined. . . . They use safety pins as earrings in place of blades of grass and combs made out of umbrella spokes instead of bamboo . . . women we know reuse the plastic fibres of rice bags, rolling them into twine with which to make traditional netbags. (1986: 8)

In another telling example, Michael O'Hanlon records how beer has come to symbolize modernity for many, yet is consumed in ways identical to the ritual consumption of pork fat and carries many of the same symbolic connotations as fat (such as promoting growth and fertility) in the context of the Wahgi Pig Festival (1993: 41–42). These examples challenge the idea that the bourgeoisie is recreating "a world after its own image," as Marx and Engels (1967) would have it, for they call into question the assumed link between globalization and cultural homogenization (Howes 1996; Classen and Howes 1996b).

Interestingly, money itself has been appropriated by some Papua New Guineans, not just as a neutral medium of exchange or means of acquiring commodities, but as one more curious new object to be incorporated into local cultural practices and discourses (Akin and Robbins 1999). The national government has taken pains to impress upon its citizens that the national currency has replaced traditional forms of "money," such as shells. "In this country, metal coins and paper notes are replacing things such as shells, clay pots, feathers and pigs, which earlier were used to buy things which men and women needed" (quoted in Foster 1998: 64). As a visual reminder of this transition the bills of Papua New Guinea are illustrated with such traditional wealth objects as shells, pots, and pigs—and the basic unit of currency is called "kina," which means shell money in the Melpa language. Government publications, however, stress that money is not really a material object, like a shell, but is rather a symbol of "the value of the work or goods which people bring into existence by their efforts" (quoted in Foster 1998: 66).

Notwithstanding, money in the form of coins and bills is inescapably material, and it is evaluated and employed in terms of its materiality by many Papua New Guinean peoples. Michael Nihill reports that the Anganen of the Southern Highlands liken 20-kina notes to pearlshells. The red notes are deemed to resemble pearlshells that are "invigorated" by being polished with red ochre by Anganen men. By extension they also resemble vigorous, decorated male bodies. Thus Nihill writes that "brilliant body decoration, bright red pearlshells, and crisp, pristine 20-kina notes are all of inherent merit and beauty" (1989: 154). In effect, therefore, the new bills have taken on the role of objects of aesthetic and cultural value, similar to the shells they were meant to replace.

If new products, and even the money with which they are purchased, can be accommodated within traditional sensory and symbolic orders, these new products also seem to be showing a tendency to occupy the more positively valued positions of those orders. Thus consumer goods are often presented and seen as being neater and cleaner than traditional goods. One of the desirable qualities of Johnson's Baby Powder is that it comes in a smooth, neat plastic container, seemingly free of any of the mess and fuss of production. Similarly, PK chewing gum is promoted as a clean, fresh alternative to the widespread practice of chewing and spitting "messy, unhealthy" betel nut. In one government-sponsored ad, a picture of smiling boys chewing PK is juxtaposed with an image of the cancerous mouth that allegedly results from chewing betel nut (see Foster 1996/97: 10; 1992: 37–43). From this perspective, where traditional goods disgust by being disorderly, crude, and subject to decay, modern commodities please by being self-contained, smooth, and clean: forever fresh and new. One sees here again the image of the trickster throwing off his old, diseased skin to reveal a shining, clean new self underneath; and now the old skin represents old, messy, decaying traditional goods and the new self all the attractive, pristine products that shine on the shelves of the trade-stores.

Paper and coin currencies are themselves promoted as neater and cleaner than the old forms of wealth. Unlike a pig, money is said to be easy to exchange at a store "for a radio set or a guitar"; and, as a booklet produced by the Reserve Bank of Australia further explains: "Money does not decay or go bad like such things as taro, sugar and tobacco. . . . Even when notes become soiled and worn, they can always be exchanged at a bank for clean fresh ones" (quoted in Foster 1996/97: 65). By this very comparison, of course, money seems to become one more, if eminently superior, material good in lieu of an abstract medium of exchange.

The processes by which consumer products are incorporated into New Guinean societies draw attention to the fact that the introduction of such products does not necessarily mean that a Western-style consumer culture will supplant local traditions, nor that a visualist emphasis on display will supplant local sensory orders. Rather, the new products may appeal to the extent to which they can fit into or complement existing sensory and social beliefs and practices. Instead of consumer culture replacing traditional ways of life, traditional ways of life may subsume consumer culture. Thus baby powder may not imply a whole new regime of baby care so much as it suggests an alternative means of ritual purification, and money need not be conceptualized as an abstract symbol of wealth but rather as a cleaner, more portable pig.

However, if consumer products do indeed come to seem more generally pleasing and desirable than local products, then a dependence on a market economy is produced that will inevitably alter the traditional links between sensory relations and social relations in Papua New Guinea. A bag purchased in a store may apparently have all of the desired sensory attributes of a bilum and more. For example, one bilum-maker interviewed by MacKenzie (1991: 133) was proud at having woven a bag so neatly that people thought it had been made by a machine.[7] Still, it will not bring with it crucial traces of and ties to the person who produced it.

On the "Transcendence of Sensuousness" in Capitalist Exchange

According to Marx's analysis in *Capital,* every commodity "may be looked at from the points of view of quality and quantity" (1954: 43). In its qualitative aspect, a commodity is "an assemblage of many properties," both natural and human-added, that satisfies a particular need or want, as in the way a coat satisfies the need for warmth (or a bilum the need for a carrying device). The material properties of the commodity, and the labor expended in its creation, constitute its use-value. The quantitative aspect of a commodity emerges only when it is exchanged for some other commodity of an equal magnitude of value. This exchange relation constitutes its exchange-value, but the latter has nothing to do with its physical form. "The value of commodities is the very opposite of the coarse materiality of their substance, not an atom of matter enters into its composition" (54). Commodities "as values" thus possess a "phantom-like objectivity." This "ghostly" or "supersensible" character of commodities "as values" is due to the process of abstraction by which they become substitutable one for another in the "interminable series of value equations" that make up the capitalist value system (69). Marx gives the following hypothetical by way of illustration:

20 yards of linen $=$ 1 coat or $=$ 10 lbs. tea or $=$ 40 lbs. coffee or $=$ 1 quarter corn or $=$ 2 ounces gold or $=$ 1/2 ton iron or $=$ &c. (68)

How could the actual material properties or actual individual labor that went into the production of any of these commodities have any influence on their substitutability for each other in this value chain? Their materiality makes them incommensurable, whereas the fact of their exchangeability homogenizes them all through introducing "something common," a "third term" capable of expressing their value. The "third term" is not, as one might think, money (see Marx 1954: 97). According to Marx, what underwrites all of these substitutions is the fact that commodities are ultimately "congelation[s] of undifferentiated human labour" in different magnitudes (68).

It cannot be too strongly emphasized that it is not the quality or individual character of the labor-time that goes into a commodity that matters to its exchange-value, but only the duration of that labor-time, and not the actual duration, but only the "socially necessary" or general average labor-time required for the production of the type of commodity in question (Marx 1954: 48–53, 80). The abstraction that characterizes a commodity's exchange-value is thus, in the final analysis, grounded in social convention, in "averages"—not that this makes its value any less an abstraction. The same goes for the currencies and weights in terms of which magnitudes of value (i.e., prices) are expressed, and for the manner in which commodities appear to move relative to each other on the stock exchange. In the latter case, according to Marx (80), the social relations between individual producers come to appear as relations between the commodities themselves.

The phantasmagoric or spectral character of Marx's account of capitalist exchange-value is well brought out in the following quotation from Thomas Keenan.

What remains after the radical reduction of difference, after the vanishing of all "atoms" of use value or [individual] productive labor? Its name is ghost, *gespenstige Gegenständlichkeit*, spectral, haunting, surviving objectivity. . . . In the rigor of the abstraction [by which commodities become "values"], only ghosts survive. The point is to exchange them . . . Because they resemble one another, as all ghosts do, having no phenomenal or sensible features by which to distinguish "themselves," the operation of which they are the remnant can finally occur. Thanks to their resemblance, the conditions of exchange are met—the very exchange that leaves them, atomless, behind. (1993: 168)

There is some question as to the truth-value of Marx's analysis of commodities from only two perspectives (i.e., use-value and exchange-value) and his exclusive reliance on a labor theory of value to account for the magnitudes in which things are exchanged. For example, Maureen MacKenzie argues that the Telefol "do not share the same principles of value determination as Marx" (1991: 127). A bilum, for example, is valued

not simply because it crystallizes productive energy in a measurable amount. Rather it embodies the endeavour of a particular woman, and objectifies her relationship with whomever she has made that bilum for. . . . Where labour is considered, it is not its *duration* but *quality* that is important. (127–28)

Marx would probably have had little difficulty dispensing with this objection. Telefol society, he would have noted, belongs with those other

ancient social organisms of production [that] are, as compared to bourgeois society, extremely simple and transparent [in that they are] founded either on the immature development of man individually, who has not yet severed the umbilical cord that unites him with his fellowmen in a primitive tribal community, or [as in the Asiatic mode of production] upon direct relations of subjection. (1954: 84)

In other words, the bonds between persons and between persons and things in precapitalist societies are not subject to the same abstraction that one finds in capitalist society, where the presumed equality (i.e., interchangeability) of commodities as of persons rules exchange. Furthermore, it is not the gift relation (as among the Telefol) but the wage relation (which is actually the guise behind which "surplus value" is extracted from the labor process) that is the defining relation of capitalist society.

Commodities as Bundles of Sensory and Social Relations

In order to advance our analysis, we must therefore set aside particularist objections like those of MacKenzie, at least for the time being, and examine Marx's account of value determination in relation to capitalist society itself. Questions of truth-value persist nonetheless. To begin with, for Marx "objectification" (viz., the end product of the labor process) could mean only one thing—alienation (Dant 1999: 10). However, as recent research in the anthropology of consumption has revealed, goods also "objectify" the symbolic order of society. According to Grant McCracken:

> One of the most important ways in which cultural categories are substantiated is through the material objects of a culture. . . . [Objects are] created according to the blueprint of culture and to this extent they make the categories of the blueprint material. (1988: 74)

Thus, commodities do not only conceal the social relations of their production, as Marx would have it. The system of objects also constitutes a framework in terms of which class and other social distinctions can be and are *expressed* through consumption—that is, through the "assemblages" that different consumers construct by selecting some goods and not others as expressive of their identity and sense of social location.[8]

What is more, it is by virtue of their material, sensuous characteristics that goods are able to express social relations. Marshall Sahlins gives the example of how gender differences are articulated in the North American clothing system.

The masculine fabric is relatively coarse and stiff, usually heavier, the feminine soft and fine; apart from the neutral white, masculine colors are darker, feminine light or pastel. The line in men's clothing is square, with angles and corners; women's dress emphasizes the curved, the rounded, the flowing and the fluffy. Such elements of line, texture, and the like are the minimal constituents, the objective contrasts which convey social meaning. (1976: 190–91)

Sahlins's objection to Marx's account of value determination consists in this: "Conceiving the creation and movement of goods solely from their pecuniary quantities (exchange-value), one ignores the cultural code of concrete properties governing . . . what is in fact produced" (1976: 166). Conversely, by assuming "that use-values transparently serve human needs, that is, by virtue of their evident properties, [Marx] gave away the meaningful relations between men and objects essential to the comprehension of production in any historical form" (169).

The sensory and social relations embodied in commodities are constitutive of what could be called their sign-value. The sensuous contrasts and relations that a given object bodies forth serve to set it off from other objects belonging to the same cultural category and so empower it to signify the social characteristics or "life-style" of its consumer. It will be appreciated how Marx's value chains (e.g., "20 yards of linen = 1 coat or = 10 lbs. tea"), which were intended to dazzle the reader by accentuating the heterogeneity of use-values and the homogeneity of exchange-values, occlude the sign-value of commodities. Marx's value chains focus on equivalencies across different categories of goods and ignore the play of difference within any given category. Marx never compares the cut or texture of two coats, for example. Only "1 coat = 10 lbs. tea or = 1/2 ton iron." To the extent that it ignores the differences in the similarities (or use-value) to concentrate on the similarities in the differences (or exchange-value), Marx's theory of value determination is therefore incomplete. Significantly, these two dimensions are actually fused in the constitution of the sign-value of the commodity, as we have just seen.

Two preliminary conclusions can be drawn. First, had Marx not been so preoccupied with exposing the social relations he took to be concealed in and by the commodity-form, he might have been more appreciative of the numerous ways in which commodities are everywhere appropriated to *express* relations of solidarity or individuation between persons. Second, had Marx not taken such a reductionistic view of the usefulness of objects, he might have been more appreciative of the complex ways in which their sensuous characteristics may be *coded* culturally.

A third line of critique has to do with the dim view Marx took of consumption. Thus, in "Money, or the Circulation of Commodities" (chap. 3 of *Capital*), Marx invites us to accompany the owner of some commodity to "the scene of action, the market." There we watch as "the social circulation of matter" unfolds (i.e., the conversion of commodity x into money and the reconversion of the money into commodity y). "When once a commodity has found a resting place, where it can serve as a use-value," Marx (1954: 106) writes, "it falls out of the sphere of exchange into that of consumption. But the former sphere alone interests us at present"—as indeed it does throughout *Capital.* Why? Because "So far as [a commodity] is a value in use, there is nothing mysterious about it" (77). By its properties it is capable of satisfying human wants, that is all.

Marx was wrong to treat the sphere of consumption as a "resting place." It is no less a "scene of action" than the market or the factory floor. Indeed, it has become a commonplace of contemporary approaches to the study of consumer action that "consumption needs to be seen as a production in that as consumers appropriate goods . . . there is a 'making' through their particular ways of using or making sense of them" (Dant 1999: 36).[9] We have already seen abundant evidence of this notion of consumption as production in our discussion of the Melanesian mode of domestication, but it is no less true of many Western modes of consumption (Lee 1993; Klein 2000).

Marx's obliviousness with respect to the social significance of the sphere of consumption was directly linked to his elevation, in classic nineteenth-century fashion, of the sphere of production. "Marx focussed on work as a primary source of meaning, dignity and self-development for modern man" (Berman 1999: 20). This presumption remains prevalent today, with the result that all the creativity evidenced by Papua New Guineans in their domestication of transnational commodities would count for nothing in the eyes of latter-day Marxists. As for Marx himself, he would have regarded the history of cargo cults in Melanesia and salience of sensuous signifiers as explicable in terms of Melanesian religion being a "primitive," "fetishistic" religion—that is, "a religion of sensuous desire" (see Pietz 1993; Pels 1998).

Primitive fetishism had its counterpart in bourgeois society, according to Marx, but in the latter it is no longer idols that are revered but commodities. Bourgeois society being several social steps up from primitive society, however, the bourgeoisie is supposed to revere commodities as abstractions rather than as sensuous objects, as exchange-values rather than as use-values. (The famous section in *Capital* on "The Fetishism of Commodities" is best read as Marx calling upon his contemporaries to come to their reason, and not, as it were, their senses.) In fact, at the moment in which a commodity becomes an object of exchange, for Marx, "all sensuous characteristics are extinguished," and it becomes a "supersensible" item in an accounting ledger or on the stock market (see Keenan 1993: 165, 181).

Ironically, therefore, given his understanding of fetishism as a "religion of sensuous desire," Marx did not perceive how in capitalist society it might also take the form of a cult of sensuous desire in which commodities are not just utilitarian articles or suprasensible items of exchange, nor "mistakenly" perceived as self-moving, but rather potent bundles of sensory symbolism and social relations. As noted previously, the industrial capitalism that reigned during Marx's time foregrounded production and free-market exchange, just as it privileged a utilitarian attitude toward the value of commodities. These processes and attitudes tend to marginalize the more sensuous or aesthetic characteristics of the commodity. Now, however, the processes of consumption appear to drive the forces of production (Bradley and Nolan 1998; Parr 1999), and "sense appeal" has become an essential attribute of commodities. It could indeed be argued that our current interest in sensory values is an offshoot of twentieth-century consumer capitalism in which self-indulgence and sensory satisfaction have replaced self-discipline and sensory deprivation as guiding social principles. In the consumer society the most seemingly utilitarian of objects, from paper clips to lemon squeezers, come in a variety of colors and shapes to entice consumers and offer an illusion (at least) of personal choice.

While consumer capitalism is undoubtedly bent on seducing the senses of the consumer through its marketing techniques, packaging, and products, the consumer need not be passive in her or his response. It is not just "primitive" Papua New Guineans who in their "ignorance" invent new uses for consumer products, using baby powder to purify the dead or lipstick to paint facial designs. As intimated previously, Western consumers may also make creative uses of products in ways never imagined by their manufacturers. The drink Kool-Aid, an icon of the mid-twentieth-century middle-class family, is used as a flamboyant hair dye by youths intent on challenging the staid norms of that era. Barbie and Ken dolls, intended to socialize girls into conventional gender roles, are collected and displayed as cult icons by the American gay community. In these cases certain "appealing" sensory and social attributes of commodities are creatively appropriated by consumers to elicit a new set of symbolic meanings. For example, the bright colors of Kool-Aid drinks, which are meant to signify tastiness and an endearing childish delight in gaudy hues, instead signify social rebellion, aesthetic freedom, and faddish trendiness when they appear on the heads of young men and women. As in Papua New Guinea, Western consumers may appropriate commodities for their own ends and even use them to challenge the system that produced them (though ultimately perhaps supporting it).

When Marx described the bourgeoisie as being alienated from their senses under capitalism he could not have foreseen all the new forms in which the senses would return to the bourgeoisie in future phases of capitalism. Nor could Marx, as a result of his progressive renunciation of the Feuerbachian doctrine of "sense-certainty" (on which more in the next section), have appreciated the ways in which the sensory signs of commodities can encode crucial social values. True to the conventional Western division of body and mind, Marx imagined the impending communist utopia to be a place where one could engage in the simple physical labors of fishing or cattle-rearing during the day and in complex critical analysis at night (see Marx and Engels 1947: 22). Marx did not realize, as his onetime mentor Fourier did, as the peoples of Papua New Guinea do, and as twenty-first-century consumers increasingly do, that the life of the senses is not separate from the life of the mind and that procuring and consuming food and other commodities can themselves be a form of critical analysis.

The Specter of the Senses in Marx

Louis Althusser (1969) has argued that an "epistemological break" occurs in the development of Marx's thought in 1845, which separates the "ideological problematic" of Marx's early work, such as the *Economic and Philosophic Manuscripts of 1844*, from the "scientific problematic" of Marx's mature works, most notably *Capital*, which was published in 1867. In what follows, we shall come to discern how, as part of this epistemological break, Marx distanced himself from sensory concerns and considerations.

Marx's early work shows considerable insight into the social and historical construction of the senses. In *The German Ideology*, for example, Marx writes that "the sensuous world . . . is, not a thing given direct from all eternity, remaining ever the same, but the product of industry and of the state of society . . . in the sense that it is a historical product" (Marx and Engels 1947: 35). Marx arrives at this insight by way of critiquing Feuerbach for identifying reality with sensation and ignoring the social factors involved in the creation of any particular sensory world. Thus, when Feuerbach tells us that we may find certainty by looking at a cherry tree, Marx retorts:

> The cherry-tree, like almost all fruit-trees was, as is well known, transplanted by commerce into our zone, and therefore only *by* this action of a definite society in a definite age [it has become "sensuous certainty" for Feuerbach]. (Marx and Engels 1947: 35)

This attack on Feuerbach was probably inspired by Marx's reading of Fourier, who was highly sensitive to the effects of commerce on the "sensescape."

By integrating Feuerbach's philosophical notion of the senses as ways of knowing with Fourier's political economy of the senses, Marx's early work seemed to promise that the senses would occupy the same prominence in Marxist theory as they had in the work of

Fourier and Feuerbach. In Marx's later work, however, the senses seem to wither away and to retain only a phantasmal presence. What alienated Marx from his senses?

One answer is that Marx did not feel comfortable with the intense sensuality of Fourier's and Feuerbach's philosophies. As has often been pointed out, Marx was a bourgeois moralist (for all his attacks on bourgeois society) and had elevated notions of human fulfillment (see Wheen 1999: 74), whence his inability to stomach either the apparent sensory libertinism of Fourier, with its utopian amatory revels, or the apparent sensory reductionism of Feuerbach, with its championing of food as the essence of life. Marx himself was "properly vague and philosophical when he depicted man's relationship to the sensate world of objects, human and natural" (Manuel 1995: 167).

Similarly to most nineteenth-century thinkers (including the anthropologists discussed in chap. 1 of this book), Marx ranked taste, touch, and smell as "primitive" senses in comparison to the more "civilized" senses of sight and hearing. His work, indeed, suggests that the hoped-for revolution (i.e., the coming-to-be of socialist society) would involve an elevation from the "lower" senses—the physical realm of the worker who "only feels himself freely active in his animal functions—eating, drinking, procreating" (Marx 1987: 74)—to the "higher" senses of sight and hearing—"a musical ear, an eye for beauty of form" (108)—and then beyond, to "criticiz[ing]" (Marx and Engels 1947: 22) and the abstract world of thought.

While dreaming of a social revolution, Marx was evidently not ready for a sensory revolution. Not so Fourier, who turned the conventional Western hierarchy of the senses on its head by rating taste and touch as the highest senses. For Fourier the interest of the working classes in "eating, drinking, procreating" was not so much evidence of their degradation as it was of the physical and social primacy of taste and touch. Fourier's utopia, Harmony, is consequently rich in satisfactions for these two favored senses. These satisfactions, however, are not all of an immediate physical nature. Fourier held that taste and touch could provide the basis for valuable intellectual stimulation and development. Thus in Harmony, for example, the "gastrosopher," or gustatory savant, replaces the

European philosopher, to, in Fourier's opinion, the benefit of all (Classen 1998: 24–30).

While more staid than Fourier in his sensory imaginary, Feuerbach also had a high regard for the "lower" senses, and particularly for taste. His best-known phrase, in fact, is "Man is what he eats," and he meant this not only in a physiological sense but in a social sense: "Human fare is the foundation of human culture and disposition" (cited in Hook 1958: 270). In *Principles of the Philosophy of the Future,* Feuerbach further held that "even the lowest senses, smell and taste, [can] elevate themselves in man to intellectual and scientific acts" (1966: 69). Indeed, Feuerbach, in words reminiscent of Fourier, calls philosophers fools "who fail to see that your teeth have long ago cracked the nut upon which you are still breaking your heads" (cited in Hook 1958: 269). For Feuerbach, "food is the beginning of wisdom." However, from a conventional standpoint, and one that Marx apparently held too, Feuerbach's, like Fourier's, enthusiasm for the "lower" senses constituted "'degenerate' sensationalism" and the least enlightening aspect of his philosophy (Hook 1958: 267–71).[10]

Marx's marginalization of the senses in his theory of capitalist exchange might well have been reinforced by his own personal circumstances. For example, Marx continually strove to rise above the often pressing need to feed, clothe, and house himself and his family and concentrate on the intellectual pursuits he valued so highly (Stallybrass 1998). Even more distressing, in later life Marx constantly suffered from malodorous, disfiguring boils or carbuncles that erupted all over his body causing him great mental and physical anguish.

> He was confronted three or four times a day with the dreadful evidence of physical corruption. The appalling odors, the red sores, the swelling and the pus were all revealed when the bandages were removed, and there seemed to be no way of keeping them under control. (Payne 1968: 347)

Marx's letters repeatedly convey his disgust at being at the mercy of a diseased, repulsive body that prevents him from pursuing his researches and writings (see Padover 1979: 174–76, 206, 414; Payne

1968: 342–50).[11] One of the treatments prescribed for his boils, indeed, was to abstain from intellectual labor (Manuel 1995: 81).

Significantly, Marx's epidermal ailments occur in the "scientific" phase of his work in which the body and the senses are largely left behind as subjects for theoretical elaboration. "He wrote the last few pages of Volume One [of *Capital*] standing at his desk when an eruption of boils around the rump made sitting too painful" (Wheen 1999: 294). It would not be surprising, under these circumstances, for Marx to harbor a distaste, and even an enmity, for his body, and for corporeality in general.

Ultimately, however, the primary reason for Marx's refusal to engage with the senses in his later work had to do with his growing desire to appear scientific (and therefore suitably "disembodied"). Sensory qualities tended to be dismissed by the science of his day—in which Marx was widely read—as unimportant and subjective compared to such quantifiable characteristics as measure and weight. The result was a world that Alfred North Whitehead has described as "a dull affair, soundless, scentless, colourless; merely the hurrying of material" (cited in Classen 1998: 5). The notion governing this scientific transcendence of sensoriality was that underlying principles must needs be abstracted from sensory appearances. When Marx begins to think of his economic theories as constituting a science (in *Capital* he presents himself as the founder of a new science) he takes on some of the incorporeal language and attitudes of the scientist. Indeed, Marx's sociology has been described as "possessed by analogies to the physical sciences" (Manuel 1995: 113; see, e.g., Marx 1954: 19, 45, 79).

One lacuna that results from Marx's transcendence of sensuality is that, unlike Fourier, he is never able or willing to present a concrete vision of the utopia that will result from his economic reforms. (As noted previously, in *The German Ideology* he briefly posits "a pastoral realm of freedom in which socialist man may be able to hunt, fish, and criticize as he pleases" [Kemple 1995: 22; Marx and Engels 1947: 22], but this sketch is nowhere developed further.) Another is that, as we have seen, Marx passes over the fact that the sensuous properties of commodities are the medium through which cultural codes are expressed. This omission is all the more glaring in light of Marx's insistence on the importance of *practice* as a means of changing social reality and of his earlier criticism of Feuerbach as concerned with "sensory thinking" to the neglect of "sensibility as a practical . . . activity" and sensory objects as socially mediated (see Hook 1958: 293–95). In fact, Marx's dismissive characterization of the use-value of commodities as "transparent" means that one can pass right through all of the sensory signs that may be encoded in them.[12] The mystery, for Marx, does not reside in the ways an object is used or experienced—"so far as it is a value in use there is nothing mysterious about it" (1954: 76)—only in what happens when it is exchanged. And at that point, according to Marx, the commodity strips off its sensuous form to become only an atomless ghost (Keenan 1993: 173–74): "As use-values, commodities are, above all, of different qualities, but as exchange-values they are merely different quantities, and consequently do not contain an atom of use-value" (Marx 1954: 45). Marx is never quite able to present commodities as completely disembodied, however. Even in their ghostly form Marx describes them as offering phantasmal seductions—they cast "wooing glances" (at money)—and spectral warnings—they admonish consumers not to mistake them as use-values (1954: 112, 87).

Significantly, the one sensory field that Marx assiduously mines for examples and metaphors in his scientific (or quantity over quality) phase is that of sight. Marx's visual references are due in part to the close association of sight with reason and science. While he uses visual metaphors to refer to intellectual clarity, however, the characteristic of sight that most attracts Marx is its capacity to distort and deceive, to turn things upside down and create mirror images. This illusory quality of sight enables him to make analogies to social and economic processes that he believes also deceive our understanding through false appearances. Thus, for example, in *The German Ideology* he writes:

> If in all ideology men and their circumstances appear upside-down as in a *camera obscura*, this phenomenon arises just as much from their historical life-process as the inversion of objects on the retina does from their physical life-process. (Marx and Engels 1947: 14)

In *Capital* references to visual delusions are multiplied, and we enter a world of "false semblances" and "mirrors," with only Marx to guide us to the truth that shines behind the mask of appearances (Wheen 1999: 305–6). "Scientific truth is always paradox," Marx states, "if judged by every-day experience, which catches only the delusive appearance of things" (1973: 42).

In his later work, therefore, Marx rejects the sensory certainty of Feuerbach and replaces it with scientific certainty. Whereas Feuerbach tells us we may find certainty by looking at a cherry tree (and, later in his philosophical development, by eating the cherries), Marx tells us that sensory experience is illusory, but that the scientific laws that underlie it, the laws of dialectical materialism, are not. In *Capital*, therefore, the senses become ghosts that remind us of the spectral world of appearances but do not obstruct our penetration of the underlying economic realities, according to Marx.

Finally, the rapidity with which Marx strips commodities of their sensuous form in order to discuss them as pure exchange-values may reflect a personal desire to shed his own "false" carbuncled skin in order to reveal the powerful force of his intellect. However, even Marx's skin takes on a spectral role in relation to his work. He describes his physical ailments as having influenced his writing, and Engels points to certain passages in *Capital* where Marx's "carbuncles have left their mark" (Marx and Engels 1987, XLII: 382). Thus, ghostly traces of Marx's own problematic physical form are left on his "scientific" exposition of the forces of the market (contrary to Derrida 1994). "At all events," Marx commented to Engels, "I hope the bourgeoisie will remember my carbuncles until their dying day" (1987, XLII: 383).

Notes

1. Notable works in history include Corbin (1986, 1995, 1998), Camporesi (1988, 1994), Leppert (1993), Classen (1998, 2001), Parr (2001), and Harvey (2002); in philosophy, Ihde (1983), Ullmer (1985), MacKendrick (1999), Korsmeyer (1999), and Rée (1999); in geography, Tuan (1974, 1995), Porteous (1990), Pocock (1993), Rodaway (1994), and Zui (2000); in sociology, Bourdieu (1984), Weinstein and Weinstein (1984), Synnott (1993), Miller (1997), and Gronow (1997); in law, Hibbitts (1992), Bently and Flynn (1996), and Manderson (2000); in medicine, Sacks (1987), Bynum and Porter (1993), and Wilson (1999); and in literature, Vinge (1975), Eagleton (1990), Rindisbacher (1992), Van Sant (1993), McSweeney (1998), Syrotinski and Maclachlan (2001), and Danius (2002). In film (e.g., Marks 2000) and performance (e.g., Schechner 2001), and above all in the visual arts, there has been a phenomenal rise in the number of artists and critics interested in contesting or subverting the "aesthetic gaze" by incorporating other senses into the aesthetic experience: Molesworth (1993), Fisher (1997, 1999a, 1999b), Drobnick (1988, 2000, 2002), Hall (1999), and Di Benedetto (2001). This list, which is meant to be illustrative only, is confined to book-length monographs and the occasional seminal review article appearing in English.

On intersensory relations as viewed through the prism of psychology see Marks (1982), Rivlin and Gravelle (1984), Romanyshyn (1989), and Stein and Meredith (1993). It bears noting that there is also a developing literature on multisensoriality in marketing (e.g., Zaltman and Coulter 1995; Bradley and Nolan 1998; Pine and Gilmore 1998). The significance of this growing commercialization of the sensorium will be explored in chapter 8.

2. The sensual turn in scholarship may otherwise be related to the "linguistic turn" (as represented by the work of Richard Rorty [1979]) finally having spent itself—there being, literally, nothing more to say. Or it could be because, as Terry Eagleton suggests:

> The body [and, therefore, the senses] has been at once the focus for a vital deepening of radical politics [after Foucault 1973, 1979], and a desperate displacement of them. There is a glamorous kind of materialism about body talk, which compensates for certain more classical [i.e., Marxist] strains of materialism now in dire trouble. (1993: 7)

Or perhaps, to turn Eagleton on his head, the sensual turn is an effect of the sheer sensuousness of contemporary existence—that is, of the hyperaesthesia of late modern consumer capitalism where the glittering sense-appeal of commodities eclipses any analysis of them (or their consumers) in terms of their use- or even exchange-value. All of these explanations remain highly speculative, however. What is needed is concrete histories of the engagement with the senses and sensuousness in each of the disciplines of the human sciences, as I propose to do for anthropology here.

3. In *Look, Listen, Read*, Lévi-Strauss's project—viz., to "formulate a logic of sense impressions in which considerations of relation and opposition [are] in the foreground" (1997: 131)—comes full circle. The detour represented by his lengthy exploration of the sensory codes of Amerindian myths in *Mythologiques* closes by rejoining the debate over the unity of the arts in eighteenth- and nineteenth-century French intellectual circles (which may just have been at the back of Lévi-Strauss's mind all along). There are many illuminating examples of Lévi-Strauss's penchant for rapid flight from sensuous experience to the "elevated" realm of structural analysis in this text, as when he writes of "colored hearing" (a particular form of synaesthesia) that it is "based on the homologies perceived between the differences . . . not the immediately perceived sensory correspondences" (1997: 95, 138).

4. Even the unity of the senses in synaesthesia turns out, on closer analysis, to be shot through with patterns of domination and subversion (see Marks 1982 and for a more social perspective Classen 1998). Where Lévi-Strauss would recognize only one relationship between the modalities, that of homology, the anthropology of the senses recognizes many. The same critique can be applied to Lévi-Strauss's mentor, Maurice Merleau-Ponty, whose doctrine of the synergy and intertranslatability of the senses in his *Phenomenology of Perception* similarly covers up the differential elaboration and potential disunity of the senses in cultural practice.

CHAPTER I

1. The suggestion that the Dani color vocabulary is a product of *physical* thinking, as opposed to visual thinking, is supported by A. R. Luria's research on the assignment of names to colors among Russian peasants. Luria records that nonliterate subjects tended to identify the color samples they were shown in terms of *objects* like "pig's dung" or "cotton in bloom" and *actions* like "rubbed." Literate subjects, by contrast, tended to identify the color samples with *categorical* names such as "brown" or "yellow." The two groups' responses were thus distributed along an "object-category continuum" (Luria 1976: 24–26). By analogy, the Dani would belong with the nonliterate peasants at the object end of this continuum.

2. This discussion of taste and smell lexicons is based on Kuipers (1991,

personal communication) in the case of the Weyéwa; Dupire (1987) in the case of the Sereer Ndut; and Richard Doty (1986) and Thomas Lamarre (personal communication) in the case of the Japanese language. For a further discussion of the intricacies of olfactory and gustatory classification, and the methodological problems involved in their study, see Classen, Howes, and Synnott (1994), Dubois (1997), Dubois and Rouby (1997) and Dubois, Ruby, and Sicard (1997).

3. It is instructive to consider Hall's approach to literature. There is a section on "literature as a key to perception" in *The Hidden Dimension*. Here, rather than "interpret" various pieces of literature, Hall analyzes them as "a source of data on man's use of his senses"; and rather than study the literary conventions governing a particular writer's style and use of imagery, Hall treats the latter as "highly patterned systems which release memories" (1969: 94–100). As we shall see presently, the tendency since the textual revolution has been just the opposite. For example, James Boon analyzes the culture of Bali as if it were reducible to a literary convention, that of romance, in *The Anthropological Romance of Bali*.

4. At the same time, some of the most influential and seemingly original contributions to contemporary social theory, such as Benedict Anderson's *Imagined Communities* or Jean Baudrillard's "society of the simulacrum" (1983), are little more than footnotes to McLuhan's philosophy. The reception of McLuhan's ideas was admittedly hampered by his elliptical style of writing and "mosaic" approach to cultural analysis. In retrospect, it is tempting to see these traits as expressions of a certain *postmodernisme avant la lettre*. However, they are better understood as expressions of McLuhan's distinctly Canadian constitution (see Howes 1992).

5. It should be noted that McLuhan and Carpenter collaborated in the work of the Centre for Culture and Technology at the University of Toronto throughout the 1950s and coedited the Centre's journal, *Explorations* (see Carpenter and McLuhan 1960). Their network of research associates included E. T. Hall (whose work is discussed in the main text), Dorothy Lee, Northrop Frye, and many other luminaries.

6. Other notable precursors and contributors to the anthropology of the senses from within French anthropology include (as I have discussed elsewhere) Maurice Leenhardt (1979) and his archaeology of sense perception among the Canaque of New Caledonia (Howes 1988), Pierre Bourdieu (1984) and his social critique of the judgment of taste (Howes and Lalonde 1991), Jacqueline Rabain (1979) and her in-depth study of the education of the senses among the Wolof of Senegal (Howes 1991: 183–85), and David Le Breton (1990; Méchin, Bianquis, and Le Breton 1998) and his analysis of the objectification of the body and senses in modernity (Howes 1995).

7. The primary/secondary textuality distinction is modeled after Walter Ong's account of the differences between "primary orality" (oral culture, speaking in person) and "secondary orality" (electronic culture, communication by telephone or television) in *Orality and Literacy*. To elaborate, in the

first or "primary" stage of the textual revolution, the idea was that other cultures could be treated "as texts." This interpretive position had to be defended against the competing definitions of culture put forward by Functionalism, Structuralism, Cultural Materialism, and so forth. In the second stage, the stage of secondary textuality, there is no more debate over the merits of different theoretical approaches, because the focus has shifted from theory to style (see van Maanen 1988: ix–x; Howes 1990b: 66). One of the more perplexing effects of this shift is that the assumption that an ethnography is the record of an ethnographer's experience in the field (mediated by a particular theoretical scheme and set of interests) no longer holds. As Stephen Tyler states in the chapter entitled "Post-modern Ethnography" in *Writing Culture:* "No experience preceded the ethnography. The experience was the ethnography" (1986: 138).

CHAPTER 2

1. Michael Jackson's work is conventionally viewed as belonging to the anthropological literature on "embodiment" (Csordas 1990, 1994). However, Jackson's emphasis on *habitus* in the "unity of body-mind-*habitus*" also represents a departure from the embodiment paradigm by signaling the importance of attending to the sensuous reaction of people to place, or what Christopher Fletcher (2002) calls "emplacement." Fletcher criticizes the embodiment paradigm for its "exclusion of the context of places where people live, and their intimate interactions with their immediate surroundings, such that the individual appears to exist indifferently to, and independently from, the place in which [she or he] dwells" (2002: 27–28). This critique is advanced within the framework of a fascinating study of the condition known as "environmental sensitivity" (ES) and how this disorder relates to the "cultural landscape" of Nova Scotia, Canada. Interestingly, Fletcher finds evidence of an "ecological subjectivity" among ES sufferers. For an analogous study that focuses on the soundscape in place of the smellscape of illness experience see Chuengsatiansup (1999).

2. There may even be a fourth level of meaning to bird sounds for the Kaluli, given that bird calls also signify and evoke a range of emotional states and are used in ritual to mobilize emotions in determinate ways, as the better part of Feld's *Sound and Sentiment* is dedicated to showing.

3. To put the last point a little more strongly, vision has long been the sense of choice for theorizing (as suggested by the very etymology of the word *theory*, which comes from the Greek *theorèin,* "to gaze upon") (Jonas 1970; Keller and Grontkowski 1983; Jay 1993). It is time for this privilege to end, so that other senses can come to the fore and also become "directly in their practice theoreticians," as Marx would say. To paraphrase another line of Marx's, theorists have only speculated about the world in different ways: the point is, however, to make sense of it. Thus, rather than "visualize the-

ory" (e.g., Taylor 1994; Grimshaw 2001), the task of anthropology should be to *sensualize* it. Otherwise, particularly given the meteoric rise of visual anthropology in recent years, "the film sense" may simply take over where the "text-organ" left off, if it hasn't already (see, e.g., Klima 2001).

4. While one of the defining characteristics of modernity is the cultural separation of the senses into self-contained fields, these distinctions are increasingly dissolved in late modern consumer capitalism where marketers present their products as appealing and satisfying across sensory domains (chap. 8).

5. Other subfields of anthropology that have been significantly enriched by the sensual turn include, in addition to those mentioned in the main text, archaeology (Houston and Taube 2000), material culture (Carp 1997; Kuechler 1987; Dant 1999), and the anthropology of place (Rodman 1992; Gell 1995; Feld 1996; Fletcher 2002), media (Marks 2000; Askew and Wilk 2002; Verrips 2002), disability (Classen 1998), tourism (Little 1991; Harrison 2002), and dance (Ness 1992; Bull 1997). The subfield that has remained the most impervious is psychological anthropology, perhaps because of its cognitivist orientation. For example, in a major review of models in the field, Bradd Shore devotes just two pages to "Nonlinguistic Models" under which he groups "olfactory," "sound image," and "visual image" models (1996: 59–60, 67). There is no evidence in Shore's work of any understanding of the importance of intersensory relationships. Nevertheless, even psychological anthropology may eventually be brought to its senses, thanks to the exemplary work of Douglas Hollan (2001) and Kathryn Linn Geurts (2003).

6. As noted previously, Merleau-Ponty's doctrine of the synergy and intertranslatability of the senses in his *Phenomenology of Perception* covers up the potential disunity of the senses in cultural practice. What is more, Merleau-Ponty became increasingly absorbed with the visual in his later works, such as *The Primacy of Perception* and *The Visible and the Invisible,* making it questionable how much he actually understood of the contribution of the "other" senses to perception in the first place. As for James Gibson's theory of the senses as "perceptual systems," this theory is marred by the same preoccupation with analyzing vision as in Merleau-Ponty and the same obliviousness to the senses in social context.

7. Ranke's example should be a warning to those who set so much theoretical store by the concept of mimesis (e.g., Taussig 1993; Stoller 1995).

8. Unfortunately, the clarion call of "exoticization" is sounded the moment there is any mention of sensory alterity, and the suggestion that one must approach cultures on their own sensory terms is dismissed as discouraging "dialogue" (see Klima 2001). This is anthropology as the denial of diversity. Another common failing is slipping back into the audiovisual groove, as when Tim Ingold acknowledges that taste and smell "raise a whole gamut of problems of their own" but then neglects to deal with them further (2000: 254). It does not appear to trouble Ingold that the "environ-

ment" he describes in *The Perception of the Environment* is basically one of just two senses, sight and hearing. Nor does he appear to be aware of the epistemological imperialism of his position. Ingold insists on the truth of Merleau-Ponty's musings on the senses over against any of the alternative constructions revealed by research in the anthropology of the senses. This move precludes any meaningful consideration of any real alternatives to Western epistemology, which is unfortunate given that there is so much to be learned from the example of the Desana, the Kaluli, the Ongee, etc.

9. In such chapters as "Pens and Needles" and "The Scented Womb and the Seminal Eye," Classen (1998) explores how at various times and with varying degrees of success women have either contested, transgressed, or strategically occupied the sensory stereotypes imposed on them by men. Taking her cue from Classen, Elysée Nouvet has shown how women belonging to Pentecostalist churches in northern Nicaragua transgress the sensory bounds of their social position through trancing (i.e., glossolalia) (Nouvet 2001; see also Newman 1999).

10. At "Uncommon Senses," an international conference on the senses in art and culture held at Concordia University in April 2000, there were numerous experiments of this kind, such as Richard Schechner's "Rasaboxes" theater workshop (Schechner 2001: 39–45). Of particular note was the performance series and art exhibition curated by Jennifer Fisher and Jim Drobnick (a.k.a. Displaycult). Insightful reviews of the ways in which the performances and installations engaged and extended the senses of conference participants include Asselin (2000), van Hoof (2000), and Carter and Ovenden (2001). My favorite intervention was the Sensorial Overload Clinic staged by Valérie Lamontagne.

CHAPTER 3

1. The areas excluded from direct involvement in the kula include Goodenough and the western half of Fergusson, as well as the mainland of Papua New Guinea and the isles of the Louisiade Archipelago (but see Lepowsky 1993: 209–10). While not formally included in this study, certain ethnographic data from these island societies have been integrated into the present analysis where they corroborated other evidence or helped bridge a gap in the record.

2. The diversity within Trobriand culture is almost as pronounced as the differences between it and other Massim cultures. For a transformational analysis of this diversity see *From Muyuw to the Trobriands* (Damon 1990).

3. The image of the kula as a switchboard or electronic circuit finds expression in other ways as well. For example, one very senior man from Koyagaugau who (in 1990) was commonly regarded as having the most complete knowledge there is of all the intersecting "paths" that make up the kula and the valuables that traverse them bore the nickname "the Computer."

4. The qualification "in most cases" is necessary because there are a few women on Dobu who currently engage in kula exchange with women on Fergusson and Duau, and there is no reason to think they did not do so traditionally. The "public profile" of women is generally higher in the western and southern Massim than in the northern and eastern parts of the region. For example, Róheim describes how women often orchestrate mortuary and marriage feasts on Duau (southern Massim), whereas Munn states that the distribution of food is entirely in the hands of men on Gawa (eastern Massim). The situation in the Trobriands (northern Massim) is the same as in the east, although in the Trobriands at least women have carved out a separate sphere of exchange for themselves. The objects of this female exchange system are grass skirts and banana-leaf bundles as opposed to yams and kula valuables (see Róheim 1932; Munn 1986: 53; Weiner 1976: 91; see also Lepowsky 1993: 209–14).

5. Darkness, solidity, and heaviness are not exclusively negative attributes. They figure as desirable attributes in the context of gardening and in the ritual to "anchor" the year's crop of yams in the village storehouses (Malinowski 1965 I: 220–23; Munn 1986: 80–82). However, the very fact that the garden magician describes himself as "anchoring" or "mooring" the yams first in the garden and later in the storehouse is indicative of where values tend to center—namely, in seafaring. Seafaring "encompasses" gardening both spatially and in the scale of values. On "encompassment" see Barraud (1979).

6. On smell as a medium of "subliminal suggestion" elsewhere in the Melanesian world see Stephen (1987) and Gell (1977).

7. Other evidence supporting the suggestion that olfaction (being in good odor) is valued over gustation (eating fully) includes the image of abundance in the Massim: the image of the surplus food at a feast, which ends up never being consumed and instead just rots away in a storehouse.

CHAPTER 4

1. On the food taboos of pregnant women see Malinowski (1929: 227–28), of mourners see Fortune (1963: 11–12), of sorcerers see Fortune (1963: 295) and Austen (1945: 30), and of carvers see Scoditti (1982: 82).

2. According to some speakers of Kilivila, from Omarakana in Kiriwina, whom I met at Budoya, the taste of salt water is classified as *yayana* (bitter). They used *bwena* (in place of *sumakenia*) for "sweet," *yayana* for "bitter, salty," and *pupuya* for "sour." I was also given *subisubi* in place of *yayana* as the word for "hot" (as in the taste of chillies or ginger). On the "bitterness" of salt water on Dobu see Fortune (1963: 266).

3. This resemblance between the smell of pig cooking and the smell of human cooking was remarked upon to me in the case of a discussion of a ritual suicide that was committed by a woman from Budoya who jumped into

the Dei'dei hot spring in 1976. What people remembered most about this tragic event was that her boiled flesh smelled "just like pig."

4. Interestingly, one of McLuhan's research associates, Dorothy Lee, argued on the basis of her analysis of the language of the Trobriands that the Trobrianders do not attach significance to lineal patterns, such as rings, only nonlineal ones (1959). As regards the kula, she writes that "every occasion in which a kula object participates becomes an ingredient of its being and swells its value; all of these occasions are enumerated with great satisfaction, but the lineal course of the traveling kula object is not important" (117).

5. The wave motif also agrees with (and was partly inspired by) Michael Young's analysis of the shape of social life on Goodenough Island (1983: 265–68).

6. People with speech defects are accordingly stereotyped as mentally deficient (Malinowski 1929: 289; see further Battaglia 1990: 57).

7. The dependency of verbal structures on physical structures has also been discussed by Harwood (1976) in "Cicero in the Trobriands." He suggests that the place-names that figure in Trobriand myths function as segmentors and series producers, as well as *topoi* in the Ciceronian sense, hence "mnemonic devices." The difficulty with Harwood's account is that it treats the landscape as a framework for organizing myth without recognizing how myth is itself constitutive of the landscape (see Tuan 1974, 1995).

8. The analysis presented here invites comparison with Battaglia's analysis of personhood, specifically the "channeled person" on Sabarl.

> Sabarl develop a sense of self, and recognize their own self-worth as generative persons, to the extent that they are able to construct and reconstruct new channels of social relationship. . . . Threats to this condition are construed primarily as physical blockages: if the ears, eyes, mouth, or brain are "obstructed" or "closed" (*kaus*), social exchange is critically impaired. . . . The channeled person—one who is physically, intellectually, and emotionally "open" to engaging in the flow of relations—is a living sign for Sabarl of an absence of blockages and reflects health in society itself. (1990: 57)

CHAPTER 5

1. Matrimonial alliance is not the only form of alliance Kwoma know. There is also "friendship" alliance. Kwoma men form such personal trading partnerships or "friendships" on the basis of totemic linkages with men in other Kwoma clans as well as men in neighboring non-Kwoma groups, most notably the Manambu (Bowden 1997: xvii, 117–18; 1991; Harrison 1993: 40–43). Among the Kwoma themselves, this relationship is symbolized by the gift of a "friendship netbag" (*ma kwow*). Friendship relationships with

individuals of non-Kwoma groups are the principal means by which the Kwoma acquire shells and shell valuables (i.e., currency items) for ceremonial decoration and exchange. Friends are also obliged to warn each other of impending raids, refrain from taking part themselves in a raid on a friend's village, and provide refuge in the event of an attack. These friendship relationships could be likened to kula partnerships, since they involve the same sort of mutual exchange and trust, except that they are in fact an expression of the totemic system, and the men involved in them refer to each other and their immediate relatives by the same kinship terms as they use for own clan members. In other words, the totemic system allows for there to be a duplication of agnation that transects the otherwise divisive principle of patrilineal filiation. In this regard, friendship relations are not really exchange relations at all such as one finds between affines (or between kula partners, for example): rather they are "fictive" agnatic relations. For a general theory of "friendship" (or as he calls them, "brotherhood") relations as complementary to affinal relations see Turner (1978a, 1978b).

2. As Williamson goes on to argue, gender is an acquired characteristic, according to Kwoma notions. Individuals are not classified by sex on the basis of their genitals, but rather on the basis of the substances associated with one or the other gender category, such as "hot" (male) and "cold" (female) blood. As these substances are alterable (for example, the temperature of the blood in a man's body can be changed by his eating hot food), so too is a person's gender alterable in theory. In practice, however, it seems that this theory applies more to men than to women, since the latter are deemed to be colder by nature. This instability of gender identity, and particularly the idea of its changeability as a function of the absorption of substances (odors, foods) that are normally associated with the opposite sex, is quite widespread in Papua New Guinea (see Meigs 1984; Gillison 1993).

3. The ambivalent regard in which the social division of the sexes and of knowledge is held by the Kwoma has parallels elsewhere in Papua New Guinea. Two especially profound and pertinent treatments of this problematic are those by Donald Tuzin (1980, 1997) and Maureen MacKenzie (1991).

4. Unless otherwise indicated, the discussion of the yam harvest ceremonies in this section is based on Bowden's reconstruction of these rituals in *Yena* and my own conversations with Kwoma individuals.

5. The association of sight with boundaries is illustrated in the way the Kwoma word for "to see" (*he*) is also the word for "surface" (Bowden 1997: 58). But perhaps the strongest testimony to this association is the ritual practice of "wiping the eyes" (*miyi bachi*) in order to sever a relationship with someone (134).

6. The perspectivalism of the Kwoma visual regime is also reflected linguistically in the numerous set phrases the Kwoma language contains for designating different points of view, such as "look after" (*hehar*), "look down" (*meyi he*), "look down into" (*mala he*), and so on (Bowden 1997: 289).

7. Lingual symbolism is highly complex in the Sepik: besides the extended tongue of the *yena* head there is the flicked tongue, which carries a different range of meanings (see Lewis 1990).

8. There is another possible interpretation for the smallness of the ears on the *yena* head. This has to do with the secretive nature of all of the most important aural communications in Kwoma society. Knowledge of spells, like knowledge of cult secrets, is only powerful to the extent it remains limited to the ken of a few. One does not need big ears to hear a secret; neither does one want other people to overhear. The tiny ears on the *yena* sculptures may therefore be said to reflect the importance attached to selective hearing by the Kwoma.

This would explain a fact that I otherwise found quite puzzling: the storage of many sculptures in plain view of noninitiates on the assumption that there was no danger in this exposure as long as the noninitiates did not know the names of any of the figures. The men with whom I discussed these figures would make a point of whispering their names to me, as if I were being drawn into some conspiracy, while the women demurely turned their heads away. Does this mean that knowing the name of a cult figure is somehow more important than simply viewing it? I would caution against this conclusion because, as we have seen, the power of the *yena* figures is supposed to reside in (or be activated by) their paint. When they are not freshly painted, their color looks drained, and so, accordingly, is their power.

CHAPTER 6

1. There is probably some connection between potting and rituals of initiation, which involve an analogous transformation of substance. On the association between blood and clay see Kaufmann (1972: 173–75, 191–93).

2. It is nevertheless possible to anticipate what such research on the sexing of the senses will turn up in the case of the Kwoma. Kwoma women would appear to have elaborated their sense of touch through weaving string bags and weaving and sewing shell pendants (which are a form of currency). Weaving is a "synthetic" or integrative act, and the products of this craft (the bags and pendants) may also be described as "synthetic"—in that they figure prominently in bridewealth transactions. Thus, women weave Kwoma society together, or attempt to do so anyway: the divisiveness of the men prevents them from succeeding. The looping patterns that the women use would, on this analysis, perform a similar function to the complex geometric designs in Caduveo facial painting (Lévi-Strauss 1992).

3. Adam Reed (1999) presents a fascinating analysis of "modes of vision" and their social consequences in Bomana prison, on the outskirts of Port Moresby. He reports that male inmates characterize Bomana as a "dark place" and observe that in Bomana their bodies grow fat and strong. It will

be appreciated how these sensuous facts would mean contrasting things depending on the speaker's background. An inmate who hails from the Middle Sepik would attach very different significance to fattening and visual concealment than one who comes from the Massim. Unfortunately, Reed does not address the question of how the sensory backgrounds of inmates from different regions of Papua New Guinea might have impacted their experience of Bomana. Nor does he explore the interplay of sound and silence in Bomana, although he is at least sensitive to this issue (see Reed 1999: 55, n. 2). Thus, interesting and important as Reed's contribution is to Western debates on the visual constitution of the individual and society, it fails to make as much sense as it could of personhood in the Melanesian context.

CHAPTER 7

1. Róheim also questioned the accuracy of Malinowski's Trobriand ethnography on certain points. For example, he argued that the role of the mother's brother was less central than Malinowski claimed (Róheim 1950: 167).

2. Malinowski refers to the eyes as "the primary motive" of sexual excitation (1929: 166) but then immediately slips into a discussion of his informant's statements concerning the alluring power of genital odors. The material discussed in chapter 3 likewise points to the role of smell in Trobriand erotica being more capacious than that of vision.

3. The question arises of whether the Western scientific debate over the existence of pheromones should be regarded as indicative of a generalized "denial of nasality" in Western culture. On this issue see Classen, Howes, and Synnott (1994); Le Guérer (1990); and Drobnick (2000).

4. The analysis presented here invites comparison with the idea of the child's "birth into language" in the work of Jacques Lacan (1966, 1977). According to Lacan, the child's "birth into language" involves, among other things, learning to use the pronouns "I" and "he" or "she" correctly. This occurs during what is called the "mirror phase" of psychosexual development. Lacan's use of mirror imagery betrays the Western roots of his psychology. In the Trobriands, the first experience of selfhood is achieved not through sight, but through smell. Lacan's theory of psychosexual development would thus probably need to be subjected to as extensive a rewrite as Freud's, in order for it to capture the dynamics of growing into one's senses and one's self the Trobriand way.

5. Ronald Provencher (1979) has shown that orality vastly outweighs sexuality as a focus of cultural elaboration and anxiety among Malays. Malay society then is one in which orality figures as the ultimate stage of the developmental process, as in the Trobriands, instead of the primary stage, as in

the West. It would be wrong to interpret this oral fixation as a sign of arrested development, Provencher argues, and I would agree. Psychoanalysis must recognize that just as there are different paths to maturity, depending on one's culture, so there may be different cultural definitions of maturity (see Howes 1991: 182–85).

6. In *Les pouvoirs de l'odeur*, the historian of ideas Annick Le Guérer (1998) has made a painstaking effort to excavate all the references to smell in Freud's collected works and, while the harvest may be small, make a narrative out of them. Le Guérer goes on to trace how the power of smell has been sidelined (*mis à l'écart*) in the work of Freud's disciples and followers. While Le Guérer and I arrived at our conclusions independently, they are remarkably complementary.

7. A further example of Freud's elision of nasality can be found in his 1927 "Fetishism" essay (Freud 1953 XXI), if we follow Jay Geller (1992). Freud introduces this essay by discussing the case of a young man with a fixation on shiny noses. Apparently, the youth could produce a shine on his nose (albeit not one perceptible to others) at will. Curiously, however, Freud never comes back to this case in the ensuing elaboration of his theory of the fetish object as a substitute for the woman's (the mother's) absent penis. He simply drops (or forgets) the case, whereas he could (and should) have used it to clinch his argument by pointing to the widespread idea of the nose as a substitute for or sign of the male penis. Equally puzzling, still following Geller, is the absence from Freud's essay of any discussion of odor as a motivating factor in fetish object choice, given that fetishisms related to smell are far more prevalent than nose fetishes per se, and that Freud was certainly familiar with the literature on olfactory fetishes.

Freud's theory of fetishism, then, is one in which "every trace of smell has been removed"; moreover, it is structured by a "shift in sensory registers from the olfactive to the visual" (Geller 1992: 432). Geller reads Freud's essay as (unconsciously) exemplifying the very substitutive process it is supposed to be theorizing, and he goes on to relate the elisions and shifts to "a transvaluation of a figure of Jewish denigration: the Jewish nose." According to Geller, Freud's obviation of the topic of olfactory fetishism, his failure to remark on the obvious connection between the nose and the male member, and the very connection that the essay seeks to establish (i.e., fetish object = absent [read: invisible] female member) were all motivated by Freud's yearning to transcend his Jewish identity—an identity that was fixed in terms of circumcision, the so-called *foeter Judaicus*, and the Jewish nose as a marker of racialized difference.

8. German literature after Freud confirms this point. In Patrick Süskind's novel *Perfume*, the protagonist, a murderer by the name of Grenouille, fits the stereotype of the overscented individual as "idiot" and "pervert" perfectly (see Classen, Howes, and Synnott 1994: 4; see further Rindisbacher 1992).

1. The diathetical is a mode of social analysis that juxtaposes social facts without attempting to resolve them into a noncontradictory, synthetic (or dialectical) totality (see Howes 1992).

2. *"Sense-perception* (see Feuerbach) must be the basis of all science," wrote Marx (1987: 111).

3. The particular relationship between the department store and the female consumer is explored by Rémy Saisselin (1984), among others, most notably Rachel Bowlby (1985).

4. Gregory has been criticized for essentializing and exaggerating the distinction between commodities (produced for sale) and gifts (produced for exchange) (see Carrier 1994).

5. "Could it be . . . that we are entranced by cargo cults because we are, at heart, commodity fetishists? That cargo cults are so titillating and seductive because we imagine the natives to be exercised by our own secret desires?" wonders Lamont Lindstrom (1993: 9) by way of introduction to his penetrating deconstruction of the very notion of "cargo cults." Also of relevance in this connection is the extensive literature on New Guinea big men as protocapitalists and the appearance of capitalism's triumph in New Britain, among other places (see Errington and Gewertz 1995: 133–55; Finch 1997; Gewertz and Errington 1999).

6. The sales techniques of the traveling vendors are documented in the 1996 film *Advertising Missionaries,* directed by Chris Hilton and Gauthier Flauder (Aspire Films).

7. Imported suitcases are now sometimes preferred to *bilums* because they are "ratproof, mothproof and lockable" (MacKenzie 1991: 151).

8. Thus, Mary Douglas observes that "goods in their assemblage [by a given consumer] present a set of meanings, more or less coherent, more or less intentional. They are read by those who know the code and scan them for information" (Douglas and Isherwood 1979: 5).

9. Many different approaches to the study of consumer action have emerged in recent years. Thus, consumption is conceptualized as appropriation (Miller 1987), diversion (de Certeau 1984), creolization (Howes 1996), symbolic recontextualization (Lee 1993), or transformation (Coote, Morton, and Nicholson 2000), and in any event not the passive reception of the meanings and intentions or uses invested in commodities by their producers or sellers (such as remains the prevailing view in the studies of "consumer behavior" that go on in business schools). In general terms:

These approaches attempt to explicate the non-economic features of consumption and avoid reductions to the point of sale and the identity of the individual consumer. They shift focus to the context in which the object is to be located and describe consumption in terms of the use of the thing in that context. Commodities do not have a pre-defined use-value, and even the sign value of an object is not determined by the discourse of advertising. Its use is variable and negotiable . . . and its precise form varies according to specific context. (Dant 1999: 36)

Marx's famous critique of Herr Grün's notion of "productive consumption" (see Marx and Engels 1947: 159–64) cannot be applied to the approaches discussed here because Marx's attack only goes to the economic features of consumption.

10. There is no intrinsic reason why Feuerbach's focus on gustation should be considered beneath philosophy, or "degenerate," as Sidney Hook (1958) pretends. Hindu philosophy, for example, is an extended meditation on processes of gustation (Pinard 1991; Schechner 2001), and "eating" provides the idiom in which many social and intellectual processes are experienced and expressed among the Hausa, Mawri, Songhay, and Tuareg, among others (Ritchie 1991; Masquelier 2001; Stoller 1997; Stoller and Olkes 1990; Rasmussen 1996).

11. The best Marx could say about his boils was that they were "really a form of proletarian sickness," thus identifying his own body with the brutalized, socially repellent body of the worker (Payne 1968: 348).

12. Marx considered the use-value of his own intellectual productions, his "laws," to be similarly clear—"these laws [work] with iron necessity toward inevitable results" (1954: 19)—and he adamantly opposed any reinterpretation of his theories.

References

Ackerman, Diane. 1990. *A Natural History of the Senses.* New York: Random House.

Akin, David, and Joel Robbins, eds. 1999. *Money and Modernity: State and Local Currencies in Melanesia.* Pittsburgh: University of Pittsburgh Press.

Althusser, Louis. 1969. *For Marx.* Trans. Ben Brewster. New York: Pantheon.

Anderson, Benedict. 1983. *Imagined Communities: Reflections on the Origin and Spread of Nationalism.* London: Verso.

Anonymous. 1953. Russian Sensory Images. In *The Study of Culture at a Distance,* ed. Margaret Mead and Rhoda Métraux, 162–69. Chicago: University of Chicago Press.

Anzieu, Didier. 1986. *Freud's Self-Analysis.* Trans. Peter Graham. Madison, CT: International Universities Press.

Appadurai, Arjun. 1996. *Modernity at Large: Cultural Dimensions of Globalization.* Minneapolis: University of Minnesota Press.

Askew, Kelly, and Richard Wilk, eds. 2002. *The Anthropology of Media: A Reader.* Oxford: Blackwell.

Asselin, Olivier. 2000. Une critique de la vision pure. *Spirale* 179 (July/August): 31–32.

Austen, Leo. 1934. Procreation among the Trobriand Islanders. *Oceania* 5:102–13.

———. 1945. Cultural Changes in Kiriwina. *Oceania* 16:15–60.

Barraud, Cécile. 1979. *Tanebar-Evav: une société de maisons tournée vers le large.* Cambridge: Cambridge University Press.

Barth, Fredrik. 1975. *Ritual Knowledge among the Baktaman of New Guinea.* New Haven: Yale University Press.

Battaglia, Debbora. 1983. Projecting Personhood in Melanesia: The Dialectics of Artefact Symbolism on Sabarl Island. *Man* (n.s.) 18:289–304.

———. 1990. *On the Bones of the Serpent: Person, Memory and Mortality in Sabarl Island Society.* Chicago: University of Chicago Press.

Baudelaire, Charles. 1962. *Curiosités esthétiques.* Paris: Garnier Frères.

———. 1975. *Selected Poems.* Trans. John Richardson. Harmondsworth: Penguin.

Baudrillard, Jean. 1983. *Simulations.* Trans. P. Foss, P. Patton, and P. Beitchman. New York: Semiotext(e).

Becker, Alton. 1979. Communicating Across Diversity. In *The Imagination of Reality,* ed. Alton Becker and Aram Yengoyan. Norwood, NJ: Ablex.

Bell, David, and Gill Valentine. 1997. *Consuming Geographies: We Are What We Eat.* London: Routledge.

Benjamin, Walter. 1969. *Illuminations.* Trans. Harry Zohn. New York: Schocken.

————. 1973. *Charles Baudelaire: A Lyric Poet in the Era of High Capitalism.* Trans. Harry Zohn. London: New Left Books.

Bently, Lionel, and Leo Flynn, eds. 1996. *Law and the Senses: Sensational Jurisprudence.* London: Pluto Press.

Berlin, Brent, and Paul Kay. 1969. *Basic Color Terms.* Berkeley: University of California Press.

Berman, Marshall. 1999. *Adventures in Marxism.* London: Verso.

Bettelheim, Bruno. 1956. *Symbolic Wounds.* London: Thames and Hidson.

Biersack, Aleta. 1987. Moonlight: Negative Images of Transcendence in Paiela Pollution. *Oceania* 57:178–93.

Bijlmer, H. J. T. 1923. *Anthropological Results of the Dutch Scientific Central New-Guinea Expedition.* Leiden: E. J. Brill.

Bleek, Wilhelm, and Lucy Lloyd. 1911. *Specimens of Bushmen Folklore.* London: George Allen.

Boon, James A. 1977. *The Anthropological Romance of Bali, 1597–1972.* New York: Cambridge University Press.

————. 1983. Functionalists Write Too: Frazer/Malinowski, and the Semiotics of the Monograph. *Semiotica* 46 (2/4): 131–50.

Boorstin, Daniel. 1962. *The Image.* New York: Atheneum.

Bourdieu, Pierre. 1977. *Outline of a Theory of Practice.* Trans. Richard Nice. Cambridge: Cambridge University Press.

————. 1984. *Distinction: A Social Critique of the Judgement of Taste.* Trans. Richard Nice. Cambridge: Harvard University Press.

Bowden, Ross. 1983. *Yena: Art and Ceremony in a Sepik Society.* Oxford: Pitt Rivers Museum.

————. 1984. Art and Gender Ideology in the Sepik. *Man* (n.s.) 19:445–58.

————. 1987. Sorcery, Illness and Social Control in Kwoma Society. In *Sorcerer and Witch in Melanesia,* ed. Michele Stephen, 183–208. New Brunswick, NJ: Rutgers University Press.

————. 1990. The Architecture and Art of Kwoma Ceremonial Houses. In *Sepik Heritage: Tradition and Change in Papua New Guinea,* ed. Nancy Lutke-haus, Christian Kaufmann, William Mitchell, Douglas Newton, Lita Osmundsen, and Meinhard Schuster, 480–90. Durham, NC: Carolina Academic Press.

————. 1991. Historical Ethnography or Conjectural History? *Oceania* 61:218–38.

————. 1997. *A Dictionary of Kwoma: A Papuan Language of North-East New Guinea.* Canberra: Pacific Linguistics.

Bowlby, Rachel. 1985. *Just Looking: Consumer Culture in Dreiser, Gissing and Zola.* New York: Methuen.

Bradley, Stephen, and Richard Nolan, eds. 1998. *Sense and Respond: Capturing Value in the Network Era*. Boston: Harvard Business School Press.

Brady, Erika. 1999. *A Spiral Way: How the Phonograph Changed Ethnography*. Jackson: University Press of Mississippi.

Brindley, Marianne. 1984. *The Symbolic Role of Women in Trobriand Gardening*. Pretoria: University of South Africa.

Brome, Vincent. 1984. *Freud and His Disciples: The Struggle for Supremacy*. London: Caliban Productions.

Bromilow, William E. 1929. *Twenty Years among Primitive Papuans*. London: Epworth.

Brown, Donald. 1991. *Human Universals*. New York: McGraw-Hill.

Buckley, Thomas, and Alma Gottlieb, eds. 1988. *Blood Magic: The Anthropology of Menstruation*. Berkeley: University of California Press.

Bull, Cynthia Jean Cohen. 1997. Sense, Meaning and Perception in Three Dance Cultures. In *Meaning in Motion: New Cultural Studies of Dance*, ed. Jane Desmond, 269–87. Durham, NC: Duke University Press.

Burridge, Kenelm. 1960. *Mambu: A Study of Melanesian Cargo Movements and Their Social and Ideological Background*. New York: Harper Torchbooks.

———. 1969. *New Heaven, New Earth: A Study of Millenarian Activities*. Oxford: Basil Blackwell.

Bynum, W. F., and Roy Porter, eds. 1993. *Medicine and the Five Senses*. Cambridge: Cambridge University Press.

Campbell, Shirley. 1983. Attaining Rank: A Classification of Kula Shell Valuables. In *The Kula: New Perspectives on Massim Exchange*, ed. Jerry Leach and Edmund Leach, 229–48. Cambridge: Cambridge University Press.

Camporesi, Piero. 1988. *The Incorruptible Flesh: Bodily Mutation and Mortification in Religion and Folklore*. Trans. Tania Croft-Murray. Cambridge: Cambridge University Press.

———. 1994. *The Anatomy of the Senses: Natural Symbols in Early Modern Italy*. Trans. Allan Cameron. Cambridge: Polity Press.

Carp, Richard M. 1997. Perception and Material Culture: Historical and Cross-Cultural Perspectives. *Historical Reflections/Réflexions historiques* 23 (3): 269–300.

Carpenter, Edmund. 1972. *Oh, What a Blow That Phantom Gave Me!* Toronto: Bantam.

———. 1973. *Eskimo Realities*. New York: Holt, Rinehart and Winston.

Carpenter, Edmund, and Marshall McLuhan, eds. 1960. *Explorations in Communication*. Boston: Beacon Press.

Carrier, James. 1994. *Gifts and Commodities: Exchange and Western Capitalism since 1700*. London and New York: Routledge.

Carter, Jennifer, and Colleen Ovenden. 2001. Finding Sense in New Places: Vital Signs in Contemporary Art Practice. *Material Culture* (spring/summer): 69–75.

Chamberlain, Alexander. 1905. Primitive Hearing and Hearing-Words. *American Journal of Psychology* 16:119–30.

References

Chowning, Ann. 1960. Canoe Making among the Molima of Fergusson Island. *Expedition* 3 (1): 32–39.

Chuengsatiansup, Komatra. 1999. Sense, Symbol and Soma: Illness Experience in the Soundscape of Everyday Life. *Culture, Medicine and Psychiatry* 23:273–301.

Classen, Constance. 1990. Sweet Colors, Fragrant Songs: Sensory Models of the Andes and the Amazon. *American Ethnologist* 17 (4): 722–35.

———. 1991. Literacy as Anti-Culture: The Andean Experience of the Written Word. *History of Religions* 30 (4): 404–21.

———. 1993a. *Inca Cosmology and the Human Body.* Salt Lake City: University of Utah Press.

———. 1993b. *Worlds of Sense: Exploring the Senses in History and across Cultures.* London and New York: Routledge.

———. 1997. Foundations for an Anthropology of the Senses. *International Social Science Journal* 153:401–12.

———. 1998. *The Color of Angels: Cosmology, Gender and the Aesthetic Imagination.* London and New York: Routledge.

———. 2001. The Senses. In *Encyclopedia of European Social History from 1350 to 2000,* ed. Peter Stearns, vol. 4, 355–64. New York: Charles Scribner's Sons.

Classen, Constance, and David Howes. 1996a. Making Sense of Culture: Anthropology as a Sensual Experience. *Etnofoor* 9 (2): 86–96.

———. 1996b. The Dynamics and Ethics of Cross-Cultural Consumption. In *Cross-Cultural Consumption,* ed. David Howes, 178–94. London and New York: Routledge.

———. 1998. Vital Signs: The Dynamics of Traditional Medicine in Northwestern Argentina. In *The Third Wave of Modernization in Latin America,* ed. Lynne Phillips, 141–54. Wilmington, DE: Jaguar Books.

Classen, Constance, David Howes, and Anthony Synnott. 1994. *Aroma: The Cultural History of Smell.* London and New York: Routledge.

Clifford, James. 1986. Introduction: Partial Truths. In *Writing Culture: The Poetics and Politics of Ethnography,* ed. James Clifford and George Marcus, 1–26. Berkeley: University of California Press.

———. 1988. *The Predicament of Culture.* Cambridge: Harvard University Press.

Clifford, James, and George Marcus, eds. 1986. *Writing Culture: The Poetics and Politics of Ethnography.* Berkeley: University of California Press.

Coote, Jeremy, Chris Morton, and Julia Nicholson. 2000. *Transformations: The Art of Recycling.* Oxford: Pitt Rivers Museum.

Corbin, Alain. 1986. *The Foul and the Fragrant: Odor and the French Social Imagination.* Trans. Miriam Kochan, Roy Porter, and Christopher Prendergast. Cambridge: Harvard University Press.

———. 1995. *Time, Desire and Horror: Towards a History of the Senses.* Trans. Jean Birrell. Cambridge: Polity Press.

————. 1998. *Village Bells: Sound and Meaning in the Nineteenth-Century French Countryside.* Trans. Martin Thom. New York: Columbia University Press.

Csordas, Thomas. 1990. Embodiment as a Paradigm for Anthropology. *Ethos* 18:5–47.

————. 1994. Introduction: The Body as Representation and Being-in-the-World. In *Embodiment and Experience: The Existential Ground of Culture and Self,* ed. Thomas Csordas, 1–24. Cambridge: Cambridge University Press.

Cummings, Neil, and Marysia Lewandoska. 2000. *The Value of Things.* Basel: Birkhauser.

Damon, Frederick H. 1990. *From Muyuw to the Trobriands: Transformations along the Northern Side of the Kula Ring.* Tucson: University of Arizona Press.

Danius, Sarah. 2002. *The Senses of Modernism: Technology, Perception, and Aesthetics.* Ithaca: Cornell University Press.

Dant, Tim. 1999. *Material Culture in the Social World.* Buckingham: Open University Press.

de Certeau, Michel. 1984. *The Practice of Everyday Life.* Trans. Steven Rendall. Berkeley: University of California Press.

De Kerckhove, Derrick. 1995. *The Skin of Culture: Investigating the New Electronic Reality.* Toronto: Somerville House.

Debord, Guy. 1977. *The Society of the Spectacle.* Detroit: Red and Black.

Derrida, Jacques. 1994. *Specters of Marx: The State of the Debt, the Work of Mourning, and the New International.* New York and London: Routledge.

Descombes, Vincent. 1986. *Objects of All Sorts: A Philosophical Grammar.* Baltimore: Johns Hopkins University Press.

Desjarlais, Robert R. 1992. *Body and Emotion: The Aesthetics of Illness and Healing in the Nepal Himalayas.* Philadelphia: University of Pennsylvania Press.

————. 1997. *Shelter Blues: Sanity and Selfhood among the Homeless.* Philadelphia: University of Pennsylvania Press.

Di Benedetto, Stephen. 2001. Stumbling in the Dark: Facets of Sensory Perception and Robert Wilson's H.G. Installation. *New Theatre Quarterly* 67 (3): 273–84.

Dorfman, Ariel. 1983. *The Empire's Old Clothes: What the Lone Ranger, Babar, and Other Innocent Heroes Do to Our Minds.* New York: Pantheon Books.

Doty, Richard. 1986. Cross-Cultural Studies of Taste and Smell Perception. In *Chemical Signs in Vertebrates,* ed. David Duvall et al. New York: Plenum.

Douglas, Mary. 1966. *Purity and Danger: An Analysis of Concepts of Pollution and Taboo.* London: Routledge and Kegan Paul.

————. 1982. *Natural Symbols: Explorations in Cosmology.* 2d ed. New York: Pantheon.

Douglas, Mary, and Baron Isherwood. 1979. *The World of Goods: Towards an Anthropology of Consumption.* New York: W. W. Norton.

Drobnick, Jim. 1998. Reveries, Assaults and Evaporating Presences: Olfactory Dimensions in Contemporary Art. *Parachute* 89:10–19.

————. 2000. Inhaling Passions: Art, Sex and Scent. *Sexuality and Culture* 4 (3): 37–56.

————. 2002. Volatile Architectures. In *Crime and Ornament,* ed. Bernie Miller. Toronto: YYZ Books.

Dubois, Danielle. 1997. Cultural Beliefs as Non-trivial Constraints on Categorization: Evidence from Colors and Odors. *Behavioral and Brain Sciences* 20:188.

Dubois, Danielle, and Catherine Rouby. 1997. Une approche de l'olfaction: du linguistique au neuronal. *Intellectica* 24:9–20.

Dubois, Danielle, Catherine Rouby, and Georges Sicard. 1997. Catégories sémantiques et sensorialités: de l'espace visuel à l'espace olfactif. *Enfance* 1:141–50.

Dundes, Alan. 1980. *Interpreting Folklore.* Bloomington: Indiana University Press.

Dupire, Marguerite. 1987. Des goûts et des odeurs. *L'Homme* 27 (4): 5–25.

Eagleton, Terry. 1990. *The Ideology of the Aesthetic.* Oxford: Basil Blackwell.

————. 1993. It Is Not Quite True That I Have a Body, and Not Quite True That I Am One Either. *London Review of Books* 15 (10): 7–8.

Errington, Frederick, and Deborah Gewertz. 1995. *Articulating Change in the "Last Unknown."* Boulder: Westview.

Eves, Richard. 1998. *The Magical Body: Power, Fame and Meaning in a Melanesian Society.* Amsterdam: Harwood Academic.

Ewen, Stuart. 1988. *All Consuming Images: The Politics of Style in Contemporary Culture.* New York: Basic Books.

Fabian, Johannes. 1983. *Time and the Other: How Anthropology Makes Its Object.* New York: Columbia University Press.

Farquhar, Judith. 2002. *Appetites: Food and Sex in Post-Socialist China.* Durham, NC: Duke University Press.

Featherstone, Michael, ed. 1990. *Global Culture.* London: Sage.

Feld, Steven. 1982. *Sound and Sentiment: Birds, Weeping, Poetics and Song in Kaluli Expression.* Philadelphia: University of Pennsylvania Press.

————. 1984. Sound Structure as Social Structure. *Ethnomusicology* 28 (3): 383–409.

————. 1986. Orality and Consciousness. In *The Oral and the Literate in Music,* ed. Y. Tokumaru and O. Yamaguti, 18–28. Tokyo: Academia Music.

————. 1988. Aesthetics as Iconicity of Style, or, "Lift-Up-Over Sounding," Getting into the Kaluli Groove. *Yearbook for Traditional Music* 20:74–113.

————. 1991. Sound as a Symbolic System. In *The Varieties of Sensory Experience,* ed. David Howes, 79–99. Toronto: University of Toronto Press.

————. 1996. Waterfalls of Song: An Acoustemology of Place Resounding in Bosavi, Papua New Guinea. In *Senses of Place,* ed. Steven Feld and Keith Basso, 91–135. Santa Fe: School of American Research Press.

Feldman, Allen. 1994. From Desert Storm to Rodney King via ex-Yugoslavia: On Cultural Anaesthesia. In *The Senses Still,* ed. Nadia Seremetakis, 87–107. Boulder: Westview.

Feuerbach, Ludwig. 1966. *Principles of the Philosophy of the Future.* Trans. Manfred Vogel. Indianapolis: Bobbs-Merrill.

Finch, John. 1997. From Proletarian to Entrepreneur to Big Man: The Story of Noya. *Oceania* 68:123–33.

Finnegan, Ruth. 1988. *Literacy and Orality: Studies in the Technology of Communication.* Oxford: Basil Blackwell.

Fisher, Jennifer. 1997. Relational Sense: Towards a Haptic Aesthetics. *Parachute* 87 (summer): 4–11.

———. 1999a. Speeches of Display: The Museum Audioguides of Sophie Calle, Andrea Fraser, and Janet Cardiff. *Parachute* 94 (spring): 24–31.

———. 1999b. Performing Taste. In *Food Culture: Tasting Identities and Geographies in Art,* ed. Barbara Fischer, 29–47. Toronto: YYZ Books.

Fletcher, Christopher M. 2002. *Equivocal Illness and Cultural Landscape in Nova Scotia, Canada.* Ph.D. diss., Université de Montréal.

Fliess, Wilhelm. 1979. *Les relations entre le nez et les organes génitaux de la femme, présentées selon leurs significations biologiques.* Trans. Anne Berman. Paris: Presses Universitaires de France.

Forge, Anthony. 1970. Learning to See in New Guinea. In *Socialization: The Approach from Social Anthropology,* ed. Philip Mayer, 269–91. London: Tavistock.

———. 1971. Art and Environment in the Sepik. In *Art and Aesthetics in Primitive Societies,* ed. Carol Jopling, 290–314. New York: E. P. Dutton.

———. 1979. The Problem of Meaning in Art. In *Exploring the Visual Art of Oceania,* ed. Sidney Mead. Honolulu: University Press of Hawaii.

Fortune, Reo. 1963. *Sorcerers of Dobu.* New York: E. P. Dutton.

Foster, Robert J. 1992. "Take Care of Public Telephones": Moral Education and Nation-State Formation in Papua New Guinea. *Public Culture* 4 (2): 31–45.

———. 1995. Print Advertisements and Nation Making in Metropolitan Papua New Guinea. In *Nation Making: Emergent Identities in Postcolonial Melanesia,* ed. Robert J. Foster, 151–81. Ann Arbor: University of Michigan Press.

———. 1996/97. Commercial Mass Media in Papua New Guinea: Notes on Agency, Bodies, and Commodity Consumption. *Visual Anthropology Review* 12 (2): 1–17.

———. 1998. Your Money, Our Money, the Government's Money: Finance and Fetishism in Melanesia. In *Border Fetishisms: Material Objects in Unstable Spaces,* ed. Patricia Spyer, 60–90. New York: Routledge.

Foucault, Michel. 1973. *The Birth of the Clinic.* Trans. A. M. Sheridan Smith. New York: Random House.

———. 1979. *Discipline and Punish: Birth of the Prison.* Trans. A. M. Sheridan Smith. New York: Vintage Books.

Fourier, Charles. [1851] 1968. *The Passions of the Human Soul and Their Influence on Society and Civilization.* Trans. John Morell. New York: A. M. Kelley.

Freud, Sigmund. 1953. *The Complete Psychological Works.* Trans. James Strachey. London: Hogarth Press.

—. 1961. *Civilization and Its Discontents.* Trans. James Strachey. New York: W. W. Norton.

Galbraith, John Kenneth. 1958. *The Affluent Society.* Boston: Houghton Mifflin.

—. 1967. *The New Industrial State.* Boston: Houghton Mifflin.

Gardi, Rene. 1960. *Tambaran: An Encounter with Cultures in Decline in New Guinea.* London: Constable.

Geary, James. 2002. *The Body Electric: An Anatomy of the New Bionic Senses.* London: Weidenfeld and Nicholson.

Geertz, Clifford. 1973. *The Interpretation of Cultures.* New York: Basic Books.

—. 1983. *Local Knowledge.* New York: Basic Books.

—. 1988. *Works and Lives: The Anthropologist as Author.* Stanford: Stanford University Press.

Gell, Alfred. 1977. Magic, Perfume, Dream. . . . In *Symbols and Sentiments: Cross-Cultural Studies in Symbolism,* ed. I. M. Lewis, 25–38. London: Academic.

—. 1979. Reflections on a Cut Finger: Taboo in the Umeda Conception of the Self. In *Fantasy and Symbol,* ed. Sidney Hook, 133–48. London: Academic.

—. 1995. The Language of the Forest: Landscape and Phonological Iconism in Umeda. In *The Anthropology of Landscape,* ed. Ed Hirsch and Michael O'Hanlon, 232–54. Oxford: Clarendon.

Geller, Jay. 1992. "A Glance at the Nose": Freud's Inscription of Jewish Difference. *Imago* 49 (4): 427–44.

Geurts, Kathryn Linn. 2003. *Culture and the Senses: Bodily Ways of Knowing in an African Community.* Berkeley: University of California Press.

Gewertz, Deborah, and Frederick Errington. 1991. *Twisted Histories, Altered Contexts: Representing the Chambri in a World System.* Cambridge: Cambridge University Press.

—. 1999. *Emerging Class in Papua New Guinea: The Telling of Difference.* Cambridge: Cambridge University Press.

Gibson, James J. 1966. *The Senses Considered as Perceptual Systems.* Boston: Houghton Mifflin.

—. 1979. *The Ecological Approach to Visual Perception.* Boston: Houghton Mifflin.

Gillison, Gillian. 1993. *Between Culture and Fantasy: A New Guinea Highlands Mythology.* Chicago: University of Chicago Press.

Gilman, Sander. 1993. *The Case of Sigmund Freud: Medicine and Identity at the Fin de Siècle.* Baltimore: Johns Hopkins University Press.

Glass, Patrick. 1986. The Trobriand Code: An Interpretation of Trobriand War Shield Designs. *Anthropos* 81:47–63.

—. 1988. Trobriand Symbolic Geography. *Man* (n.s.) 23:56–76.

Gonzalez-Crussi, Frank. 1989. *The Five Senses.* New York: Harcourt Brace Jovanovich.

Goody, Jack. 1977. *The Domestication of the Savage Mind.* Cambridge: Cambridge University Press.

————. 1986. *The Logic of Writing and the Organization of Society.* Cambridge: Cambridge University Press.

Gosden, Chris, and Chantal Knowles. 2001. *Collecting Colonialism: Material Culture and Colonial Change.* Oxford: Berg.

Gourlay, K. A. 1975. *Sound Producing Instruments in Traditional Society: A Study of Esoteric Instruments and Their Role in Male-Female Relations.* Canberra: Australian National University Press.

Gregory, Chris. 1983. Kula Gift Exchange and Capitalist Commodity Exchange: A Comparison. In *The Kula: New Perspectives on Massim Exchange,* ed. Jerry Leach and Edmund Leach, 103–17. Cambridge: Cambridge University Press.

Grimshaw, Anna. 2001. *The Ethnographer's Eye: Ways of Seeing in Modern Anthropology.* Cambridge: Cambridge University Press.

Gronow, Jukka. 1997. *The Sociology of Taste.* London and New York: Routledge.

Haddon, Alfred, ed. 1903. *Reports of the Cambridge Anthropological Expedition to the Torres Strait.* Cambridge: Cambridge University Press.

Hall, Edward T. 1966. *The Hidden Dimension.* Garden City, NY: Doubleday.

————. 1977. *Beyond Culture.* New York: Anchor Books.

Hall, James. 1999. *The World as Sculpture.* London: Chatto and Windus.

Harrison, Julia. 2002. *Being a Tourist: Finding Meaning in Pleasure Travel.* Vancouver: University of British Columbia Press.

Harrison, Simon. 1985. Concepts of the Person in Avatip Religious Thought. *Man* (n.s.) 20:115–30.

————. 1990. *Stealing People's Names: History and Politics in a Sepik River Cosmology.* Cambridge: Cambridge University Press.

————. 1993. *The Mask of War: Violence, Ritual and the Self in Melanesia.* Cambridge: Cambridge University Press.

Harvey, Elizabeth, ed. 2002. *Sensible Flesh: Touch in Early Modern Culture.* Philadelphia: University of Pennsylvania Press.

Harwood, Frances. 1976. Myth, Memory, and the Oral Tradition: Cicero in the Trobriands. *American Anthropologist* 78:783–96.

Haug, Wolfgang. 1986. *Critique of Commodity Aesthetics: Appearance, Sexuality and Advertising in Capitalist Society.* Trans. Robert Bock. Minneapolis: University of Minnesota Press.

Herle, Anita. 1998. The Life-histories of Objects: Collections of the Cambridge Anthropological Expedition to the Torres Strait. In *Cambridge and the Torres Strait: Centenary Essays on the 1898 Anthropological Expedition,* ed. Anita Herle and Sandra Rouse, 77–105. Cambridge: Cambridge University Press.

Herzfeld, Michael. 2001. *Anthropology: Theoretical Practice in Culture and Society.* Oxford: Blackwell.

Hibbitts, Bernard J. 1992. "Coming to Our Senses": Communication and Legal Expression in Performance Cultures. *Emory Law Journal* 41 (4): 873–960.

Hodgkinson, Frank. 1982. *Sepik Diary.* Victoria: Richard Griffin.

Hollan, Douglas. 2001. Developments in Person-Centered Ethnography. In *The Psychology of Cultural Experience,* ed. Carmella Moore and Holly Mathews, 48–67. Cambridge: Cambridge University Press.

Hook, Sidney. 1958. *From Hegel to Marx.* New York: Humanities Press.

Houston, Stephen, and Karl Taube. 2000. An Archaeology of the Senses: Perception and Cultural Expression in Ancient Mesoamerica. *Cambridge Archaeological Journal* 10 (2): 261–94.

Howes, David. 1986. Le sens sans parole: Vers une anthropologie de l'odorat. *Anthropologie et Sociétés* 10 (3): 29–45.

————. 1988. On the Odour of the Soul: Spatial Representation and Olfactory Classification in Eastern Indonesia and Western Melanesia. *Bijdragen tot de Taal-, Land- en Volkenkunde* 124:84–113.

————. 1990a. Les techniques des sens. *Anthropologie et Sociétés* 14 (2): 99–115.

————. 1990b. Controlling Textuality: A Call for a Return to the Senses. *Anthropologica* 32 (1): 55–73.

————, ed. 1991. *The Varieties of Sensory Experience: A Sourcebook in the Anthropology of the Senses.* Toronto: University of Toronto Press.

————. 1992. What Is Good for Anthropology in Canada? In *Fragile Truths: Twenty-five Years of Sociology and Anthropology in Canada,* ed. William Carroll, Linda Christiansen-Ruffman, Raymond Currie, and Deborah Harrison. Ottawa: Carleton University Press.

————. 1995. The Senses in Medicine. *Culture, Medicine and Psychiatry* 19:125–33.

————. 1996. Introduction: Commodities and Cultural Borders. In *Cross-Cultural Consumption: Global Markets, Local Realities,* ed. David Howes, 1–16. London and New York: Routledge.

————. 2001. e-Legislation: Law-Making in the Digital Age. *McGill Law Journal* 47 (1): 39–57.

Howes, David, and Constance Classen. 1991. Conclusion: Sounding Sensory Profiles. In *The Varieties of Sensory Experience,* ed. David Howes, 257–88. Toronto: University of Toronto Press.

Howes, David, and Marc Lalonde. 1991. The History of Sensibilities: Of the Standard of Taste in Mid-Eighteenth Century England and the Circulation of Smells in Post-Revolutionary France. *Dialectical Anthropology* 16:125–35.

Ihde, Don. 1983. *Sense and Significance.* Atlantic Highlands, NJ: Humanities Press.

Illich, Ivan, and Barry Sanders. 1989. *ABC: The Alphabetization of the Popular Mind.* New York: Vintage.

Ingold, Tim. 2000. *The Perception of the Environment: Essays on Livelihood, Dwelling and Skill.* London and New York: Routledge.

Isbell, Billie Jean. 1985. The Metaphoric Process: "From Culture to Nature and Back Again." In *Animal Myths and Metaphors in South America,* ed. Gary Urton, 285–313. Salt Lake City: University of Utah Press.

Iyer, Pico. 1989. *Video Nights in Katmandhu and Other Reports from the Not-So-Far East.* New York: Vintage.

Jackson, Michael. 1983a. Knowledge of the Body. *Man* (n.s.) 18:327–45.

———. 1983b. Thinking through the Body: An Essay on Understanding Metaphor. *Social Analysis* 14:127–48.

———. 1989. *Paths toward a Clearing: Radical Empiricism and Ethnographic Inquiry.* Bloomington: Indiana University Press.

———. 1998. *Minima Ethnographica: Intersubjectivity and the Anthropological Project.* Chicago: University of Chicago Press.

Jacob, Suma. Assessing Putative Human Pheromones. In *Olfaction, Taste and Cognition,* ed. Catherine Rouby, Benoist Schaal, and Daniele Dubois, 178–95. Cambridge: Cambridge University Press.

James, Alison. 1996. Cooking the Books: Global or Local Identities in Contemporary British Food Cultures? In *Cross-Cultural Consumption,* ed. David Howes, 77–92. London and New York: Routledge.

Jay, Martin. 1988. Scopic Regimes of Modernity. In *Vision and Visuality,* ed. Hal Foster, 3–27. Seattle: Bay Press.

———. 1993. *Downcast Eyes: The Denigration of Vision in Twentieth-Century French Thought.* Berkeley: University of California Press.

Jonas, Hans. 1970. The Nobility of Sight: A Study in the Phenomenology of the Senses. In *The Philosophy of the Body,* ed. Stuart Spicker. Chicago: Quadrangle Books.

Jones, Ernest. 1925. Mother-Right and the Sexual Ignorance of Savages. *International Journal of Psycho-Analysis* 6:109–30.

Kahn, Miriam. 1986. *Always Hungry, Never Greedy: Food and the Expression of Gender in a Melanesian Society.* Cambridge: Cambridge University Press.

Karp, Ivan, and K. Maynard. 1983. Reading *The Nuer. Current Anthropology* 24:481–92.

Kaufmann, Christian. 1968. Uber Kunst und Kult bei den Kwoma und Nukuma (Nord-Neuguinea). *Verhandlungen der Naturforschenden Gesellschaft in Basel* 79 (1): 63–111.

———. 1972. *Das Topferhandwerk der Kwoma in Nord-Neuguinea: Beitrage zur Systematik primarer Topfereiverfahren.* Basel: Pharos-Verlag.

———. 1979. Art and Artists in the Context of Kwoma Society. In *Exploring the Visual Art of Oceania,* ed. Sidney Mead. Honolulu: University Press of Hawaii.

———. 1990. Swiss and German Ethnographic Collections as Source Materials. In *Sepik Heritage: Tradition and Change in Papua New Guinea,* ed. Nancy Lutkehaus, Christian Kaufmann, William Mitchell, Douglas Newton, Lita Osmundsen, and Meinhard Schuster, 587–95. Durham, NC: Carolina Academic Press.

Kaufmann, Robert. 1979. Tactility as an Aesthetic Consideration in African Music. In *The Performing Arts: Music and Dance,* ed. John Blacking and Joann Kealiinohomoku, 251–54. The Hague: Mouton.

Keenan, Thomas. 1993. The Point Is to (Ex)Change It: Reading *Capital*

Rhetorically. In *Fetishism as Cultural Discourse,* ed. Emily Apter and William Pietz, 152–85. Ithaca: Cornell University Press.

Keesing, Roger. 1997. Experienced Bodies as Contested Sites. *Visual Anthropology Review* 13 (1): 40–51.

Keifenheim, Barbara. 1999. Concepts of Perception, Visual Practice, and Pattern Art among the Cashinahua Indians (Peruvian Amazon Area). *Visual Anthropology* 12:27–48.

Keil, Charles, and Steven Feld. 1994. *Music Grooves: Essays and Dialogues.* Chicago: University of Chicago Press.

Keller, Evelyn Fox, and Christine Grontkowski. 1983. The Mind's Eye. In *Discovering Reality,* ed. Sandra Harding and Merrill Hintikka, 207–24. Dordrecht: Reidel.

Kemple, Thomas. 1995. *Reading Marx Writing: Melodrama, the Market, and the "Grundrisse."* Stanford: Stanford University Press.

Kirmayer, Lawrence. 1992. The Body's Insistence on Meaning: Metaphor as Presentation and Representation of Illness Experience. *Medical Anthropological Quarterly* 6 (4): 323–46.

Klima, Alan. 2001. The Telegraphic Abject: Buddhist Meditation and the Redemption of Mechanical Reproduction. *Comparative Studies in Society and History* 43:552–82.

Klein, Naomi. 2000. *No Logo: Taking Aim at the Brand Bullies.* Toronto: Vintage.

Knight, Chris. 1991. *Blood Relations: Menstruation and the Origins of Culture.* New Haven: Yale University Press.

Korsmeyer, Carolyn. 1999. *Making Sense of Taste.* Ithaca: Cornell University Press.

Kuechler, Suzanne. 1987. Malangan: Art and Memory in a Melanesian Society. *Man* 22:238–55.

Kuipers, Joel. 1991. Matters of Taste in Weyéwa. In *The Varieties of Sensory Experience,* ed. David Howes, 111–27. Toronto: University of Toronto Press.

Kuklick, Henrika. 1991. *The Savage Within: The Social History of British Social Anthropology, 1885–1945.* Cambridge: Cambridge University Press.

————. 1998. Fieldworkers and Physiologists. In *Cambridge and the Torres Strait: Centenary Essays on the 1898 Anthropological Expedition,* ed. Anita Herle and Sandra Rouse, 158–80. Cambridge: Cambridge University Press.

Kurtz, Stanley. 1991. Polysexualization: A New Approach to Oedipus in the Trobriands. *Ethos* 19:68–101.

————. 1992. *All the Mothers Are One: Hindu India and the Cultural Reshaping of Psychoanalysis.* New York: Columbia University Press.

————. 1993. A Trobriand Complex. *Ethos* 21:79–103.

Lacan, Jacques. 1966. *Ecrits.* Paris: Seuil.

————. 1977. *The Four Fundamental Concepts of Psychoanalysis.* Trans. Alan Sheridan. Harmondsworth: Penguin.

Laderman, Carol. 1987. The Ambiguity of Symbols in the Structure of Healing. *Social Science and Medicine* 24 (4): 293–301.

————. 1991. *Taming the Wind of Desire: Psychology, Medicine, and Aesthetics in Malay Shamanistic Performance.* Berkeley: University of California Press.

————. 1994. The Embodiment of Symbols and the Acculturation of the Anthropologist. In *Embodiment and Experience: The Existential Ground of Culture and Self,* ed. Thomas Csordas, 183–97. Cambridge: Cambridge University Press.

Laderman, Carol, and Marina Roseman, eds. 1996. *The Performance of Healing.* New York and London: Routledge.

Lakoff, George, and Mark Johnson. 1980. *Metaphors We Live By.* Chicago: University of Chicago Press.

Lassiter, Luke. 2001. From "Reading Over the Shoulders of Natives" to "Reading Alongside Natives," Literally: Toward a Collaborative and Reciprocal Ethnography. *Journal of Anthropological Research* 57:137–51.

Law, Lisa. 2001. Home Cooking: Filipino Women and Geographies of the Senses in Hong Kong. *Ecumene* 8 (3): 264–83.

Le Breton, David. 1990. *Anthropologie du corps et modernité.* Paris: Presses Universitaires de France.

Le Guérer, Annick. 1990. Le declin de l'olfactif: mythe ou réalité? *Anthropologie et Sociétés* 14 (2): 25–46.

————. 1998. *Les pouvoirs de l'odeur,* new ed. Paris: Editions Odile Jacob.

Leach, Edmund. 1976. *Culture and Communication.* Cambridge: Cambridge University Press.

Leach, Jerry. 1983. Introduction. In *The Kula: New Perspectives on Massim Exchange,* ed. Jerry Leach and Edmund Leach, 1–12. Cambridge: Cambridge University Press.

Leach, Jerry, and Edmund Leach, eds. 1983. *The Kula: New Perspectives on Massim Exchange.* Cambridge: Cambridge University Press.

Leavitt, John, and Lynn Hart. 1990. Critique de la "raison" sensorielle: L'élaboration esthétique des sens dans une société himalayenne. *Anthropologie et Sociétés* 14 (2): 77–98.

Lederman, Rena. 1986. Changing Times in Mendi: Notes Towards Writing Highland New Guinea History. *Ethnohistory* 33 (1): 1–30.

Lee, Dorothy. 1959. *Freedom and Culture.* New York: Prentice-Hall.

Lee, Martyn. 1993. *Consumer Culture Reborn: The Cultural Politics of Consumption.* London: Routledge.

Leenhardt, Maurice. 1979. *Do Kamo: Person and Myth in the Melanesian World.* Trans. B. Miller Gulati. Chicago: University of Chicago Press.

Lepowsky, Maria. 1982. A Comparison of Alcohol and Betel Nut Use on Vanatinai (Sudest Island). In *Through a Glass Darkly: Beer and Modernization in Papua New Guinea,* ed. Mac Marshall, 325–42. Boroko: Institute of Applied Social and Economic Research, Monograph no. 18.

————. 1993. *Fruit of the Motherland: Gender in an Egalitarian Society.* New York: Columbia University Press.

Leppert, Richard. 1993. *The Sight of Sound: Music, Representation and the History of the Body.* Berkeley: University of California Press.

Levin, David Michael, ed. 1993. *Modernity and the Hegemony of Vision.* Berkeley: University of California Press.

Lévi-Strauss, Claude. 1966. *The Savage Mind.* Chicago: University of Chicago Press.

————. 1969. *The Raw and the Cooked: Introduction to a Science of Mythology,* vol. 1. Trans. John Weightman and Doreen Weightman. New York: Harper and Row.

————. 1981. *The Naked Man: Introduction to a Science of Mythology,* vol. 4. Trans. John Weightman and Doreen Weightman. New York: Harper and Row.

————. 1992. *Tristes Tropiques.* Trans. John Weightman and Doreen Weightman. Harmondsworth: Penguin.

————. 1997. *Look, Listen, Read.* Trans. Brian Singer. New York: Basic Books.

Lévy-Bruhl, Lucien. 1978. *The Notebooks on Primitive Mentality.* Trans. Peter Rivière. New York: Harper Torchbooks.

Lewis, Gilbert. 1975. *Knowledge of Illness in a Sepik Society.* Cambridge: Cambridge University Press.

————. 1980. *Day of Shining Red.* Cambridge: Cambridge University Press.

————. 1986. The Look of Magic. *Man* (n.s.) 21:414–37.

————. 1990. Gestures of Support. In *Sepik Heritage: Tradition and Change in Papua New Guinea,* ed. Nancy Lutkehaus, Christian Kaufmann, William Mitchell, Douglas Newton, Lita Osmundsen, and Meinhard Schuster, 255–65. Durham, NC: Carolina Academic Press.

Lidz, T., and R. W. Lidz. 1989. *Oedipus in the Stone Age: A Psychoanalytic Study of Masculinization in Papua New Guinea.* Madison, CT: International Universities Press.

Liep, John. 1994. Recontextualization of a Consumer Good: The Ritual Use of Johnson's Baby Powder in Melanesia. In *European Imagery and Colonial History in the Pacific,* ed. Toon van Meijl and Paul van der Grijp, 64–75. Starbruken: Verlag für Entwicklungspolitik Breitenbach GmbH.

Lindstrom, Lamont. 1993. *Cargo Cult: Strange Stories of Desire from Melanesia and Beyond.* Honolulu: University of Hawaii Press.

LiPuma, Edward. 2000. *Encompassing Others: The Magic of Modernity in Melanesia.* Ann Arbor: University of Michigan Press.

Little, Kenneth. 1991. On Safari: The Visual Politics of a Tourist Representation. In *The Varieties of Sensory Experience,* ed. David Howes, 148–63. Toronto: University of Toronto Press.

Lock, Margaret. 1993. Cultivating the Body: Anthropology and Epistemologies of Bodily Practice and Knowledge. *Annual Review of Anthropology* 22:133–55.

Lowe, Donald. 1982. *History of Bourgeois Perception.* Chicago: University of Chicago Press.

Luria, A. R. 1976. *Cognitive Development.* Trans. M. Lopez-Morillas and L. Solotaroff. Cambridge: Harvard University Press.

Macintyre, Martha. 1983. Warfare and the Changing Context of "Kune" on Tubetube. *Journal of Pacific History* 18:11–34.

————. 1987. Nurturance and Nutrition: Change and Continuity in Concepts of Food and Feasting in a Southern Massim Community. *Journal de la Société des Océanistes* 84 (1): 51–59.

MacKendrick, Carmen. 1999. *Counterpleasures.* Albany: State University of New York Press.

MacKenzie, Maureen A. 1991. *Androgynous Objects: String Bags and Gender in Central New Guinea.* Philadelphia: Harwood Academic.

Malinowski, Bronislaw. 1923. The Problem of Meaning in Primitive Languages. In *The Meaning of Meaning*, C. K. Ogden and I. A. Richards, 296–336. London: Routledge and Kegan Paul.

————. 1924. Psychoanalysis and Anthropology. *Psyche* 4:293–332.

————. 1929. *The Sexual Life of Savages in North-Western Melanesia.* New York: Harcourt, Brace and World.

————. 1960. *Sex and Repression in Savage Society.* London: Routledge and Kegan Paul.

————. 1961. *Argonauts of the Western Pacific.* New York: E. P. Dutton.

————. 1965. *Coral Gardens and Their Magic.* Vols. I and II. Bloomington: Indiana University Press.

————. 1967. *A Diary in the Strict Sense of the Term.* London: Athlone Press.

Manderson, Derek. 2000. *Songs Without Music: Aesthetic Dimensions of Law and Justice.* Berkeley: University of California Press.

Manuel, Frank. 1995. *A Requiem for Karl Marx.* Cambridge: Harvard University Press.

Marcus, George. 1998. *Ethnography through Thick and Thin.* Princeton: Princeton University Press.

Marcus, George, and Dick Cushman. 1982. Ethnographies as Texts. *Annual Review of Anthropology* 11:25–69.

Marcus, George, and Michael Fischer. 1986. *Anthropology as Cultural Critique.* Chicago: University of Chicago Press.

Marks, Laura. 2000. *The Skin of the Film: Intercultural Cinema. Embodiment and the Senses.* Durham, NC: Duke University Press.

Marks, Lawrence. 1982. *The Unity of the Senses.* New York: Academic.

Marx, Karl. 1954. *Capital: A Critique of Political Economy,* vol. I. Trans. Samuel Moore and Edward Aveling. London: Lawrence and Wishart.

————. 1973. *Wages, Price and Profit.* Peking: Foreign Languages Press.

————. 1987. *Economic and Philosophic Manuscripts of 1844.* Trans. Martin Milligan. Buffalo: Prometheus Books.

Marx, Karl, and Frederick Engels. 1947. *The German Ideology.* Ed. R. Pascal. New York: International Publishers.

————. 1967. *The Communist Manifesto.* Intro. A. J. P. Taylor. Harmondsworth: Penguin.

————. 1987. *Collected Works.* New York: International Publishers.

Masquelier, Adeline. 2001. *Prayer Has Spoiled Everything: Possession, Power, and Identity in an Islamic Town of Niger.* Durham, NC: Duke University Press.

Masson, Jeffrey, ed. 1985. *The Complete Letters of Sigmund Freud to Wilhelm Fliess, 1887–1904.* Cambridge: Harvard University Press.

Mauss, Marcel. 1966. *The Gift: Forms and Functions of Exchange.* London: Routledge and Kegan Paul.

———. 1979. Body Techniques. In *Sociology and Psychology Essays,* trans. Ben Brewster, 95–123. London: Routledge and Kegan Paul.

Mayer, Jessica. 1982. Body, Psyche and Society: Conceptions of Illness in Ommura, Eastern Highlands, Papua New Guinea. *Oceania* 52:240–59.

McCracken, Grant. 1988. *Culture and Consumption: New Approaches to the Symbolic Character of Consumer Goods and Activities.* Bloomington: Indiana University Press.

McDowell, Nancy. 1980. It's Not Who You Are But How You Give That Counts: The Role of Exchange in Melanesian Society. *American Ethnologist* 7:57–64.

McLuhan, Marshall. 1962. *The Gutenberg Galaxy.* Toronto: University of Toronto Press.

———. 1964. *Understanding Media.* New York: New American Library.

McLuhan, Marshall, and Quentin Fiore. 1967. *The Medium Is the Massage.* New York: Bantam.

McSweeney, Kerry. 1998. *The Language of the Senses: Sensory-Perceptual Dynamics in Wordsworth, Coleridge, Thoreau, Whitman, and Dickinson.* Montreal and Kingston: McGill-Queen's University Press.

Mead, Margaret. 1956. *Sex and Temperament in Three Primitive Societies.* New York: New American Library.

Mead, Margaret, and Gregory Bateson. 1942. *Balinese Character: A Photographic Analysis.* New York: New York Academy of Sciences.

Mead, Margaret, and Rhoda Métraux. 1953. Introduction. In *The Study of Culture at a Distance,* ed. Margaret Mead and Rhoda Métraux, 3–53. Chicago: University of Chicago Press.

Méchin, Colette, Isabelle Bianquis, and David Le Breton, eds. 1998. *Anthropologie du sensoriel: Les sens dans tous les sens.* Paris: L'Harmattan.

Meigs, Anna. 1984. *Food, Sex and Pollution: A New Guinea Religion.* New Brunswick, NJ: Rutgers University Press.

Merleau-Ponty, Maurice. 1962. *Phenomenology of Perception.* Trans. C. Smith. London: Routledge.

———. 1964. *The Primacy of Perception.* Evanston: Northwestern University Press.

———. 1968. *The Visible and the Invisible.* Evanston: Northwestern University Press.

Métraux, Rhoda. 1953. Resonance in Imagery. In *The Study of Culture at a Distance,* ed. Margaret Mead and Rhoda Métraux, 343–62. Chicago: University of Chicago Press.

Miller, Daniel. 1987. *Material Culture and Mass Consumption.* Oxford: Blackwell.

Miller, William Ian. 1997. *The Anatomy of Disgust.* Cambridge: Harvard University Press.

Mintz, Sidney. 1986. *Sweetness and Power: The Place of Sugar in Modern History.* New York: Penguin.

Molesworth, H. 1993. Before *Bed. October* 63:69–82.

Montague, Susan. 1983. Trobriand Gender Identity. *Mankind* 14 (1): 33–45.

Munn, Nancy. 1977. The Spatiotemporal Transformations of Gawa Canoes. *Journal de la Société des Océanistes* 33:39–51.

———. 1983. Gawan Kula: Spatio-temporal Control and the Symbolism of Influence. In *The Kula: New Perspectives on Massim Exchange,* ed. Jerry W. Leach and Edmund Leach, 227–308. Cambridge: Cambridge University Press.

———. 1986. *The Fame of Gawa: A Symbolic Study of Value Transformation in a Massim (Papua New Guinea) Society.* New York: Cambridge University Press.

Myers, Charles. 1903. Smell. In *Reports of the Cambridge Anthropological Expedition to the Torres Strait,* ed. A. C. Haddon, vol. 2. Cambridge: Cambridge University Press.

Ness, Sally Ann. 1992. *Body, Movement and Culture: Kinesthetic and Visual Symbolism in a Philippine Community.* Philadelphia: University of Pennsylvania Press.

Newman, Deena. 1999. The Western Psychic as Diviner: Experience and the Politics of Perception. *Ethnos* 64 (1): 82–106.

Newton, Douglas. 1971. *Crocodile and Cassowary: Religious Art of the Upper Sepik River, New Guinea.* New York: Museum of Primitive Art.

———. 1975. *Massim: Art of the Massim Area, New Guinea.* New York: Museum of Primitive Art.

Nihill, Michael. 1989. The New Pearlshells: Aspects of Money and Meaning in Anganen Exchange. *Canberra Anthropology* 12 (1–2): 144–59.

———. 2000. Gift Exchange as Sensory Experience among the Anganen. *Oceania* 71 (2): 110–28.

Nouvet, Elysée. 2001. *El mundo, God and the Flesh: Experiencing Sacredness in a Nicaraguan Church.* M.A. diss., Concordia University.

O'Hanlon, Michael. 1989. *Reading the Skin: Adornment, Display and Society among the Wahgi.* London: British Museum.

———. 1992. Unstable Images and Second Skins: Artefacts, Exegesis and Assessments in the New Guinea Highlands. *Man* (n.s.) 27:587–608.

———. 1993. *Paradise: Portraying the New Guinea Highlands.* London: British Museum.

Ong, Walter J. 1967. *The Presence of the Word.* New Haven: Yale University Press.

———. 1977. *Interfaces of the Word.* Ithaca: Cornell University Press.

———. 1982. *Orality and Literacy.* New York: Methuen.

———. 1991. The Shifting Sensorium. In *The Varieties of Sensory Experience,* ed. David Howes, 25–30. Toronto: University of Toronto Press.

Padover, Saul, ed. 1979. *The Letters of Karl Marx.* Englewood Cliffs, NJ: Prentice-Hall.

References

Pandya, Vishvajit. 1993. *Above the Forest: A Study of Andamanese Ethnoanemology, Cosmology, and the Power of Ritual.* Delhi: Oxford University Press.

Parr, Joy. 1999. *Domestic Goods: The Material, the Moral and the Economic in the Postwar Years.* Toronto: University of Toronto Press.

————. 2001. Notes for a More Sensuous History of Twentieth-Century Canada: The Timely, the Tacit and the Material Body. *Canadian Historical Review* 82 (4): 720–45.

Payne, Robert. 1968. *Marx.* New York: Simon and Schuster.

Pels, Peter. 1998. The Spirit of Matter: On Fetish, Rarity, Fact, and Fancy. In *Border Fetishisms: Material Objects in Unstable Spaces,* ed. Patricia Spyer, 91–121. London and New York: Routledge.

Pietz, William. 1993. Fetishism and Materialism: The Limits of Theory in Marx. In *Fetishism as Cultural Discourse,* ed. Emily Apter and William Pietz, 119–51. Ithaca: Cornell University Press.

Pinard, Sylvain. 1991. A Taste of India: On the Role of Gustation in the Hindu Sensorium. In *The Varieties of Sensory Experience,* ed. David Howes, 221–30. Toronto: University of Toronto Press.

Pine, B. Joseph, II, and James H. Gilmore. 1998. Welcome to the Experience Economy. *Harvard Business Review* 76 (4): 97–105.

Pocock, Douglas. 1993. The Senses in Focus. *Area* 25 (1): 11–16.

Porteous, J. Douglas. 1990. *Landscapes of the Mind: Worlds of Sense and Metaphor.* Toronto: University of Toronto Press.

Provencher, Roland. 1979. Orality as a Pattern of Symbolism in Malay Psychiatry. In *The Imagination of Reality,* ed. A. Becker and I. Yengoyan. Norwood, NJ: Ablex.

Rabain, Jacqueline. 1979. *L'enfant du lignage.* Paris: Payot.

Rasmussen, Susan. 1995. *Spirit Possession and Personhood among the Kel Ewey Tuareg.* Cambridge: Cambridge University Press.

————. 1996. Matters of Taste: Food, Eating, and Reflections on "The Body Politic" in Tuareg Society. *Journal of Anthropological Research* 52:61–83.

————. 1999. Making Better "Scents" in Anthropology: Aroma in Tuareg Sociocultural Systems and the Shaping of Ethnography. *Anthropological Quarterly* 72 (2): 55–73.

Rée, Jonathan. 1999. *I See a Voice: Deafness, Language, and the Senses—A Philosophical History.* New York: Metropolitan Books.

Reed, Adam. 1999. Anticipating Individuals: Modes of Vision and Their Social Consequences in a Papua New Guinea Prison. *Journal of the Royal Anthropological Institute* (n.s.) 5:43–56.

Reichel-Dolmatoff, Gerardo. 1978. Desana Animal Categories, Food Restrictions, and the Concept of Color Energies. *Journal of Latin American Lore* 4 (2): 243–91.

————. 1981. Brain and Mind in Desana Shamanism. *Journal of Latin American Lore* 5 (1): 73–98.

————. 1985. Tapir Avoidance in the Colombian Northwest Amazon. In

Animal Myths and Metaphors in South America, ed. Gary Urton, 107–43. Salt Lake City: University of Utah Press.

Richards, Graham. 1998. Getting a Result: The Expedition's Psychological Research, 1898–1913. In *Cambridge and the Torres Strait: Centenary Essays on the 1898 Anthropological Expedition,* ed. Anita Herle and Sandra Rouse, 136–57. Cambridge: Cambridge University Press.

Ricoeur, Paul. 1970. The Model of the Text: Meaningful Action Considered as a Text. *Social Research* 38:529–62.

Rindisbacher, Hans. 1992. *The Smell of Books: A Cultural-Historical Study of Olfaction in Literature.* Ann Arbor: University of Michigan Press.

Ritchie, Ian. 1991. Fusion of the Faculties: A Study of the Language of the Senses in Hausaland. In *The Varieties of Sensory Experience,* ed. David Howes, 192–202. Toronto: University of Toronto Press.

Rivlin, Robert, and Karen Gravelle. 1984. *Deciphering the Senses.* New York: Simon and Schuster.

Robbins, Richard. 1998. *Global Problems and the Culture of Capitalism.* Boston: Allyn and Bacon.

Rodaway, Paul. 1994. *Sensuous Geographies.* London: Routledge.

Rodman, Margaret. 1992. Empowering Place: Multilocality and Multivocality. *American Anthropologist* 94 (1): 640–55.

Róheim, Géza. 1932. Psycho-analysis of Primitive Cultural Types. *International Journal of Psycho-analysis* 13:1–224.

———. 1948. Witches of Normanby Island. *Oceania* 18 (4): 279–308.

———. 1950. *Psychoanalysis and Anthropology.* New York: International Universities Press.

———. 1954. Cannibalism in Duau, Normanby Island. *Mankind* 4 (12): 487–95.

Romanyshyn, Robert. 1989. *Technology as Symptom and Dream.* London: Routledge.

Root, Deborah. 1996. *Cannibal Culture: Art, Appropriation, and the Commodification of Difference.* Boulder: Westview.

Rorty, Richard. 1979. *Philosophy and the Mirror of Nature.* Princeton: Princeton University Press.

Roscoe, Paul. 1990. Male Initiation among the Yangoru Boiken. In *Sepik Heritage: Tradition and Change in Papua New Guinea,* ed. Nancy Lutkehaus, Christian Kaufmann, William Mitchell, Douglas Newton, Lita Osmundsen, and Meinhard Schuster, 402–13. Durham, NC: Carolina Academic Press.

Roseman, Marina. 1991. *Healing Sounds from the Malaysian Rainforest.* Berkeley: University of California Press.

Sacks, Oliver. 1987. *The Man Who Mistook His Wife for a Hat and Other Clinical Tales.* New York: Perennial Library.

Sahlins, Marshall. 1976. *Culture and Practical Reason.* Chicago: University of Chicago Press.

Saisselin, Rémy G. 1984. *The Bourgeois and the Bibelot.* New Brunswick, NJ: Rutgers University Press.

References

267

Schechner, Richard. 2001. Rasaesthetics. *The Drama Review* 45 (3): 27–50.

Schieffelin, Edward L. 1976. *The Sorrow of the Lonely and the Burning of the Dancers.* New York: St. Martin's Press.

Schur, Max. 1972. *Freud: Living and Dying.* New York: International Universities Press.

Scoditti, Giancarlo. 1977. A Kula Prowboard: An Iconological Interpretation. *L'Uomo* 1 (2): 199–232.

———. 1982. Aesthetics: The Significance of Apprenticeship on Kitawa. *Man* (n.s.) 17:74–91.

———. 1983. Kula on Kitava. In *The Kula: New Perspectives on Massim Exchange,* ed. Jerry W. Leach and Edmund Leach, 249–73. Cambridge: Cambridge University Press.

———. 1984/85. The Use of "Metaphors" in Kitawa Culture, Northern Massim. *Oceania* 55:50–70.

Seeger, Anthony. 1981. *Nature and Society in Central Brazil: The Suyà Indians of Mato Grosso.* Cambridge: Harvard University Press.

———. 1987. *Why Suyà Sing: A Musical Anthropology of an Amazonian People.* Cambridge: Cambridge University Press.

Senft, Gunter. 1986. *Kilivila: The Language of the Trobriand Islands.* The Hague: Mouton de Gruyter.

Seremetakis, C. Nadia, ed. 1994. *The Senses Still: Memory and Perception as Material Culture in Modernity.* Boulder: Westview.

Sheldon, Roy, and Egmont Arens. 1976. *Consumer Engineering: A New Technique for Prosperity.* New York: Arno Press.

Shipley, Thorne. 1995. *Intersensory Origin of Mind: A Revisit to Emergent Evolution.* London and New York: Routledge.

Shore, Bradd. 1996. *Culture in Mind: Cognition, Culture, and the Problem of Meaning.* New York: Oxford University Press.

Silas, Ellis. 1926. *A Primitive Arcadia: Being the Impressions of an Artist in Papua.* London: T. Fisher Unwin.

Simon, B., ed. 1957. *Psychology in the Soviet Union.* Stanford: Stanford University Press.

Smith, David M. 1998. An Athapaaskan Way of Knowing: Chipewyan Ontology. *American Ethnologist* 25 (3): 412–32.

Spiro, Melford. 1982. *Oedipus in the Trobriands.* Chicago: University of Chicago Press.

———. 1992. Oedipus Redux. *Ethos* 20:358–76.

Stallybrass, Peter. 1998. Marx's Coat. In *Border Fetishisms: Material Objects in Unstable Spaces,* ed. Patricia Spyer, 183–207. London and New York: Routledge.

Stein, Barry, and M. Alex Meredith. 1993. *The Merging of the Senses.* Cambridge: MIT Press.

Stephen, Michele. 1987. Master of Souls: The Mekeo Sorcerer. In *Sorcerer and Witch in Melanesia,* ed. Michele Stephen, 41–80. New Brunswick, NJ: Rutgers University Press.

Stoddart, D. Michael. 1990. *The Scented Ape: The Biology and Culture of Human Odour.* Cambridge: Cambridge University Press.

Stoller, Paul. 1984. Sound in Songhay Cultural Experience. *American Ethnologist* 11 (3): 559–70.

———. 1989. *The Taste of Ethnographic Things: The Senses in Anthropology.* Philadelphia: University of Pennsylvania Press.

———. 1994. Ethnographies as Texts, Ethnographers as Griots. *American Ethnologist* 21 (2): 353–66.

———. 1995. *Embodying Colonial Memories: Spirit Possession, Power and the Hauka Movement in West Africa.* New York: Routledge.

———. 1997. *Sensuous Scholarship.* Philadelphia: University of Pennsylvania Press.

Stoller, Paul, and Cheryl Olkes. 1987. *In Sorcery's Shadow: A Memoir of Apprenticeship among the Songhay of Niger.* Chicago: University of Chicago Press.

———. 1990. La sauce épaisse: Remarques sur les relations sociales songhais. *Anthropologie et Sociétés* 14 (2): 57–76.

Strathern, Andrew. 1989. Melpa Dream Interpretation and the Concept of Hidden Truth. *Ethnology* 28 (4): 301–16.

———. 1996. *Body Thoughts.* Ann Arbor: University of Michigan Press.

Strathern, Marilyn. 1988. *The Gender of the Gift.* Cambridge: Cambridge University Press.

Sullivan, Lawrence E. 1986. Sound and Senses: Toward a Hermeneutics of Performance. *History of Religions* 26 (1): 1–33.

Süskind, Patrick. 1986. *Perfume.* London: Hamish Hamilton.

Synnott, Anthony. 1991. Puzzling over the Senses: From Plato to Marx. In *The Varieties of Sensory Experience,* ed. David Howes, 61–76. Toronto: University of Toronto Press.

———. 1993. *The Body Social: Symbolism, Self and Society.* London and New York: Routledge.

Synnott, Anthony, and David Howes. 1992. From Measurement to Meaning: Anthropologies of the Body. *Anthropos* 87:147–66.

Syrotinski, Michael, and Ian Maclachlan, eds. 2001. *Sensual Reading: New Approaches to Reading in Its Relations to the Senses.* London: Associated University Presses.

Tambiah, Stanley. 1968. The Magical Power of Words. *Man* (n.s.) 3:175–203.

Taussig, Michael. 1993. *Mimesis and Alterity: A Particular History of the Senses.* London and New York: Routledge.

Taylor, Lucien, ed. 1994. *Visualizing Theory: Selected Essays from V.A.R., 1990–1994.* New York: Routledge.

Tester, Keith, ed. 1994. *The Flâneur.* London and New York: Routledge.

Theroux, Paul. 1992. *The Happy Isles of Oceania: Paddling the Pacific.* New York: Putnam.

Thomas, Nicholas. 1991. *Entangled Objects: Exchange, Material Culture, and Colonialism in the Pacific.* Cambridge: Harvard University Press.

———. 1995. *Oceanic Art.* London: Thames and Hudson.

Thornton, E. M. 1984. *The Freudian Fallacy*. Garden City, NY: Doubleday.

Thune, Carl Eugene. 1980. *The Rhetoric of Remembrance: Collective Life and Personal Tragedy in Loboda Village*. Ann Arbor, MI: University Microfilms International.

Tomas, David. 1996. *Transcultural Space and Transcultural Beings*. Boulder: Westview.

Tuan, Yi-Fu. 1974. *Topophilia*. Englewood Cliffs, NJ: Prentice-Hall.

———. 1995. *Passing Strange and Wonderful: Aesthetics, Nature and Culture*. Tokyo and New York: Kodansha International.

Turner, David H. 1978a. *Dialectics in Tradition: Myth and Social Structure in Two Hunter-Gatherer Societies*. London: Royal Anthropological Society, Occasional Paper no. 36.

———. 1978b. Ideology and Elementary Structures. *Anthropologica* 20 (1–2): 223–47.

Turner, Victor W. 1967. *The Forest of Symbols: Aspects of Ndembu Ritual and Belief*. Ithaca: Cornell University Press.

Tuzin, Donald. 1972. Yam Symbolism in the Sepik. *Southwestern Journal of Anthropology* 28:230–54.

———. 1980. *The Voice of the Tambaran*. Berkeley: University of California Press.

———. 1995. Art and Procreative Illusion in the Sepik: Comparing the Abelam and the Arapesh. *Oceania* 65:289–303.

———. 1997. *The Cassowary's Revenge: The Life and Death of Masculinity in a New Guinea Society*. Chicago: University of Chicago Press.

Tyler, Stephen. 1984. The Vision Quest in the West or What the Mind's Eye Sees. *Journal of Anthropological Research* 40:23–42.

———. 1986. Post-modern Ethnography. In *Writing Culture*, ed. James Clifford and George Marcus, 122–40. Berkeley: University of California Press.

———. 1987. *The Unspeakable: Discourse, Dialogue and Rhetoric in the Postmodern World*. Madison: University of Wisconsin Press.

Ullmer, Greg. 1985. *Applied Grammatology: Post(e)-Pedagogy from Jacques Derrida to Joseph Beuys*. Baltimore: Johns Hopkins University Press.

Van Esterik, Penny. 2000. *Materializing Thailand*. Oxford: Berg.

van Hoof, Marine. 2000. Signes de Vie: Vital Signs. *Vie des arts* 179:71.

van Maanen, John. 1988. *Tales of the Field: On Writing Ethnography*. Chicago: University of Chicago Press.

Van Sant, Ann Jessie. 1993. *Eighteenth-Century Sensibility and the Novel: The Senses in Social Context*. Cambridge: Cambridge University Press.

Verrips, Jojada. 2002. Haptic Screens and Our Corporeal Eye. *Etnofoor* 15 (1/2): 21–46.

Vinge, Louise. 1975. *The Five Senses: Studies in a Literary Tradition*. Lund, Sweden: Royal Society of Letters at Lund.

Visser, Margaret. 1991. *The Rituals of Dinner*. New York: HarperCollins.

Webster, Steven. 1983. Ethnography as Storytelling. *Dialectical Anthropology* 8:185–205.

Weiner, Annette B. 1976. *Women of Value, Men of Renown: New Perspectives in Trobriand Exchange.* Austin: University of Texas Press.

———. 1978. The Reproductive Model in Trobriand Society. *Mankind* 11:175–86.

———. 1983. From Words to Objects to Magic: Hard Words and the Boundaries of Social Interaction. *Man* (n.s.) 18:690–709.

———. 1988. *The Trobrianders of Papua New Guinea.* New York: Holt, Rinehart and Winston.

Weinstein, Deena, and Michael Weinstein. 1984. On the Visual Constitution of Society: The Contributions of Georg Simmel and Jean-Paul Sartre to a Sociology of the Senses. *History of European Ideas* 5 (4): 349–62.

Wheen, Francis. 1999. *Karl Marx.* London: Fourth Estate.

Whiting, John M. W. 1938. *Inculcation and Social Control in a New Guinea Society.* Doctoral diss., Yale University.

———. 1941. *Becoming a Kwoma: Teaching and Learning in a New Guinea Tribe.* New Haven: Yale University Press.

———. 1970. *Kwoma Journal.* New Haven: Human Relations Area Files.

Whiting, John M. W., and Stephen Reed. 1938/39. Kwoma Culture: Report on Field Work in the Mandated Territory of New Guinea. *Oceania* 9:170–216.

Wikan, Unni. 1990. *Managing Turbulent Hearts: A Balinese Formula for Living.* Chicago: University of Chicago Press.

Williams, T. R. 1966. Cultural Structuring of Tactile Experience in a Borneo Society. *American Anthropologist* 68:27–39.

Williamson, Margaret Holmes. 1979a. Cicatrization of Women among the Kwoma. *Mankind* 12:35–41.

———. 1979b. Who Does What to the Sago? *Oceania* 49 (3): 210–20.

———. 1983. Sex Relations and Gender Relations: Understanding Kwoma Conception. *Mankind* 14 (1): 13–23.

———. 1990. Gender and the Cosmos in Kwoma Culture. In *Sepik Heritage: Tradition and Change in Papua New Guinea,* ed. Nancy Lutkehaus, Christian Kaufmann, William Mitchell, Douglas Newton, Lita Osmundsen, and Meinhard Schuster, 385–94. Durham, NC: Carolina Academic Press.

Wilson, Frank. 1999. *The Hand: How Its Use Shapes the Brain, Language, and Human Culture.* New York: Vintage Books.

Wober, Mallory. 1966. Sensotypes. *Journal of Social Psychology* 70:181–89.

———. 1975. *Psychology in Africa.* London: International Africa Institute.

Wordsworth, William. 1959. *The Prelude, or Growth of a Poet's Mind.* Ed. E. de Selincourt. Oxford: Clarendon Press.

Worsley, Peter. 1970. *The Trumpet Shall Sound: A Study of "Cargo" Cults in Melanesia.* London: Paladin.

Wright, K. 1994. The Sniff of Legend. *Discover* (April): 60–67.

Yans-McLaughlin, Virginia. 1986. Science, Democracy, and Ethics: Mobilizing Culture and Personality for World War II. In *Malinowski, Rivers, Benedict and Others: Essays on Culture and Personality*, ed. George Stocking, 184–217. Madison: University of Wisconsin Press.

Young, Michael. 1971. *Fighting with Food: Leadership, Values and Social Control in a Massim Society*. Cambridge: Cambridge University Press.

———. 1983. *Magicians of Manumanua: Living Myth in Kalauna*. Berkeley: University of California Press.

———. 1987. The Tusk, the Flute and the Serpent: Disguise and Revelation in Goodenough Mythology. In *Dealing with Inequality: Analysing Gender Relations in Melanesia and Beyond*, ed. Marilyn Strathern, 229–54. Cambridge: Cambridge University Press.

Zaltman, Gerald, and Robin Coulter. 1995. Seeing the Voice of the Customer: Metaphor-Based Advertising Research. *Journal of Advertising Research* 3:35–51.

Zemp, Hugo, and Christian Kaufmann. 1969. Pour une transcription automatique des "langages tambourinés" mélanésiens. *L'Homme* 9 (2): 38–88.

Zui, Daniel Z. 2000. Visuality, Aurality, and Shifting Metaphors of Geographical Thought in the Late Twentieth Century. *Annals of the Association of American Geographers* 90 (2): 322–43.

Index

friendship alliance, 135, 171, 242–43n. 1

functionalist analysis, 85, 238n. 7

Gawa, 61, 70, 83–84, 115–16, 121, 241n. 4

gaze. *See* sight

Geertz, Clifford, 3, 17–21, 25–27, 33

Gell, Alfred, xiii, 241n. 6

Geller, Jay, 246n. 7

gender, 55, 121–23, 133–34, 139–40, 148–49, 243n. 2, 244n. 2

genitals, 137, 182–83, 194, 197

Geurts, Kathryn Linn, xiii, 239n. 5

Gibson, James, 239n. 6

gift exchange, xvii, 213, 224, 247n. 4. *See also* commodity exchange; kula exchange

Gilman, Sander, 202

Gilmore, James H., 212

ginger, 98–99, 121, 149–50

Glass, Patrick, 117

globalization, 208, 219

Goodenough Island, 61, 69, 240n. 1, 242n. 5

Goody, Jack, 113

Gregory, Chris, 213, 247n. 4

Grimshaw, Anna, 45

gustation. *See* taste

habitus, 31–32, 238n. 1

Haddon, Alfred, 10

Hall, Edward T., 14, 17, 26, 237nn. 3, 5

hardness, xx, 130, 133, 156, 162–63, 169

Harrison, Simon, 158–59

Harwood, Frances, 242n. 7

Haug, Wolfgang, 211

Hausa, 42, 248n. 10

Haus tambaran. *See* men's house

hearing, xvii, xviii, xx, 4–7, 16, 19, 41, 113–16, 121, 145–46, 158–59, 170–71, 240n. 8, 244n. 8. *See also* auditory discrimination; Kwoma

sensory order; Massim sensory order; sound

Hegel, G. W. F., 205

hegemony of vision, xii, 22, 45

hermeneutics, 18, 21, 28. *See also* textualist

Hilton, Chris, 247n. 6

Hindu, 248n. 10

Hollan, Douglas, 239n. 5

Holmes, Oliver Wendell, 210–11

Hook, Sidney, 248n. 10

hunting, 134, 172, 210–11, 232

hyperaesthesia, 211, 236n. 2

hypervisualism, xiii

Iatmul, 124

iconographic approach, 156

Illich, Ivan, 113

illness, 31–32, 39–40, 131, 162

incest taboo, 135, 184–85, 187

individuation, 118–19, 181, 226

industrial capitalism, 206, 208, 212, 227. *See also* consumer capitalism

information theory, 52–53, 93

Ingold, Tim, xiii, 239–40n. 8

insanity, 114–15

intellect, 115, 120

interpretive anthropology, 18. *See also* textualists

intersensory relationships, xx–xxi, 16–17, 36, 48, 53, 76–77, 106–8, 145–46, 160, 235n. 1, 236n. 4, 239n. 5

Jackson, Michael, xiii, 29–34, 36, 40–41, 113, 238n. 1

James, Henry, 210

Japanese culture, 9, 14

Jones, Ernest, 175

Kahn, Miriam, 100

Kaluli, xvii, 36–39, 217, 240n. 8

Kasabwaibwaileta, 72, 167, 218

Kaufmann, Christian, 124, 142, 244n. 1

Kaufmann, Robert, 47

mind, xxi, xxii, 5, 30, 50, 93, 98–99, 105, 228

mindja (Kwoma ceremonial section, initiate, ritual, sculpture), 126, 144

mint plant, 74, 89, 185, 193, 196

mirror, 118–19, 233, 245n. 4

mnemonic devices, 46, 242n. 7

modernity, 47, 219, 237n. 6

Montague, Susan, 69

mortuary ritual, 178–79

Mount Hagen, xvii

mourning, 177–79, 217–18

mouth, 120, 153

movement, xii, 8, 38, 70, 91, 106, 156. *See also* dance

Munn, Nancy, xiii, xvii, xix, 61, 70, 82, 84, 87, 92, 98, 110–11, 119, 169, 241n. 4

music, 7, 47–48, 217

Myers, Charles, 5

myth, xx, 139–40, 146, 184–85, 187, 218, 242n. 7

name, 77–78, 83, 113, 114, 122, 168, 172

nasality, xv, 177, 182, 193, 200, 202–3, 245n. 3. *See also* psychosexual development

nasal reflex neurosis. *See* naso-genital relationship

nasal symbolism, 155–56. *See also* phallic symbolism

nasal taboo, 200

naso-genital relationship, 197, 203

Navajo, 8

Ness, Sally Ann, 51

neuroses, 196

Newton, Douglas, 152

Nihill, Michael, 219

nonverbal (sensual) communication, xvii–xviii, 32–33, 117

nose, 5, 12, 54, 120, 154–56, 180–82, 185, 193, 198–202, 246n. 7

Nouvet, Elysée, 240n. 9

Nukuma, 124

objects, 20, 44–45, 87, 210–11, 218–19, 224, 236n. 1. *See also* kula objects

observation, 13, 25

ocularcentrism, 141, 154

odor, xii, 5, 13–14, 46, 49, 54–56, 74–77, 131, 146–49, 155, 177–81, 183–84, 187, 189, 191, 193–95, 201, 203, 212, 215–16, 218, 231, 238n. 1, 241–42n. 3, 245n. 2; vocabulary, 9–10. *See also* smell

Oedipus complex, xv, 175–76, 183–84, 188–89, 192

O'Hanlon, Michael, xvii, 34–36, 40, 215, 219

Oken, Lorenz, 5

olfaction. *See* smell

olfactory anxiety, 181–83

olfactory discrimination, 5

Olkes, Cheryl, 41–42

Ommura, 202

Ong, Walter J., xviii, 15–17, 24, 53, 113, 119, 161, 237n. 7

Ongee, 4, 46, 51, 203, 240n. 8

onomatopoeia, 85, 87–88

orality. *See* oral societies

oral mentality, xviii, 95, 113–21

oral societies, xviii, xix, 9, 19, 51–52, 64, 113–21, 157, 237n. 7

other, 24, 46, 49

Pandya, Vishvajit, xiii, 46

Papua New Guinea, xiv, xvi, xviii, 204, 213–17, 219, 221

Pasteur, Louis, 200

penis, 132–33, 138, 140, 150, 155–56, 165, 202, 246n. 7

Pepsi-Cola, 216–17

perception, 11, 17, 21–23, 40, 50–51, 52, 84, 115, 122–23, 237n. 3, 239n. 6

performance. *See* theater

perfume, 57–58

periodicity, 194, 197–98, 202–3

Index

279

visualism, 51–52, 196, 210, 221
visuality, xx, 200
voices, 24, 28
von Trapp, Maria, 64–65

Wahgi, xvii, 34–36
warfare, 104, 149, 151, 161, 168
Washkuk Hills. *See* Kwoma
ways of seeing, 45
ways of sensing, xix, 29, 95, 106, 112
weaving, 8, 163, 213, 244n. 2
Weiner, Annette, 61, 63, 67, 69, 85, 87, 92, 93, 117
Western culture, xviii, 4–5, 42–43, 45–46, 48–51, 54, 56, 102, 115, 187, 213–15, 220, 228, 230. *See also* other; "primitive" people
Western hierarchy of the senses, 230
Wéyewa, 9, 237n. 2
Whitehead, Alfred North, 232
Whiting, John, 124, 132, 137, 164

Wikan, Unni, 20
Williams, T. R., 14
Williamson, Margaret Holmes, 124, 129–31, 133, 135, 243n. 2
witch, 121–23
Wober, Mallory, 15
Wolof, 237n. 6
women, 55, 67–68, 74, 81, 99–100, 121–23, 128–30, 145–46, 154, 170, 177, 190, 194, 198–99, 213, 223, 225, 240n. 9, 241n. 4, 244n. 2
Wordsworth, William, xxi–xxii
writing, xix, 3, 19, 22–28, 42–43, 57–58, 214

Yambon, 147
yams, 66–67, 85, 96–97, 99–100, 125–26, 150; harvest ceremony (*yena, mindja,* and *nowkwi* rituals), 126, 138, 140–44
yena head, 152–59
Young, Michael, 61, 69, 242n. 5